D1237035

CVCA Royal Library
4687 Wyoga Lake Road
Stow, OH. 44224-1011

A POET'S PARENTS

A Poet's Parents

THE COURTSHIP

LETTERS OF

EMILY NORCROSS AND

EDWARD DICKINSON

EDITED BY VIVIAN R. POLLAK

The University of North Carolina Press

Chapel Hill & London

B
Dickinson

T9599

© 1988 The University of North Carolina Press
All rights reserved
Manufactured in the United States of America

The courtship letters and other Norcross-Dickinson
family materials are reproduced by permission of the
Houghton Library, Harvard University, Cambridge, Mass.

The paper in this book meets the guidelines for
permanence and durability of the Committee on
Production Guidelines for Book Longevity of the
Council on Library Resources.

92 91 90 89 88 5 4 3 2 1

Library of Congress Cataloging-in-Publication Data

Pollak, Vivian R.
  A poet's parents.

  Bibliography: p.
  Includes index.
    1. Dickinson, Emily, 1830–1886—Biography—Family.
2. Dickinson, Emily—Correspondence. 3. Dickinson,
Edward—Correspondence. 4. Dickinson family—
Correspondence. 5. Love-letters. 6. Amherst (Mass.)—
Biography. 7. Poets, American—19th century—Biography.
I. Title.
PS1541.Z5P59 1988 811'.4 [B] 87-35868
ISBN 0-8078-1797-X

CVCA Royal Library
4687 Wyoga Lake Road
Stow, OH 44224-1011

C. 1   10-5-01   25.00

For my very dear parents,

Sylvia and Morrison Rogosa

CONTENTS

ILLUSTRATIONS

PREFACE

While preparing this edition of the courtship letters exchanged by Emily Dickinson's parents, the question I was most often asked by anyone who expressed an interest in it was the following: "Did Emily Dickinson read the letters?" To which I replied, "I don't know." Intuitively, it seems to me unlikely that Emily Dickinson would have read these letters before her mother's death in 1882, and there is no evidence that she ever read them. There is no reason to think that these letters, as literary texts, influenced the poet's style, nor have I been struck by significant verbal parallels between the letters written by her parents and Dickinson's poetry. Having said this, let me hasten to add that these letters reveal the personalities of her parents and the relationship between them more directly and with incomparably greater detail than any other biographical source. I emphasize the word *biographical* because Emily Dickinson's poetry may be said to be our single best source for understanding her parents, their relationship, and her relations with them, at least obliquely. In her poetry, Emily Dickinson attempted to "Tell all the Truth" but to "tell it slant." As I have argued elsewhere, the occasions of her poems are brilliantly obscured. To state that Emily Dickinson's poetry is inconceivable without her parents, their relationship, and her relations with them is to state the obvious. But for a poet such as Dickinson who could describe herself as "Exterior—to Time," these letters may serve as a timely reminder that great art has a human history.

By anyone interested in the phenomenon of the Dickinson family as a whole, I was likely to be asked whether these letters would reveal a hitherto unforeseen sexual scandal. Perhaps unfortunately, the writers—Emily Dickinson's parents—were remarkably reticent about their sexual experience, as I explain in the Introduction. To a remarkable degree, theirs was a literary courtship, by which I mean (in part) that who had written to whom most lately was a more important source of tension between them than who had responded most vividly to a parting kiss, which seems not to have been an issue between them. That Emily Dickinson's parents should have attached such great importance to the written word—Edward Dickinson by writing, Emily Norcross by not writing—is itself noteworthy, and it could be argued that Dickinson's poems are both written and unwritten, by which I mean (in part) that her poems, perhaps more than most, foreground the tension between stated and unstated, apprehended and unapprehended actions, thoughts, and emotions.

This edition of ninety-six letters is based on a set of manuscripts acquired by Harvard University in 1950 from the estate of Martha Dickinson Bianchi, the poet's niece. Martha Dickinson Bianchi, an unreliable biographer of her aunt, was the last surviving descendant of Emily Norcross and Edward Dickinson, both of whom came from large families. Neither the poet Emily Dickinson nor her sister Lavinia ever married. Given the sexual conventions of the day, neither of them had any children, although Emily Dickinson hinted that she might be pregnant in one of the letters she wrote to a mysterious, somewhat real, somewhat fantastic lover she addressed as "Master." The poet's brother Austin had three children: Gilbert died at the age of eight, Ned died shortly before his thirty-seventh birthday without having married, and Martha Dickinson Bianchi married at thirty-six. She herself aspired to poethood, published several volumes of verse, and died childless. As an editor of Emily Dickinson's poetry, Bianchi sought to superimpose her critical preferences on the poet's texts. Happily, she was a more faithful conservator of the Dickinson family papers.

This edition contains all of the extant letters that were exchanged by Emily Norcross and Edward Dickinson during their courtship, together with three additional letters that illuminate their relationship but are not courtship letters as such. Letter 18 is a declaration of intent written by Edward Dickinson to his prospective father-in-law; Letter 73 is a plea for help written by Lavinia Norcross, the poet's maternal aunt, to the poet's mother; Letter 96 was written by Edward to Emily, his wife, after their marriage and rounds out the correspondence exchanged by the couple for the year 1828. As I explain in the headnotes to Letters 3 and 66, there appear to be two missing letters, one written by Edward, the other by Emily. With these exceptions, this edition therefore contains all of their known correspondence with each other for 1826 through 1828.

After their marriage, the Dickinsons corresponded extensively in 1838–39 when Edward was living in Boston during one of his terms in the Massachusetts legislature, though I have seen no letter written by Emily Norcross Dickinson to anyone that postdates 1844. This subsequent correspondence is interesting both for its references to their daughter Emily and for its presentation of the Dickinsons as anxious parents and as tense marriage partners. Initially, I was tempted to expand this edition of courtship letters to include all of the Dickinsons' postmarriage correspondence with each other and with their children. But the sheer bulk of such an expanded edition seemed formidable. Moreover, some of this subsequent correspondence had already been published and analyzed by Millicent Todd Bingham, Jay Leyda, Thomas H. Johnson, John Cody, and Richard B. Sewall, so that many of its more salient features were already accessible. Thus it seemed best to limit this edition to a set of letters that has the advantage of psychological coherence, despite its lack of chronological scope, and that most emphatically highlights the psychological, social, and intellectual imbalance between the poet's parents. Opposites attracted. As I suggest in the Epilogue, their marriage was apparently more gratifying to Edward than to Emily. But then so too was their courtship.

ACKNOWLEDGMENTS

I am enormously grateful to the staff of the Houghton Library of Harvard University and especially to Rodney G. Dennis, Manuscript Curator, and Melanie Wisner, the curator of the Dickinson Collection. Invaluable assistance was also provided by librarians at Amherst College, Cheyney University, Duke University, the Forbes Library in Northampton, the Jones Library in Amherst, the Monson Free Public Library, the New England Historic Genealogical Society, the Northampton Law Library, Springfield Public Library, the University of Pennsylvania, the University of Washington, Williams College, and Yale University. Edward J. Kilsdonk, then a sophomore at Amherst College, provided essential research assistance. My friend and neighbor Jean P. Zelten typed the manuscript with her usual competence and enthusiasm. A 1986 Summer Stipend from the National Endowment for the Humanities buoyed my spirits and helped me to meet some of the expenses connected with this project. I am also grateful to scholar-friends who shared their insights with me. Wendy Martin was especially helpful during the early stages of the project. In subsequent months, my interactions with Nina Auerbach, Gary Handwerk, Suzanne Juhasz, Jerome Loving, George Monteiro, Jonathan Morse, Kenneth M. Price, Ruth Shipman, and Barton Levi St. Armand were inspiriting. Iris Tillman Hill of the University of North Carolina Press took it upon herself to read and comment upon the edition as a whole. This is a better book because of her efforts. As always, my husband Bob was an important source of strength, as were my children Ed and Steve and our family's newest member, Jill Shulman-Pollak. Finally, it is a pleasure to acknowledge the lifelong inspiration of my parents, Sylvia and Morrison Rogosa, to whom this edition is dedicated.

INTRODUCTION

I

In January 1826, Edward Dickinson traveled to Monson, Massachusetts, a farming community some twenty-five miles south of Amherst. At that time, he was introduced to Emily Norcross, his future wife. On 8 February, he surprised her with a letter in which he announced his desire to form a more intimate acquaintance with her, hinting rather broadly that marriage was on his mind. A month passed before she favored him with a reply. Responding to his letter on 10 March, she explained that she had had no intimation of his romantic interest in her during his Monson visit but expressed her willingness to correspond with him, so that they might explore the possibility of a more permanent relationship. Since Edward Dickinson's subsequent visits to Monson were infrequent and Emily Norcross was singularly averse to visiting him in Amherst, the letters they exchanged before their marriage on 6 May 1828 played an important part in the development of their relationship.

In *The Life of Emily Dickinson*, Richard B. Sewall provides some tantalizing excerpts from the letters that were written by Emily Dickinson's parents to each other during their protracted courtship. Sewall's analysis of these letters is equally tantalizing, but while completing my own book, *Dickinson: The Anxiety of Gender*, I became aware of certain ellipses and ambiguities in his presentation.[1] I then contacted the curator of the Dickinson family manuscripts at the Houghton Library, Harvard University, who provided me with photocopies of key letters in the correspondence. As I read these sample letters, it was apparent to me that the correspondence as a whole was likely to be a rich source for Dickinson biography. Having by now transcribed and annotated these letters, which remain virtually unpublished, I hope that such an edition will interest not only literary scholars but also students of nineteenth-century American social history. For example, this correspondence will illuminate some of the social and sexual conflicts experienced not only by the poet but also by her brother Austin. Austin Dickinson's scandalous liaison with one of the first editors of Emily Dickinson's poetry, Mabel Loomis Todd, was

1. See Richard B. Sewall, *The Life of Emily Dickinson*, 2 vols. (New York: Farrar, Straus and Giroux, 1974), 1:47–51, 76–78.

discussed at some length by Sewall.[2] More recently, however, this relationship has been reexamined by Peter Gay, in *The Bourgeois Experience Victoria to Freud: Education of the Senses*, and by Polly Longsworth, in *Austin and Mabel: The Amherst Affair and Love Letters of Austin Dickinson and Mabel Loomis Todd*.[3] The Norcross-Dickinson correspondence does not explain how the poet's parents nurtured such unconventional children, but it does identify issues of vital importance to them from the inception of their relationship, issues that can be shown to have influenced their children's subsequent development.

In all, Edward Dickinson and Emily Norcross exchanged ninety-three extant letters during their courtship. His is the dominant voice: he wrote sixty-nine of the letters, she wrote twenty-four. His letters are lengthy, hers are perfunctory. Indisputably, Edward Dickinson's intellectual range was broader, his command of language superior. The extent of Emily Norcross's formal education remains to be determined, but it is known that she received a commendation for "punctual attendance, close application, good acquirements, and discreet behavior" and that she attended a girls' boarding school in New Haven in 1823.[4] Judging from her letters, these "good acquirements" did not include such language conventions as spelling, punctuation, and capitalization. Although her handwriting is elegant, her syntax is simple, her vocabulary unambitious. She was twitted by her friends for epistolary indolence, even before Edward Dickinson ran up against this problematic character trait, which unsettled him, given their lengthy separations. The poet subsequently remarked, "My Mother does not care for thought."[5]

In Monson, Emily Norcross attended "improving" lectures but tacitly rebuffed Edward's attempts to supervise her further education, although his essays on female education were being published concurrently in a local newspaper.[6] She barely glanced at the books he sent her and ignored the enthusiastic literary critiques he wrote to accompany some of them. Happily, Edward Dickinson did not look to Emily Norcross primarily for intellectual companionship and repeatedly ex-

2. Ibid., 1:170–228.

3. See Peter Gay, *The Bourgeois Experience Victoria to Freud: Education of the Senses* (New York: Oxford University Press, 1984), 1:71–108, and Polly Longsworth, *Austin and Mabel: The Amherst Affair and Love Letters of Austin Dickinson and Mabel Loomis Todd* (New York: Farrar, Straus and Giroux, 1984).

4. Sewall, *Life of Emily Dickinson*, 1:76.

5. Emily Dickinson, *The Letters of Emily Dickinson*, ed. Thomas H. Johnson, 3 vols. (Cambridge: Harvard University Press, 1958), 2:404. Hereafter cited as *Letters of Emily Dickinson*.

6. See Letter 33, n. 1 and Letter 38, n. 1 of this edition.

pressed his perfect satisfaction with their interviews, which occurred in Monson perhaps once every six weeks.

During their courtship, Emily Norcross's extended silences—her aversion to written self-expression—became contextually significant. Especially given her active social life in Monson, Edward began to feel that she was neglecting him, just as the poet was subsequently to complain of maternal neglect. Emily Norcross never succeeded in persuading him that her domestic responsibilities were so time-consuming as to prevent her from writing to him, though many of her letters advance this unlikely claim. During the winter of 1828, Edward became so frustrated by the paucity of her written self-expression, by her unwillingness to visit him in Amherst, and by her reluctance to commit herself to a reasonable marriage date, that he was tempted to sever their relationship. Yet through the intervention of her father and sister at this crucial juncture, his fears were mollified and he was persuaded to bide his time. The couple were married in Monson on 6 May 1828 in a ceremony that was unconventional because of the absence of attendants—of bridesmaids and groomsmen. Emily Norcross wanted to "stand up alone," in order to diminish the social significance of a new life about which she remained profoundly ambivalent. Though puzzled by her excessive shyness, Edward acquiesced.

In one of his last courtship letters, however, he could not resist taunting his future bride about her tenacious attachment to her parents' home. Indeed, throughout their courtship correspondence, the extent to which Emily Norcross did or did not venture beyond her parents' house and grounds was the focus of some conflict for these lovers. The pattern of home-centeredness that emerges here is a complex one. First, Emily Norcross's letters may be equated with symbolic leave-takings from her parents, siblings, and Monson friends. Unconsciously, she appears to have made this association, and Edward regarded her letters as love tokens. Second, he was threatened by her active social life in Monson, especially on those occasions such as evening lectures when she asserted herself apart from the Norcross family. Edward Dickinson appears to have assumed that a home-centered daughter would become a home-centered wife. Such exaggerated home-centeredness in a wife was necessary to his psychological well-being. Third, Emily Norcross's obstinacy in refusing to visit him in Amherst troubled him deeply, for obvious reasons. During their courtship she traveled to New York with her father, and as I have already stated she was educated in New Haven, but she had never been to Amherst before meeting Edward and visited him only once during their courtship, which began in January 1826 and ended in

May 1828. Edward's pleas that she acquaint herself with his family and her new surroundings were therefore entirely reasonable, as were his pleas that she permit them to socialize with other couples in Monson, which she also circumvented. Finally, her anxiety as their courtship tended toward its natural conclusion—her separation from her Monson home—though to some extent understandable, was insufficiently offset by her attachment to Edward. One social historian (Ellen K. Rothman, in *Hands and Hearts: A History of Courtship in America*) has observed that many young women experienced comparable anxieties before their marriages.[7] Cheerfully engaging themselves, they also attempted to postpone their marriages. Similarly, in *An American Triptych: Anne Bradstreet, Emily Dickinson, Adrienne Rich*, Wendy Martin argues that "marriage frequently caused severe homesickness and loneliness for women," who were "uprooted from a familiar and supportive environment. . . . The shift from their father's to their husband's homes meant that wives had to relinquish their primary bonds."[8] Emily Norcross's homesickness on the eve of her marriage was therefore a common cultural phenomenon, though other facts need to be considered here as well. Clearly, *both* of the poet's parents invested home-centeredness with great psychological significance even before their marriage. During the poet's childhood, Emily Norcross Dickinson found Edward's lengthy absences from home exceptionally difficult to tolerate. His feelings during these intervals were more ambivalent and to some extent remain to be determined. But examples of the importance of home-centeredness in the Dickinson family context are numerous, and home-centeredness is but one theme in the courtship correspondence of Emily Dickinson's parents that has prophetic power for her poetry.

As I suggested in the Preface, reticence about sexual desire, experience, frustration, and gratification is a notable characteristic of these letters. Repeatedly, Edward asks Emily to give him a "parting kiss," the latter word often abbreviated as "k——s" or, for the plural "k——s." On several occasions, he describes having dreamed about her in such a way as to hint at erotic fantasies. Nowhere, however, does either partner comment on the physical appearance of the other, and Edward's insistence on *parting* kisses underscores his determination to discipline his own eroticism. Yet erotic as well as affectional desires undoubtedly prompted Edward to try to advance their marriage date.

7. See Ellen K. Rothman, *Hands and Hearts: A History of Courtship in America* (New York: Basic Books, 1984), pp. 56–75.

8. See Wendy Martin, *An American Triptych: Anne Bradstreet, Emily Dickinson, Adrienne Rich* (Chapel Hill: University of North Carolina Press, 1984), pp. 151–52.

When Emily visited New York City during the spring of 1827, Edward's thoughts turned to urban prostitution:

My heart fails me to paint the scenes of too common occurance in all our cities—the abodes of death, the places where innocence has no dwelling—where virtue never comes—where some of the once most lovely of the fair creation are forced to resort to hide their shame—rather the victims of the seducer's arts are forced to congregate, and where hundreds of unsuspecting females, who have lost their honor in an unguarded [?] moment, when perhaps they thought themselves safe, are found living in the most loathsome prostitution. Such cities swarm with men of fashion—men who, while their words are fair & their manners fascinating, are bent on no other purpose but the gratification of their unhallowed passions at the expense of all that is dear in life—Good Heaven! My blood boils at the idea of seeing & knowing that such unrighteous abodes are suffered to exist—Would to God! I had the power, I would march thro' the cities of the land, rooting out these monsters of vice—these "charnel houses"—these destroyers of the health, the reputation & the morals of our most promising youth of both sexes—I would overturn & overturn, till virtue was again placed upon the throne, & all these abominable vices forced to do her homage. But I have insensibly said more than I intended— [L41]

Without doubting the sincerity of his frenzied moral outrage, I should like to suggest that Edward's inflamed rhetoric may profitably be attributed to the repression of his desire to seduce his fiancée or to be seduced by her. As depicted by Edward, New York City, unlike the quiet Connecticut Valley, is a corrupting place. Women are especially vulnerable to such corruption, although he is also concerned about the effect of prostitution on men. Given his proprietorial style, Edward was reluctant to entrust his beloved to such a shameful scene. Of course Emily returned to Monson without having visited a brothel and ignored his impassioned diatribe in her subsequent letters. When Edward exploded, Emily tended not to notice him, thereby securing a kind of space of her own.

When Emily brought herself to speak of a "parting kiss" in an 1827 letter, this expression embarrassed her (L52). Yet I am inclined to think that in person Emily Norcross was physically demonstrative. When tensions were running high in her relations with Edward, she alluded to outings that they had made together—carriage rides and the like—in order to suggest that he could not, remembering their mutual pleasure on these intimate journeys, doubt her affection for him. Yet erotic as well as affectional fears must have prompted Emily to defer their marriage; certainly, she was sensitive to the demonstrable risks of childbirth. In June 1827, for example, she described the postpartum invalidism of a friend: "Mr Stimson and Lady have lately been home with the dear child I called on her saturday last found her quite miserable poor woman thought I [,] I had rather be a spectator but I presume she is reconciled to her situation or ought to be" (L43). This almost harsh assessment of the biological risks to which married women were subjected is one of several allusions to pregnancy and childbirth in her letters. In October 1827, she describes the *husband* of her cousin Maria Flynt Coleman as "quite elated with the little stranger" (L59). In a subsequent letter, she comments lugubriously on her cousin Maria's "continued illness," observing that "there is no happiness but what is mingled with sorrow" (L62).

Unlike Austin Dickinson, who looked first to his future wife Susan Gilbert and then to his mistress Mabel Loomis Todd to rescue him from overwhelming community responsibilities, Edward Dickinson consistently speaks of his obligation to Emily Norcross and to the community.[9] A conflict between personal inclination and social convention never appears to occur to him. He expected marriage to enhance his social usefulness. In that sense, the marital relationship he imagined was antiromantic and informed by eighteenth- or early nineteenth-century ideals of social utility. Within this context of social utility, Edward Dickinson asserted considerable independence of his future wife. At no time does he assert that his psychological well-being depends exclusively on her approval—an obsessional theme in the letters that were written by Austin to the women he loved. Rather, Edward's psychological well-being depended primarily on his ability to satisfy his conscience and to a lesser degree on his professional success or failure, which probably indicates that he was more self-confident as a lawyer than as a lover. Despite the example of his formidably risk-taking father, chance has no place in his conception of his future. Naively, he asserts "times without number" that outcomes depend almost exclusively upon effort, a conception of success singularly absent in the poet Emily Dickinson's worldview. Throughout this correspondence, the word "exertions" resounds in Edward's discourse. He used the word "laborious" approvingly. Belaboring his work ethic, which he himself associated with manliness, Edward

9. There are excerpts from Austin Dickinson's courtship letters to Susan Gilbert in John Cody, *After Great Pain: The Inner Life of Emily Dickinson* (Cambridge, Mass.: Harvard University Press, 1971), pp. 192–202. However, most of Austin's letters to Susan remain unpublished. They form part of the collection of the Dickinson Family Papers in the Houghton Library of Harvard University.

Dickinson to some extent assumed that Emily Norcross's romantic interest in him depended on his professional success. Repeatedly, he discussed the state of his business with her, apparently believing that she would perceive a direct correspondence between his value as a businessman and his value as a husband.

The extent to which Edward Dickinson's future wife admired his strenuous ideology is ambiguous. Certainly, she felt herself to be more subject to the whims, needs, and desires of others. The following excerpt from a December 1826 letter is typical of her self-effacing stance:

> May I hope dear Edward that you do not think me insensible how much I am indebted to you, as I am unwilling to suppose that you think more of recieveing letters from me than I do of answering yours. I have designed writing evry evening of this week but have not succeeded untill the present in my endeavours and it is attended with some inconvenience that I leave my Mother this evening as she is quite indisposed, but for the plea-sure of conversing with you a short time I lay aside inconve-nienties [?] as you may suppose I often admit them to prevent me from executeing my purposes I was happy to hear of your safe arrival home and that your misfortune was supposed no fault of yours. I imagine I thought more of it than any one else except yourself which is perfectly natural, but have you not often heard the observation that the bitter useually accompanies the sweet, but it may not always prove true, at least may one overpower the other. [L27]

Emily's mother, Betsy Fay Norcross, had had nine children. As de-picted in the courtship letters, her health was uncertain and she died several years later. Emily's father was a wealthy man in the process of becoming wealthier who, like Edward, was interested in female educa-tion. Emily refers to him more frequently in the letters than she does to her mother, whom she tends to mention only as the victim of ill health, which also plagued other members of her immediate family. (Three of her siblings were already dead.)[10] Whether writing a letter or mailing it, Emily Norcross depended on a social network that would enable her to complete her projects. Rarely does she describe exerting herself. Her sense that she was likely to be interrupted at any moment may reflect not only her internal disorganization but a social

---

10. In *After Great Pain*, Cody emphasizes the effects on the poet's mother of a series of deaths in the Norcross family. In my judgment he overemphasizes the ex-tent to which Emily Norcross Dickinson was traumatized by these events.

reality, which perhaps accounts for the tentative and even melancholy tone of much of her discourse. In any event, her sister Lavinia—her only living sister—had a much more forceful personality.

Emily's father Joel Norcross was one of the founders and major contributors to Monson Academy, a college preparatory "high school" with a significant reputation in Massachusetts and to some extent beyond; there were male boarding students at Monson from other states and from foreign countries. Monson Academy admitted women as day students; beginning in 1818, about the time Emily Norcross would have begun attending high school, Monson had separate classes for women, whereas previously women had attended classes with men. Whether this represented a step up, down, or across for female students I am unable to say. The early records of Monson Academy were destroyed in a series of fires, but in the normal course of events Joel Norcross would have enrolled Emily at Monson. Many New England women attended such academies, even if only for several months a year.[11] Furthermore, Emily Norcross had a year's additional schooling at what appears to have been a glorified finishing school in New Haven, although according to her brother Joel Warren Norcross, she attended one of the finest female seminaries in New England.[12] Some of her female friends, however, were conscious of the school's deficiencies.[13] In any event, there is every reason to believe that Emily Norcross's formal education was equal if not superior to the formal education of Ellen Tucker Emerson who, in the letters she wrote to Ralph Waldo Emerson during their courtship—almost contemporaneous with that of the Dickinsons—exhibited a remarkable range of literary and affectional resources.[14] In short, Emily Norcross

11. "Portrait of a Family: Emily Dickinson's Norcross Connection" by Mary Elizabeth Kromer Bernhard, *New England Quarterly* 60 (September 1987): 363–81, was published just as I was readying this manuscript for the printer. Bernhard advances evidence that Emily Norcross attended Monson Academy in 1820–21 but does not speculate as to how long.

12. See Joel Warren Norcross, *History and Genealogy of the Norcross Family*, 2 vols. (1882). Unpublished manuscript in the collection of the New England Historic Genealogical Society, Boston, Massachusetts.

13. In a letter of 17 June 1826, for example, Olivia Flynt wrote to her cousin Emily, "The school is better than when we were here—only 38 scholars now—and is more strict than formerly." And on 2 August 1830 her sister Lavinia wrote, "Mr. Herrick's school—I would not give a farthing for all I shall learn" (Dickinson Family Papers).

14. See Ellen Tucker Emerson, *One First Love: The Letters of Ellen Louisa Tucker to Ralph Waldo Emerson*, ed. Edith W. Gregg (Cambridge, Mass.: Harvard University Press, 1962). Emerson's letters to Ellen Tucker are no longer extant.

appears to have had social and intellectual opportunities for self-expression she rather consistently ignored. Her sister Lavinia, for example, was a much better writer. Similarly, Louisa Van Velsor Whitman, Walt Whitman's mother, although virtually unschooled, exhibited a narrative flair in her letters that is lacking in the letters written by Emily Dickinson's mother.[15] Emily Norcross's affectless style is nevertheless occasionally redeemed by the makings of a tart wit: "Poor woman thought I [,] I had rather be a spectator."

Whitman, whose idealization of his mother is perhaps the most consistent feature of his relationship with her, observed to his biographer Horace Traubel,

> How much I owe her! It could not be put in a scale—weighed: it could not be measured—be even put in the best words: it can only be apprehended through the intuitions. Leaves of Grass is the flower of her temperament active in me. My mother was illiterate in the formal sense but strangely knowing: she excelled in narrative—had great mimetic power: she could tell stories, impersonate: she was very eloquent in the utterance of noble moral axioms—was very original in her manner, her style.[16]

Quite oppositely, the poet Emily Dickinson sought to deny her mother's influence on her. When she was almost forty, she explained to Thomas Wentworth Higginson, "I never had a mother. I suppose a mother is one to whom you hurry when you are troubled." Writing to Higginson four years later she explained, "I always ran Home to Awe when a child, if anything befell me. He was an awful Mother, but I liked him better than none." During the early stages of her correspondence with Higginson, which began in 1862, the poet also underscored her psychological isolation from the other members of her immediate family. "They are religious—except me," she explained, "and address an Eclipse, every morning—whom they call their 'Father.'" Underscoring not only her psychological isolation from her family but also her resentment at parental neglect, she described her father as "too busy with his Briefs—to notice what we do." "My father only reads on Sunday," she told Higginson in 1870. "He reads *lonely & rigorous* books."[17] Yet Emily Dickinson's poetry suggests

15. Most of Louisa Van Velsor Whitman's letters are unpublished and may be found in the Trent Collection of the Rare Book Department, William R. Perkins Library, Duke University, Durham, N.C.

16. As quoted in Horace Traubel, *With Walt Whitman in Camden* (Boston: Small Maynard, 1906), 1:227.

17. The quotations are from *Letters of Emily Dickinson*, 2:475, 517–18, 404, 473.

that the influence of both of her parents on her self-conception was very great indeed, and few poets can have spent more time in an almost unbroken original family circle (notwithstanding Austin's marriage and move into a house of his own—next door) than Emily Dickinson. As I suggested in *Dickinson: The Anxiety of Gender*, the poet revered and despised her father's patriarchal values. Rather more consistently, she viewed her mother as a negative role model for an empowered woman poet.

Dickinson's inability to identify with her mother is perhaps paralleled by Whitman's inability to identify with his father—a disaffected farmer turned carpenter. Walter Whitman, Senior, combined a hot temper and low spirits. Unsuccessful in his business ventures, he was more often the victim of "the tight bargain, the crafty lure," than the perpetrator of it, as Justin Kaplan has shrewdly remarked.[18] Yet however different the temperament and experience of the two poets, this brief comparison suggests a further range of inquiry. It now appears that most of the major American writers of the nineteenth century who flourished before or during the American Civil War encountered some kind of profound disturbance in their relationship with a parent of the same sex. Just as the works of such writers as Whitman, Poe, Emerson, Thoreau, Hawthorne, and Melville constitute a formidable critique of patriarchal culture; so too Dickinson's poetry constitutes a formidable critique of a matriarchal culture that attempted to "shut [her] up in Prose." Given Edward Dickinson's professional ambitions and the dominance of a "separate sphere" ideology for men and for women during Emily Dickinson's formative years, the poet's experience of her home was necessarily dominated by her interaction with her mother. Because she viewed her mother as having been overshadowed by her father, "*They* shut me up in Prose," she wrote (italics mine). Her poetry too is haunted by patriarchal emblems; matriarchy functions as an absence, a "Missing All," that, the poet explained, prevented her from missing "minor Things." I am not suggesting that a literally or psychologically absent parent of the same sex guarantees literary greatness. Yet for nineteenth-century American writers who flourished up to and through the turbulent years of the American Civil War, disturbances in same-sex bonding were a powerful goad to literary autonomy. Thus Emily Dickinson's family situation, whatever its unique features, takes on a kind of cultural fatality.

18. See Justin Kaplan, *Walt Whitman: A Life* (New York: Simon and Schuster, 1980), p. 62. The quotation is from Whitman's poem "There Was a Child Went Forth" in which "the father, strong, self-sufficient, manly, mean, anger'd, unjust" is characterized by "the blow, the quick loud word, the tight bargain, the crafty lure."

In certain respects the elusive Emily Norcross Dickinson has eluded the poet's biographers because she eluded the poet as well. Traditionally, Emily Norcross has been characterized as a sweetly submissive Victorian wife; Edward Dickinson has been characterized as a stern Victorian paterfamilias who unflinchingly dominated his wife and the other members of his family. The Edward Dickinson who emerges in the courtship letters is more vulnerable and more of a feminist than tradition would have it; the Emily Norcross who emerges in the courtship letters usually gets her way with Edward, although she is also confused about her own psychological ambitions. Her language is superficially compliant and nonthreatening; a casual reading of the letters does not reveal either her rigidity or her strength. In that sense the letters show that there was a significant discrepancy between her public personality and her private persona. These letters help to delineate the poet's maternal legacy, modify our understanding of male dominance and female submission in the Dickinson household, and show how conventional courtship patterns in the nineteenth century could be subtly undermined by an intellectually unambitious woman who was also a covert role rebel. Often overwhelmed by her parents and her siblings, she aspired to greater autonomy with Edward. To the extent that she achieved such autonomy, however, she did so in the name of her obligations as a member of the Norcross family. In the process, she relinquished important opportunities to interact more closely with Edward and with his family, to say nothing of his friends.

When I began this project, I entertained the desire to rehabilitate Emily Dickinson's mother. Having pursued it, I have discovered that the courtship letters ground Dickinson's perceptions of her mother in reality. Increasingly, I have come to respect the wisdom of Richard Sewall's conclusion that Dickinson's final affection for her mother was a major moral and psychological victory.[19] In 1875, on the first anniversary of her husband's death, Mrs. Dickinson suffered a paralytic stroke from which she never fully recovered. After her mother's death in 1882, the poet explained to her friend Elizabeth Holland, "We were never intimate Mother and Children while she was our Mother—but Mines in the same Ground meet by tunneling and when she became our Child, the Affection came."[20]

Feminist critics have taught us that "When a Writer Is a Daughter," female role models matter.[21] Thus despite the ferocity of her need to

19. See Sewall, *Life of Emily Dickinson*, 1:75.

20. *Letters of Emily Dickinson*, 3:754–55.

21. See especially Barbara Antonina Clarke Mossberg, *Emily Dickinson: When a Writer Is a Daughter* (Bloomington: Indiana University Press, 1982). Mossberg tends to view Emily Norcross Dickinson as a victim of nineteenth-century gender

deny her mother's rather formidable influence on her, even Emily
Dickinson had a mother. The Dickinson family letters show that this
relationship changed over time—Mrs. Dickinson flourished in the
1840s—and that the poet viewed her mother from multiple psycho-
logical perspectives. But Dickinson's cutting comments about her
mother's psychological inaccessibility were clearly grounded in some
historical reality. The courtship letters both reveal that reality and
preserve the crucially defining ambiguity of her mother's situation and
temperament. Unquestionably, they are our most valuable biographi-
cal source for reading Emily Norcross Dickinson. However, the poet's
conviction that she had been neglected by her mother was both just
and unjust, reality and myth. A shrewd, subjective, and boldly egocen-
tric observer of those who populated the house on Main Street, Am-
herst, Massachusetts, Emily Dickinson chose to dwell also in the
house of "Possibility— / A fairer House than Prose." In this second
house, the house of art, there was only one angel, only one demon,
and only *one* Emily Dickinson.

I I

My Dear Sir,
    As I have heard nothing from you since we parted at Monson,
& as an opportunity now presented itself of sending directly to
you, I thought I would just inquire how you have enjoyed yourself
since, & whether you do not occasionally wish yourself back
again, especially to attend the Chemical Lectures with the young
Lady, who lived about a mile from our quarters, & near one of
the Factories. It cannot be necessary for me to mention her name
for I think the impression she made upon your heart, was too
deep to be soon effaced.

> [Solomon Warriner, Jr.,
> to Edward on 8 February
> 1826 from Springfield]

I should be pleased to attend the Lectures again, with the Com-
pany we had last winter. We really enjoyed ourselves finely & if I
could always perform a Camp duty so easy, I should not be loth

---

ideology, whereas I am more concerned with what the poet's mother made of
those opportunities and obstacles she encountered.

to obey my country's call, whenever it should be necessary for them to call for me as *one* of the *Militia*! !

[Warriner to Edward on
17 January 1827]²²

One of the most interesting fantasies that Edward Dickinson entertained as a young man was that of his fiancée as a recluse. Rather early on in their courtship, he began to feel that Emily Norcross was taking advantage of him and that he cared more for her than she did for him. When he hinted as much—and hint was all he did since he was too insecure to risk an outright rejection—Emily pretended to ignore his feelings, or sought to reassure him by alluding to vague and unspecified obligations to her family, which was a very extended one, or to her neighbors and friends, including some young men of whom Edward might reasonably be jealous. Occasionally, there was an actual health-related emergency that concerned her: her ailing mother took a turn for the worse or a cousin in the town was thought to be gravely ill. In such situations, Edward responded with appropriate concern and counted on Emily to help out both at home and in the community. Indeed, he took pride in the skilled nursing powers he attributed to her, mistakenly I believe. More generally, Emily Norcross tried to create the impression that her time was not her own but that, given the right circumstances, her time would be Edward's. For *time* read *self*.

Although not skilled in the art of romantic negotiation, Edward was too intelligent not to sense that something was wrong. Actually, something *was* wrong in Monson. Emily's mother was dying of tuberculosis, her brother was dying of tuberculosis, and it appears that tuberculosis ran in the Norcross family. Additionally, Edward had a number of acquaintances who died suddenly in the prime of life, though his own family, unlike Emily's, was as yet untouched by the hand of death. Given the comparatively primitive medical knowledge of the day, many New Englanders probably found it difficult to distinguish

22. Warriner was a clerk in a store or a merchant in Springfield when he and Edward participated in the militia duties that originally brought Edward to Monson. There are thirty-six letters from Warriner to Edward in the Dickinson Family Papers beginning on 8 February 1826 and ending on 9 February 1829. The most tantalizing excerpt from these letters was written on 17 July 1826 and reads as follows: "We had a visit from the 2 Miss Norcross & E Whitaker [?] Saturday & of course heard from Monson—E. was well & tending [?] Tuckers [?] writing school."

between, let us say, a severe cold and an incipient case of fatal pneumonia. In any case, Edward himself had suffered from anxiety symptoms in the form of heart palpitations as a student at Yale and began to worry excessively about Emily's health. It is worth remarking here that her health was generally excellent and that she eventually outlived him by about eight years. The more important point, however, is that Edward's concern about her health intensified at crisis points in their relationship when he was habitually unable to retreat from his somewhat stultified and stultifying public persona and to tell her how bad she was making him feel. At such times he urged her to stay home.

Picture the following circumstances. A young man who has his own way to make in the world, owing in part to the fact that he is an American and owing in part to his father's craziness ("Money is distressingly scarce," Samuel Fowler wrote; "other comforts abound"),[23] falls in love with the, I think, pretty daughter of a shrewd and chary businessman whose son later describes him as the largest real estate holder in Monson, a town comparable in size and importance at that time to Amherst.[24] Though later, owing in part to Samuel Fowler's craziness, Amherst dominates. Incidentally, I use the word "crazy" or a variant on it advisedly. "Our affairs are still in a crazy situation," Edward's much-maligned mother Lucretia Gunn Dickinson wrote him while he was in college.[25] "My Life had stood—a Loaded Gun," the poet Emily Dickinson wrote subsequently, and her niece Martha Dickinson Bianchi perpetuated the legend that Grandmother Gunn's name was synonymous among her descendants with temper tantrums, though Grandmother Gunn's name should also have been synonymous with trouble.[26] I have a sense, she wrote to her son Edward in

23. Samuel Fowler Dickinson to Edward, 27 March 1823, Dickinson Family Papers.

24. So far as I can tell, Emily came to Edward with no dowry beyond some rather lovely household possessions and a perfect stove. There is an interesting letter from Edward to Joel in March 1830 which tries to interest Joel in the young couple's housing problems but Joel wouldn't bite. Edward may, however, have profited from Joel's shrewdness as an investor in real estate. See, for example, his 1835 letter to Emily asking her to get Joel to invest in Maine lands for him. See Jay Leyda, *The Years and Hours of Emily Dickinson*, 2 vols. (New Haven: Yale University Press, 1960), 1:30. For Joel's real estate holdings in Monson, see Norcross, *History and Genealogy of the Norcross Family*.

25. "They have compleated the College our affairs are still in a crazy situation" (Lucretia Gunn Dickinson to Edward on 5 December 1820, Dickinson Family Papers).

26. Lucretia Gunn Dickinson "was often referred to in moments of bad temper as 'coming out' in her high-strung grandchildren. If a door was banged—'It's not me—it's my Grandmother Gunn!' was an excuse glibly offered." See Martha

more or less these words, while he was in college, that you are reluctant to tell us what you need. Speak up. We'll try to help you out, poor as we are.[27] But Edward loved his father and didn't speak up and his mother had no money of her own, though on her deathbed she was knitting stockings for his children.[28]

Here then is Edward—not the valedictorian of his Yale class and not even the salutatorian of his class as his father was at Dartmouth in 1795, but certainly smart enough and not devoid of rhetorical powers. A trial lawyer. Someone who was invited to give patriotic speeches on the Fourth of July, as his father had done. Here is Edward, who adores his crazy father and who seeks to remember his Creator in the days of his youth as his parents were continually urging him to do in the rather touching letters they wrote him, but who is fortunately too self-protective to remember his Creator while forgetting himself. Here is Edward wearing his heart on his sleeve as his friend Solomon Warriner notes (for him, that is—Warriner also calls him "squeamish" because of his reticence; Warriner was eager for sexual gossip and Edward was not forthcoming).[29] So that everybody in Monson, according to Warriner, knows by February 1826 that Edward is madly in love with Emily.[30] And here is Emily, not madly in love with Edward by a long shot, but rather madly in love with herself. But this young couple has imbibed an ideology which holds that women are more empathetic than men, that women are more altruistic than men, that women are better nurses than men (though Edward gets up at six o'clock in the morning and writes to her after midnight, finishing one letter at two thirty A.M., and also stays up all night nursing his sick father and brother though he believes that women are peculiarly fitted for such self-sacrificing tasks). And so on and so forth. Here is Edward in love, yet committed to preparing himself for a life of "rational happiness." Under these circumstances, what happens?

Dickinson Bianchi, *Emily Dickinson Face to Face: Unpublished Letters with Notes and Reminiscences* (Hamden, Conn.: Archon, 1970), pp. 87–88.

27. "Edward it seems to me your wants are more silent than they used to be you must not suffer rather than make them known." Letter of 26 March 1823, Dickinson Family Papers.

28. See her letter of 30 November 1839 to Lavinia, beginning "My Dear Grandchild," to accompany the gift. She also offers to make another pair if the stockings she sent fit Austin or Emily better, explaining "my health continues better hope I may be able to do considerable." The letter is partly excerpted in Leyda, *The Years and Hours of Emily Dickinson*, 1:58.

29. The "squeamish" letter was written on 8 August 1827.

30. Warriner's letter of 22 February 1826, Dickinson Family Papers.

What happens is that Edward begins to fantasize about his beloved fiancée as a recluse. However, despite her somewhat saccharine tone, Emily Norcross is too self-protective to be wholly coopted by this fantasy. The appeal of this fantasy for Edward is that it places her wholly under his "protection." For *protection*, read *control*. The fantasy coincides with some of Emily Norcross's manifest behavior patterns. She is indeed home-centered, in that she is disorganized, as the poet Emily Dickinson subsequently perceives her to be. She also finds it difficult to interact with strangers such as Edward's parents and brothers and sisters. Monson is enormously convenient. Everyone knows her. She is Squire Joel's oldest daughter. She takes moonlight walks with her cousins. Her mother indulges her. Her father is possessive. And then there is the intangible factor. She is strangely shy. She finds it genuinely difficult to express herself outside of her home. But she adores her siblings, especially her sister Lavinia, and feels almost homesick without her. Reader, you are too smart to believe in psychological determinism. These courtship letters may, however, persuade you that even Emily Dickinson had a mother.

I I I

Let us prepare for a life of rational happiness. I do not expect, neither do I desire a life of *pleasure*, as some call it—I anticipate pleasure from engaging with my whole soul in my business, and passing the time which can be spared from that, in the enjoyment which arises from an unreserved interchange of sentiment with My dearest friend—

> [Edward Dickinson to
> Emily Norcross
> 19 March 1828]

Emily Norcross was not wholly coopted by Edward's recluse fantasy, but her daughter Emily was. Before launching into a discussion of this proposition, let me add a number of qualifications. First, I do not believe that Edward consciously attempted to turn his daughter into a recluse. Second, Dickinson's reclusion began gradually and was most noticeable during the last twenty years of her life, so that until she was about thirty-five her social interactions were not limited exclusively to her home. Third, Dickinson's creative energies were most remarkable before her reclusion had become inflexible, a statement which to some extent implies that in its extreme form her reclusion was not good for her as an artist and which is also based on the prior assumption that her great identity-crisis poems of the Civil War years represent a heroic attempt to transcend the pathological elements in her family experience and in her response to her family. Fourth, in that she was a great feeler, a great thinker, and a great wielder of powerful language, Dickinson was never wholly coopted by her father's fantasies—by his feelings, by his thoughts, or by his language. Fifth, Dickinson's reclusion was in some respects surprisingly social. She read widely; she conducted a voluminous, a beautiful, and a brilliant correspondence with numerous friends and acquaintances. She continued to receive old friends at home in Amherst, and even during the last twenty years or so of her life she continued to make new friends without leaving her home. She sent flowers, and poems, and baked goods to neighbors, she flirted with children and entertained them. Her sister Lavinia said that she was always on the lookout for the rewarding person.

But Emily Dickinson was coopted by her father's fantasy. For her, at least, "Great Streets of silence led away / To Neighborhoods of Pause."[31] And the funerals in the brain about which she wrote so many extravagantly remarkable poems were implicated in that fantasy and to some extent structured by the context out of which that fantasy emerged and within which it functioned. Which is to say that Dickinson's life was rich not only in words, in thoughts and feelings, and in material comforts, but also in suffering. What was the suffering?

Here too qualifications are necessary. Dickinson explained her reclusion variously to various people and to herself at different times. "No one could ever punish a Dickinson by shutting her up alone," she told her niece. Turning an imaginary key to the door of that room and pretending to lock it she explained, "It's just a turn—and freedom."[32] She wrote brilliantly about self-reliance, of which she was a formidable practitioner, and she wrote persuasively about sudden rushes of joy. She was also a breezy social satirist. Nevertheless, many if not most of Dickinson's greatest poems emerged out of her experience of a psychological prison. "I have lost the run of the roads," she explained. And "Dying is a wild Night and a new Road."[33] Though it is perhaps futile to try to sum up thus briefly the range of Dickinson's

31. Emily Dickinson, *The Poems of Emily Dickinson*, ed. Thomas H. Johnson, 3 vols. (Cambridge, Mass.: Harvard University Press, 1955), 2:810. Hereafter cited as *Poems of Emily Dickinson*.

32. The quotations are from Leyda, *The Years and Hours of Emily Dickinson*, 2:483.

33. *Letters of Emily Dickinson*, 2:523, 463.

responses to varying degrees of actual and psychological social isola-
tion, I think it useful to restate the obvious: Dickinson is a great poet
of erotic bereavement. Elsewhere I have called her the laureate of the
dispossessed.

To return now to the erotic bereavements she experienced as a con-
sequence of her interactions with her mother and her father. On a
number of different occasions Emily Dickinson stated in no uncertain
terms that she was homebound because her father preferred it that
way. And there is some objective evidence to support this view, though
there were also occasions on which Edward Dickinson was embar-
rassed by her antisocial behavior. Before working with these courtship
letters, I tended to believe that such statements as "I must omit Bos-
ton. Father prefers so" or "I do not cross my Father's ground to any
House or town"[34] were attempts to blame her father for her own
weaknesses and for her own choices. To some extent, I still believe
that these statements attach too much responsibility to Edward Dick-
inson. Nevertheless, something like this seems to have happened.

A sensitive young woman who feels rejected by her mother notices
that her father, despite his absurdly formal bearing and his prickly
disposition, is the more realistic and empathetic of her two parents,
though her father's powers of empathy are also severely limited. She
works at home, in that she helps with the cooking, especially the
baking, and generally makes herself useful in other ways, though she
dislikes housework and as time passes does less and less of it, proba-
bly in the end doing next to nothing, as her sister Lavinia takes over
and as there are more servants. More importantly, she works at home
because she is a writer and her home is thus the place where she feels
most fulfilled. Now it happens that her father worries about her exces-
sively when she is away from home, interrupts her schooling at Mount
Holyoke because of her "health," and gets frantic when she stays out
late at night even in Amherst, even next door. All in all, as time passes
she finds it easier to stay home more and more, and eventually she
stays home all the time; she has also experienced some anxiety attacks
in church, on the streets, and the like and generally suffers from a high
level of nervous tension that is exacerbated when she meets strangers,
even in her home. Now this type of compromise with the various
parameters of her situation—that she should stay home where she
feels safest and strongest—is perhaps preparing for or even enjoying a
life of rational happiness, which is not exactly a life of pleasure "as
some call it" but which is understandable and comparatively straight-
forward.

34. Ibid., 2:453, 460.

There is, however, another element in the situation which is less rational or understandable and which has to do with this Supposed Person's fantasies about her status at home. In addition to being smarter than either of her parents, she is significantly more empathetic. And the parent she empathizes with the most, as previously stated, is her father. Observing her mother's narcissistic inwardness, she begins to perceive herself unconsciously as her father's good wife. So she does more than bake bread for him, for her father only likes hers. She also tries to please him in a variety of other ways and realizes that she can please him best by staying home. On the other hand, her father doesn't want her to stay home all the time because, among other reasons, that would look odd in the community; *he* doesn't stay home all the time, and he wants her to demonstrate that she is cultivated and accomplished and socially serviceable. He also wants her to have a good time and to take advantage of the social and cultural opportunities that Amherst affords. Occasionally, he would like her to take a trip to visit friends and to see the world. The irrational part is that this Supposed Person exaggerates her father's fantasy; she also empathizes with her mother and resents his infantilization of her—of course her mother is very easy to infantilize. In any event, when she is twenty-two she writes her adored older brother, with whom she also competes for status within the family, "I wish we were children now. I wish we were *always* children, how to grow up I dont know."[35] Thereby hangs a tale.

35. Ibid., 1:241.

A NOTE ON
EDITORIAL
PROCEDURE

With several minor exceptions, I have attempted to reproduce the manuscripts as they were written, although it has been necessary to standardize the placement of headings, salutations, closings, postscripts, and the like. Emily Norcross, however, used dots to represent both periods and commas. For readability, I have used commas in some of these instances. (There are fewer than a dozen bona fide commas in the original documents.) For readability, I have also substituted some capitals for lowercase letters at the beginning of her sentences. But I have made these changes sparingly, and the other nontraditional features of her style have been faithfully preserved.

Edward employed traditional *P.S.*'s but also filled up the side margins of his letters with afterthoughts. All of these unofficial *P.S.*'s have been placed after his signature. In those instances where a word or mark of punctuation is almost illegible, I have used question marks in brackets to signal doubtful readings. Occasionally, I have also used brackets to supply clarifying information.

I

LETTERS 1–28

[1826]

*"I am sensible that
I hazard much"*

*"You may rightly conclude that
my feelings are in unison
with yours"*

Having met Emily in Monson on 1 January, Edward waited approximately five weeks before writing to her. As I indicated in the Introduction, his letter surprised her, not only because of the passage of time but also because, when they had parted, Edward's manner had been somewhat reserved. A graduate of Yale College (class of 1823), in 1825–26 Edward was a student at the Northampton Law School. I have not been able to determine who introduced him to Emily, but a likely candidate is her uncle Erasmus Norcross, a lawyer to whom Edward alludes repeatedly and enthusiastically in this correspondence. He and his wife Eliza Holbrook had been married in 1821. Erasmus was only ten years older than his niece, and his wife appears to have been a high-spirited and sociable young woman.

1
Edward to Emily Norcross
8 February 1826

Northampton, February 8, 1826

My Dear Friend,

In attempting, unsolicited, to address by so familiar a title, one with whom I have had so little opportunity of becoming acquainted, I am sensible that I hazard much—and expose myself to the charge of unwelcome intrusion. But, relying on your candor, I have thus presumed to address you upon a subject, on which reason and inclination prompt me to speak, but which delicacy & prudence and my regard for the feelings of one, from whom I received so much civility, while a comparative stranger, hardly suffer me to broach.

And while I was very agreeably disappointed in the whole aspect of things in Monson, & much better pleased with the place & the people, than I expected—and while I pay my tribute of gratitude to those who contributed to my pleasure—my amusement & instruction while engaged in the most uninteresting of every thing called business, I owe it to myself & to you, to acknowledge, that I am greatly indebted to *you* for the social enjoyment I experienced—and do not charge me with an attempt to flatter, when I say, that from our short interviews, I imbibed an attachment for you, which I shall continue to cherish, and shall regard with peculiar esteem, a person, in whom so many of the female virtues are conspicuous, and which have drawn from me, thus early, this unequivocal testimony of my respect. And should it be agreeable to you, after making what enquiries you wish respecting me, that our acquaintance should be continued & become more intimate, I should be happy to cherish a friendship, which a regard for your virtues has already inspired, and which, if reciprocated, might pro-

mote our mutual happiness. Will you please to inform me, whether
my proposal is agreeable to you? And while we ought to have a fair
understanding on subjects so intimately connected with our happi-
ness, be assured, that whatever may be your reply, I shall ever cherish
for you that peculiar esteem which is due to the amiable & virtuous. I
shall be happy to hear from you, soon. How is your health—& that of
your mother & brother, and William.¹ Accept, for the good people of
Monson, my best respects, & for yourself, my affectionate regard.

Your sincere friend,
Edward Dickinson

P.S. I have just recd a letter from Mr. Warriner, & at the same mo-
ment, a call from Col. Burbank, both of which more than any thing,
except the pleasure of hearing Parson Coleman preach at Amherst the
Sabbath after I left Monson, brought fresh to mind the scenes which
afforded so much enjoyment.—²

1. Emily Norcross was the third of nine children, but three of her siblings were
already dead in 1826. Her oldest brother Hiram was born in 1800, married
Amanda Brown in about 1822, fathered a child in 1823, and lived in a separate
house on the property of his father. His health was uncertain and he died of tu-
berculosis in 1829. Thus, in 1826, Emily Norcross was the oldest living child in
her parents' house. Her brother William Otis (born in 1806) was a student at
Yale and graduated in 1826. The preceding year he had been forced to withdraw
from college because of illness. In January 1826, Edward probably also met
Lavinia (born in 1812), Alfred (born in 1815), and Joel Warren (born in 1821).
At that time, therefore, Lavinia was almost fourteen, Alfred ten, and Joel Warren
four. The twenty-two-year-old Emily undoubtedly had some maternal responsi-
bility for her considerably younger siblings, but in this correspondence Emily
never describes herself as taking charge of her sister or brothers. Although her
mother died in 1829 at the age of fifty-two of tuberculosis, it is unclear how seri-
ous Betsy Fay Norcross's illness was perceived to be during the courtship. Neither
Emily nor Edward refers to her as terminally ill nor uses the word *consumption*
or any other diagnostic word to describe her health.

2. Mr. Warriner is S. Warriner, Jr., a native of Springfield, Massachusetts, who
was courting Emily's cousin Olivia Flynt. A Lieutenant Colonel Christopher Bur-
bank was summoned to be court-martialed in late January 1826 for having ab-
sented himself from serving in a military court in Monson earlier that month.
Otherwise he is unidentified. Assuming that this is the same Colonel Burbank, he
must have been exonerated or the penalty was light; Edward does not refer to
him as a guilty man. Parson Coleman is Edward's close friend Lyman Coleman,
who married Emily's Monson cousin Maria Flynt later in the year.

Emily waited approximately three weeks before answering Edward's letter, in part because she had been ill but also because she felt uncomfortable writing "to one with whom my acquaintance has been so short." Cautiously, she refused to commit herself to the exploratory, romantic correspondence he had proposed, especially before seeing him again.

2
Emily Norcross to Edward
1 March 1826

Monson March 1st

Respected Friend

With pleasure I acknowledge the reception of your letter which you undoubtedly presumed would be unexspected to me, as I recieved no intimations of the kind in our last interview. Yet I designed favouring you with an answer before this, had I not been afflicted with indisposition of which I have been unable to write but when I reflect that I am writing to one with whom my acquaintance has been so short, I can hardly exercise the freedom I would desire. Still I will say to you, that I realised much happiness in your society while at Monson. It likewise gave me pleasure to recieve inteligence from you, which I did not anticipate, with respect to the subject you propose and which you justly observed that our happiness was so much interested. Perhaps it would not be prudence in me to give you a definite answer at present, as I may be permited to see you again. Yet I am sensible that you have confered your friendship upon one who is undeserving. I think of no occurence in Monson that will excite your curiosity very much except that Rev Mr Coleman has again favoured us with his presence. I imagine that he is quite persevering but perhaps not unusualy so for a clergyman in speculations of the kind.[1] He has not yet address[ed] us from the desk I conclude however that his third visit will accomplish that object. Your friend Mr Petengil has left us which we regret very much.[2] Brother William writes to me that he has been very much affected with the influensy but is now recovering of it. Perhaps you may have experience[d] something of the fashion as impartiality is one of its principle characteristics. My friends at home are better than when you left Monson.[3] I shall hear from you with pleasure.

Yours with respect E Norcross

1. Emily's circuitous language is enlisted here in the service of her sense of humor. She is referring to Coleman's perseverance in courting her cousin.
2. Emily is referring to Amos Pettingell, a Yale graduate who was an instructor at Monson Academy in 1825 and for several months in 1826.

3. Both Edward and Emily use the word "friends" to include friends and relatives. Presumably she is referring to her mother and brother Hiram; in Letter 1, Edward had inquired about their health.

On 20 March, Edward took his younger brother Samuel to Monson Academy, where Samuel enrolled as a boarding student. Of course he also visited Emily again. After this visit, Edward felt awkward about writing to her before receiving another letter. He waited almost three weeks before writing Letter 3. By his count, however, this was Letter 4. (On 16 March, Edward wrote a letter that is no longer extant, which may have been destroyed or mislaid by Emily.) Therefore, one questions his claim that he emerged from his visit to Monson "in the full assurance of meeting a reciprocation of my sentiments," although "the fresh glow of cordiality which our last interview inspired" sounds genuine. Characteristically, Edward denies his doubts; his defensiveness takes the form of an assertion that he is not defensive.

Edward's concern with manliness, which he links to "exertion," is apparent in this letter and dominates much of his subsequent courtship correspondence. He also sought to delineate the separate sphere of womanliness, a subject with which he had been much concerned in Letter 1, in which he had praised Emily as a model of female excellence. In Letter 3, did Edward mean to exempt Emily from his critique of female education? Or was his belief that "the plan of education hitherto adopted, has been greatly deficient" a partly unconscious response to the fact that Emily was poorly educated? This is a difficult matter to assess, because Edward's educational program was designed to fit women for and to keep women in their proper social place—as wives, mothers, and helpmeets. Yet the tense in which he links Emily to his ideally accomplished woman is the hortative subjunctive. "May all these excellencies," he writes, "be yours." Similarly, in Letter 5, he exhorts, "May you excel in every virtue, be universally esteemed—& be an ornament to your sex." And in Letter 7 he writes, "That you may increase in all your virtues & receive the happiness due to your merits, 'is my heart's desire, fervent prayer.'—May you be all that is excellent & amiable & lovely."

Emily Norcross had neither the intellectual training nor the personal inclination to engage in abstract disputation, even when the subject at hand was the status of women. Thus, although she could be stubborn and unyielding about what seemed to her more substantive, practical matters, she refused to be drawn into feminist or antifeminist controversy. At this stage in their correspondence, her most pow-

erful weapon was silence, and her next letter was not written until a month later. In it, she expressed a vaguely inattentive "aprobation" of his views. Her ability to shrug off Edward's subtly coercive, proscriptive style was undoubtedly enhanced by the passage of time. In fairness to Edward, however, it should be noted that when speaking of the duties of both men and women, he consistently stressed service to some community—whether society at large or the family.

3
Edward to Emily Norcross
10 April 1826

Northampton, Monday Eve, April 10, 1826.

My Dear Emily,

.The pleasure of writing to our friends, is exceeded only by seeing them; and while distance prevents a frequent enjoyment of the latter, it can not deprive us of the peculiar happiness which we may, at all times, derive from the former.

And while nothing affords me a more satisfying & agreeable relief from the fatigue ever attendant on studious habits, than a free & unrestrained intercourse with my friends; so, in their absence, the same pleasure may be experienced, in a degree, by a familiar epistolary correspondence. And as it has been some weeks since our last interview, & I have not recd. any communication from you, I shall not longer lose the pleasure of writing, in waiting for intelligence from you, but send my third epistle without regard to "forms or ceremonies"—& proceed in the full assurance of meeting a reciprocation of my sentiments, in one whom I have been led to regard with so much esteem. And I should not do myself justice not to acknowledge the pleasure that I experienced in your society, while at Monson, and the fresh glow of cordiality which our last interview inspired. I shall cherish the recollection of it with that fond delight, which now succeeds the rational & virtuous intercourse between friends attached to each other by a "kindred feeling," & that sympathy of spirit, known only to those "who relish the sweets of social converse," & who realize the truth of the Poet's lines,

> "For affection bids distance defiance,"
> "Its ardor no absence can change:"
> "And the links of this *Holy Alliance*,"
> "Extend through creation's vast range."[1]

This pleasure is heightened to one whose almost constant attention to the severest duties, & the necessity of mingling with all classes of society in the performance of his business, would tend to abstract from all contemplation of those refined & pure enjoyments which are only felt in the scenes of domestic quiet—while all is still & tranquil—and where all that gives zest to life, alone is experienced. And while men enjoy a satisfaction in engaging with energy in the discharge of all the duties of the places they occupy, and feel the warmth which ambition excites, & that greatness & dignity & manliness which a laudable desire to excel in virtue & goodness & knowledge, our fellows—and while the eagerness & zeal with which men pant for honor & renown—the thirst for fame which urges them forward, and that insatiable desire of power which gives rise to innumerable wild & visionary schemes—and that ignorance of real life which induces men to build so many "airy castles," may each & all in their turn, furnish food to the mind, & yield a temporary satisfaction,—Yet the pleasure of retiring, at the close of a day crowded with business, into the bosom of [?] domestic circle, produces a calmness & happiness, which all the tumultuous joys can not equal.

I would by no means, be understood, to say that men should not make exertion—that they must not mingle with their fellow-men—that they should devote themselves to the continual enjoyment of these quiet scenes;—far from it. All men should feel that there is a vast field for exertion—that the world presented a scene in which, to be happy, men must be active & energetic. A thousand motives to energy meet them on every side—The happiness of their fellow men, by the improvement of their moral condition—the diffusion of knowledge, the establishment of useful institutions of a civil & religious & literary character, & the augmentation of the means of improvement of every description—and above all, a desire to discharge the duties of life in a manner worthy of existence—to attain the great end for which all men were endowed with faculties of so exalted a character, are sufficient to excite in the mind a disposition to exert all its powers, & to animate it in the pursuit of knowledge & virtue & happiness. There is no limit to the power of exertion—schemes the most vast, & plans the most grand and magnificent have been accomplished and still other schemes & other plans of equal magnitude present themselves. And it is truly a happy reflection that exertion meets with its reward—We live in a country & in an age when all offices & honors are held out to the deserving, and where the man of merit—the man of untiring energy & perseverance can hardly fail of promotion—& where a man of decision & determination & resolution & energy of character, seldom fails of success.—But these remarks do not apply exclusively to men. Females, also, have a sphere of action, which, tho' different entirely in its kind, from that of our own sex, is yet no less important. Scarcely any subject, if we have a right to judge from what daily presents itself to a close observer of character, is so little understood, as that of female education. And tho' all may not agree with me, in opinion, respecting it, yet it needs but little examination, to convince an unprejudiced mind, that the plan of education hitherto adopted, has been greatly deficient, in some respects, & erroneous in others. The sphere of their action is vastly different from that of the other sex. And were I to direct their mode of education, I should propose a plan which should tend the most directly to make them what, in my estimation, constitutes the perfection of female character—An amiable disposition—modest & unassuming manners—a thorough knowledge of every branch of domestic economy—good sense, cultivated & improved by a moderate acquaintance with a few of the most select works of taste, & an acquaintance & frequent intercourse with refined society & a happy contentment & equanimity of character, & a desire to promote the happiness of all around her, constitute the essence of female excellence. These, in fact, constitute the perfection of female character.—And she who possesses these qualities & qualifications is worthy of the esteem & unceasing respect of all who move in her sphere, & constitute a part of her circle of acquaintance. May all these excellencies be yours, & may you be as happy as their perfect enjoyment can make you.

I saw Mr. Stimpson & Lady, at Springfield, on my return from Monson—& also Mrs. Erasmus Norcross, at Mr. Carews, where Mr. Warriner & myself spent a part of the evening.[2]

Mr. Gillet from your place thinks of moving to Amherst—I saw him there when I returned from Monson—[3]

I feel anxious about my brother, at your Academy—and fear he will not conduct himself properly. How is it?—[4]

Will you write as soon as convenient after receiving this, if agreeable to you; for be assured that nothing will afford me more pleasure than to hear of your health & happiness—& that I shall continue to regard you with the highest esteem.

Your devoted friend Edward Dickinson

P.S. Remember me to your little sister—& your father's family—& Mrs. E. Norcross—How is you brother's health?[5]—How is Wm etc?—

1. This quotation remains to be identified. In *The Life of Emily Dickinson*, 1:45–46, Richard B. Sewall suggests that some of the poetry "quotations" may

have been written by Edward himself, but I think this unlikely. In the letters that comprise this edition, Edward quotes from the Bible and from the poetry of Shakespeare, Addison, Pope, and Young.

2. Edward and Emily already had a number of acquaintances in common. An Austin Stimpson wrote to Edward from Brimfield on 17 July 1826 and on 7 August 1826, when Edward asked him to check into the opportunities there for a lawyer. Apparently his family owned a prosperous store. Otherwise the Stimpsons are unidentified. "Mr. Carew" was presumably from Springfield. Note that Edward often refers to friends of his own age such as Warriner as "Mr."

3. Unidentified.

4. The accounts of Samuel Dickinson's experience are spotty. According to Richard B. Sewall, "Samuel Fowler, Jr., went to New York and then entered business in Savannah, Georgia" (*Life of Emily Dickinson*, 1:51n). According to Millicent Todd Bingham in *Emily Dickinson's Home: Letters of Edward Dickinson and His Family* (New York: Harper, 1955), p. 510, Samuel was born in 1811, married in 1834, had two children, and died in 1886. There is a troubled letter that he wrote to Edward in 1831 in Leyda, *The Years and Hours of Emily Dickinson*, 1:16. But in 1835, when his father's family was suffering from a variety of misfortunes, he appears to have been prosperous and generous toward his relatives. See Catharine Dickinson's letter to her brother Edward in Leyda, 1:27–28. Samuel Fowler, Jr., never attended college and Edward may have anticipated that he would not be a good student at Monson Academy.

5. Edward is referring to Hiram.

As I have already suggested, Edward's "separate sphere" philosophy tended to slight women's intellectual development and to stress "modest & unassuming manners." Yet in practice, Edward also attempted to stimulate Emily intellectually, especially during the early stages of the courtship. He hoped that she would enjoy reading twelve volumes of the Spectator *and sent her three. Since Emily was not much of a reader, this aspiration was wide of the mark.*

4
Edward to Emily Norcross
2 May 1826

Northampton May 2, 1826.

My Dear Friend,

I send you by the Stage, three volumes of the Spectator, which you will find interesting, instructive & amusing. The three first vols. are lent; otherwise I should have sent them.—But as there is no connection between them, but each volume consists of distinct, independent essays, it makes no difference which is read first.

I shall send the rest, (12 vols. in the whole) at a future time—together with such other books, as I think it will please you to read.[1]

Accept the renewed assurance of my high esteem & regard, and believe that your happiness will ever give me much pleasure.

Shall I not hear from you, soon?

Your sincere & devoted friend
E. Dickinson.

1. Edward's twelve-volume edition of the *Spectator* was published in Philadelphia in 1819. Inscribed "E. Dickinson 1825," it now forms part of the Houghton Library collection of "Books Found in the Home of Emily Dickinson at Amherst, Massachusetts, Spring, 1950."

5
Edward to Emily Norcross
3 May 1826

Northampton May 3, 1826—

My Dear Friend,

Rev. Mr. C. is now in town, & has this moment, politely reminded me that he should visit Monson to-morrow—and as politely offerred to take any commands from me to that quarter—and though I have but 15. minutes I can not let so good a chance pass, to enquire after your health, and also to remind you that you have not favored me with a letter since I saw you—

I have merely time to say that I should be gratified to hear from you, and to tell you that my desire to form a more intimate acquaintance with you, as expressed in my first letter, has not diminished—and that your happiness will always be a source of pleasure to me—in any event—and in whatever light you may regard my proposition, I shall ever esteem it a happy circumstance, that so valuable an acquaintance has been added to my circle—May you excel in every virtue, be universally esteemed—& be an ornament to your sex—& ever be happy.—

The day is beautiful—the face of nature begins to look cheering and animating—

The Supreme Court is now sitting in town—There is a Junior Exhibition in Amherst College, next week—Would it not be a pleasant ride for you & your brother, to come up—Wednesday—2 P.M.—

The time has expired—the Parson is waiting—& the hour has almost arrived when it becomes my duty to deliver a Legal Dissertation before the Society composed of the Law School, over which I have the honor to preside.¹ I must close—A bad pen & great haste, are my apology for the looks of this letter. Your devoted friend

E. Dickinson—

Parson C. & Miss Maria—a fine match?²

1. Apparently Edward was the president of the debating society at his law school.

2. This sentence is preceded by a drawing of a pointing hand, a visual device that Edward occasionally used for emphasis. Lyman Coleman and Maria Flynt were married in September 1826. Edward enjoyed the progress of their romance and often called Emily's attention to it. His statement above, in which he expresses the hope that he and Emily will be friends whether or not she accepts his "proposition" or implied proposal, is intended to flatter her and to save face for himself, should she reject him. Her silence was undermining his confidence in the understanding he thought he had discovered between them when he was in Monson on 20 March.

6
Emily Norcross to Edward
10 May 1826

Monson May 10th

Affectionate Friend

By the politeness of Rev Mr. Coleman I recieved your letter for which I feal myself quite obliged to you I am not surprised that you think it necessary to remind me that I have not written to you, but perhaps I have not been as thoughtless of the subject as you may have supposed. My inability of sending to you is my principle apology, which you may suppose is unworthy of notice I could not consistent with my present fealings send letters by mail which is the only way that I could convey them to you at all. Therefore I have thus delayed But it is quite fortunate for me however that you are not as partial to ceremony as many are.¹ Brother William is now at home which adds very much to my happiness I conclude that you are agreeably entertained this afternoon if you are present at the Exhibition I informed William of the exercises of the day, but my father is absent which renders it inconvenient for him to leave I suspect that you were not disappointed.² I was much interested in the perusal of your first letter I presume the subject is familiar to you, and I will improve this opportunity to express my aprobation of your views, and I certainly desire that you may be so happy as to participate in the excellence which you admire.³ I presume you are solicitous for you[r] brother at Monson I can say but little of him as I seldom see him except at church. I conclude he is well. We consider Mr Coleman as almost a resident I imagine he thinks cousin Maria would make but little progress in her favourite study, devinity without frequent lectures[4] my brother which has so long been ill has to day gone as far as Springfield accompanied with his favourite physician. As I have resorted to my chamber without any one persons knowing how I am occupied I fear I shall soon be enquired for. You must therfore excuse me.[5] Will you have the kindness to direct your letters to William should you write again. Your friend E Norcross

1. Emily was probably unwilling to use the mails because she wished to conceal her correspondence from the postmaster Rufus Flynt, who was her uncle. Concealing her motivation from Edward—note that she does not explain her reasoning—she indirectly equated the desire of a suitor to be reassured with excessive partiality to "ceremony." In fact Edward was both partial to ceremony and in need of reassurance. In praising Edward for his informality, Emily was perhaps attempting to instill this characteristic in him.

At the conclusion of this letter, Emily asked Edward to address future correspondence to her brother William, which he did not do. Whenever Edward could get a friend such as Coleman to hand deliver a letter, however, he took advantage of the opportunity to do so.

2. Perhaps she means that since he was not really expecting her, he could not have been disappointed by her absence.

3. Emily is being maddeningly vague but seems to be saying that she wishes Edward success in courting her. "I presume the subject is familiar to you" means something like "I assume you remember what you wrote." The subject is their marriage. "The excellence which you admire" is apparently an oblique reference to herself or to his professional ambitions or both. His "first letter" is presumably Letter 3, in which he expounded his views on the separate but equally important duties of men and women, among other subjects.

4. Emily's sense of humor surfaces again when she refers to her cousin's favorite study as divinity.

5. The sentences beginning "As I have resorted to my chamber" are difficult to interpret. Apparently Emily has two concerns: that her family will discover that she is writing to Edward and that some demand will be made on her which will prevent her from finishing her letter. Both of these concerns indicate that she had little autonomy at home, yet in other letters she sounds pleased with her life in Monson.

Strangely, Edward says nothing about Emily's letter of 10 May, which he had received. Instead, he begins with an extended meditation on the starry beauty of a May evening; discovers the hand of a benevolent Deity in the soothing atmosphere; considers the differing means by

which men seek to attain a common goal (happiness); describes hu-
man experience as "but a season of preparation for a higher and
brighter state of existence"; exults in the unprecedented opportunities
available to an ambitious American in the modern era ("never was
there a time when our country offerred more avenues to fame, fortune
& honor"); and then returns to a by now familiar theme: female
virtue. With the exception of the concluding paragraphs, this is one of
Edward's least intimate and most public letters.

7
Edward to Emily Norcross
15 May 1826

Northampton, Monday Eve, May 15, 1826

Affectionate Friend,

It is evening—and after a day of excessive heat, it is sweet to feel the refreshing breeze of Eve—and to experience that reviving influence which comes to brace us up, after the relaxing effect which the uncommon warmth of the day has produced.

At this silent hour—when the hum of business has ceased in the streets—and all nature has assumed that tranquility which a May evening scarcely fails to produce—when the fields are rendered vocal by the song of the night-bird—when the Moon is shining in majestic splendor, & gladdening all with her mild & beautiful & softened beams—while the sky is spangled with innumerable stars—the suns of other worlds—the centres of other systems—& around which revolve infinite numbers of inferior luminaries, to cheer & animate & gladden the inhabitants of other planets of equal importance with ourselves—when the budding rose—the blossoming trees & the opening flowers fill the air with a "balmy fragrance," and all enjoy peace & calmness—how pleasing to devote an hour to converse with our "friends" —to exchange the friendly salutation—& enjoy the rational gratification which ever attends the reciprocation of benevolent feeling and affectionate regard.

Never did the face of creation appear more beautiful—never did every thing put on a more lovely aspect—and in no season of the year can we see so much to lead us to a contemplation of the power & goodness & benevolence of the Author—To him who can name the rocks & plants—analyze the flowers—discover beauties in every blade of grass—to him "Who can find tongues in trees,"

"Sermons in stones, books in running brooks,"
"And good in every thing"—[1]

Who can look at the hills & vales & plains by day—& view the "hosts of heaven"—the moon & stars, by night, & in all, trace the hand of a presiding Deity, & recognize the constant care of a benevolent, ever present God, the varied landscape presents to view all that can please the fancy, gratify the taste—improve the imagination & elevate the soul & refine & purify & exalt the mind. Never was there a time when the mind is more disposed to look at the scenes around it with more undisguised simplicity & frankness—while all departments of emotion seem animated with joy, the mind can not but cast off its jealousies & suspicions, while it is happy within itself, it must view all around it with that peculiar complacency, which its inward peace will produce.—

The virtuous mind is made to feel a sentiment of expansive benevolence—and a desire to see all men happy, holds the highest place in the breast.

While the pursuit of happiness is the object of all, how various are the methods taken to obtain it? Some seek it in the haunts of dissipation—some in lives of profligacy & dissoluteness—some in "elegant leisure"—& genteel indolence—some in striving to gain the false & ephemeral honors conferred by the crowd on those who make large pretensions to popular favors—& lose sight of principle in their eagerness for vulgar applause—

But how mistaken are their conceptions—the true road to real happiness lies through a contented spirit, & a virtuous mind—a mind at ease with itself, & "all the world beside"—which delights in doing good—in seeing its fellow men enjoy solid pleasure, which rejoices at the recital of others' happiness & weeps at the tale of others' woes, & which is actuated by that purity of motive—& regulated by that correctness of principle which brings it substantial satisfaction to be able to promote, in the slightest degree, the comfort & enjoyment of all within the sphere of its influence.

In looking at life as a scene of action—it is not a fair medium to behold it thro' the glass of the Poet or the Novelist—it is a stage on which all must act a part—each in his proper sphere—& accord[ing] to his talents—it is but a season of preparation for a higher and brighter state of existence—and business is given to men to call their powers into exercise—to strengthen, enlarge & improve them—& better fit them for the employments for which they are destined—and this is a cheering thought—the idea that all our actions will have a lasting influence upon all our characters is, of itself, one would think, sufficient to stimulate to vigorous action. There is a vast field for enterprise open before us—and all that can excite the ambitious—

CVCA Royal Library
4687 Wyoga Lake Road
Stow, OH. 44224-1011

kindle the zeal—rouse to emulation, & urge us on to glorious deeds is presented to view—Talents & industry & moral worth seldom fail of their reward—and never was there a time when our country offerred more avenues to fame, fortune & honor—exertion & resolution & a principle of decision, united with an unblemished moral character will secure the confidence & love & esteem & influence of all whose respect is worth enjoying—and to obtain happiness in the world, men have but to follow straight in the paths of virtue & integrity & industry—

And while the road to happiness for your sex is somewhat different from the one which we must travel, yet some of the same principles must govern all—Women, have only to be virtuous, innocent, amiable, contented, & industrious—cultivate the domestic virtues, & acquire the graces of society—be benevolent—& do good[2] be charitable & kind to all—relieve the distressed—comfort the afflicted—pour the balm of consolation into the spirit of [the repining?] & sorrowful—& make the happiness of their friends their greatest object.—Improve their hearts & their minds—cultivate that peculiar modesty & sweetness of disposition which will procure the love & affection of the worthy & good. That you may increase in all your virtues & receive the happiness due to your merits, "is my heart's desire, fervent prayer."—May you be all that is excellent & amiable & lovely.

I expect to go to Monson, next Monday after my brother—shall go by way of Springfield on business—& be in Monson, Monday Evening—when, if agreeable, I should be happy to have another interview with you, and in repeating the assurances of my attachment for you—& my regard for the virtues which my acquaintance with you has convinced me you possess, next to hearing of your happiness, would be the pleasure of knowing that my attachment was worthy of reciprocation.

I send you a Novel, called the "Rebels," written by a Miss Francis of Medford near Boston, which, as I borrowed, I should be glad to have you read, so that I can take it, when I come. You will find it interesting. I shall direct the packet to your brother Wm. agreeably to your request.[3] Your sincere friend *E. Dickinson*
"Good night"

Tuesday Morning.
P.S. The Book which I send contains as nicely drawn distinction between virtue & vice, as almost any work of the kind that I ever read & the rewards of each could not be more strikingly illustrated. And while the purity—disinterested benevolence of character which Mr. & Mrs. Percival possessed—the nobleness & generosity & magnanimity

of spirit, of Henry Osborne & Lucretia Fitzherbert, (who finally proved to be Gertrude Wilson) and the amiableness & sweetness of Grace Osborne, united with her unrepining resignation to her hard fate, & her uncomplaining submission to her several[?] trials, excite our admiration & sympathy—the character of Somerville is calculated to excite the most unqualified disgust & indignation—and the fate he merited, every one can not but rejoice he recieved—& "Would to heaven" that such baseness may ever meet a similar reward. *D.*

1. *As You Like It* (2.1.16–17), slightly misquoted.

2. When the letter was unsealed, a small tear in the paper obscured Edward's punctuation. The tear also accounts for the reading in brackets that follows. Some of his other letters were also slightly torn when Emily unsealed them.

3. *The Rebels, or Boston Before the Revolution* was written by Lydia Maria (Francis) Child and published in 1825 before her marriage. Edward is mistaken in supposing that Emily would want to read this 304-page novel before his visit in less than a week. Although he was sending the novel under cover to William, his letter is addressed to Emily and he ignored her desire to keep their correspondence secret, as I have already suggested.

On 23 May, Edward went to Monson to take his brother Samuel home from the Academy and to visit Emily. The letter that follows is a formal proposal of marriage. By now Edward had persuaded himself that Emily possessed the necessary "qualifications" to become his "friend" for life. In declaring his carefully considered and rationally justified esteem for her virtues—virtues that would enable her to render herself and her "friends" happy—Edward erred on the side of passionlessness.

8
Edward to Emily Norcross
4 June 1826

Northampton, Sunday Afternoon, June 4, 1826.

Affectionate Friend,

I am compelled to steal a small portion of the Sabbath, (tho' between meetings,) to enable me to write a letter to send by my friend, Parson Coleman, who goes to Monson to-morrow. And it can hardly be deemed sacrilege, to devote a portion, even of holy time, to our friends—for while all business is suspended—while devotion is universal—the very silence which prevails produces a calmness which those who have mingled in the noise of business during the past week are peculiarly fitted to enjoy—It is a day of rest from the anxieties of the week—& freedom from the cares which engross the other six. And after the fatigue of a week's laborious application to study, & the exhaustion produced by the most oppressive heat, I feel a peculiar pleasure in relaxing myself in social intercourse with my friend.

And tho', from the commencement of our acquaintance, our correspondence has given me much pleasure, yet it has increased with my acquaintance—and from the good understanding which I hope exists between us, you can not suspect me of flattery, if I am plain with you. It is proper, in an intercourse like ours, that the most perfect frankness & ingenuousness should, at all times, prevail, & from what I have expressed in my former letters, you must be satisfied of the opinion which I have entertained of your character—& our last interview, which was much more free & unreserved than any former one, led me to a satisfactory conclusion respecting your qualifications, & convinced me that you possessed virtues calculated to render yourself & your friends happy.—And such reliance do I place on your candor, that I feel perfectly safe in making a most unreserved avowal of my esteem, & in declaring my wish to become a friend for life to you— feeling confident, that if my attachment is not thought worthy of reciprocation, our correspondence will remain unknown to all but ourselves.[1]

In making your conclusion respecting my proposal, you owe it to your own happiness, & the regard you have for your friends to be fully satisfied respecting the character & standing of the person from whom the proposal comes. From what sources you have gained any information of either, I know not—nor do I know that you have made any enquiries—And tho' as you remarked, when I saw you last, that we "ought to form our own opinions, or our own judgments," yet in taking a course, in forming opinions which are to affect us through our lives, it would be unjust in me not to give you a fair *opportunity* to ascertain my real character. I can refer you to any gentleman in my native town—Judge Howe, or Mr. Mills, in Northampton[2]—and almost any clergyman in the neighboring towns—for as my father's business has necessarily led me considerably abroad, my acquaintance is somewhat extensive—To any of these, or any other source you please, I am willing to refer you. Of any member of the Law school, also, I am willing you should enquire—and if it was [?] necessary, I could refer you to Gentlemen abroad in whom you might place the most perfect confidence. For my character in College, Mr. Coleman can answer.[3]—But I have discharged my duty in this respect, & I say no more.—

I have said thus much upon this topic, because, notwithstanding my settled desire to form a permanent connection with you, & my full conviction of your merits & your virtues, I do not wish you to risk yourself on my protection without you are satisfied of a reasonable expectation of having your happiness secured—and however strong my attachment may be for you, if you have good reason to believe that you expose yourself to unhappiness, thro' your life, certainly you ought to decline my addresses. It would be a source of unceasing regret to me, if I should persuade you to join yourself with me, & too late you should discover faults, or traits of character which were inconsistent with your enjoyment—Your happiness is too dear to me, to suffer me to wish, for the sake of increasing my own, to do anything which should endanger yours—and nothing can afford me more substantial pleasure than to know that you experience that degree of happiness which your amiable qualities can not fail to secure to you—& I shall rejoice, if after due consideration, you can feel a confidence in making me the guardian of your happiness, & your person. My life must be a life of business—of laborious application to the study of my profession—for no profession requires such continual devotedness & such untiring perseverance as ours. The whole course of practice & the new works on different branches of the Law are undergoing such changes & receiving such additions, that, to attain any thing like eminence, a man must be industrious & patient & persevering & constant in his attention to his professional duties. And notwithstanding the great number of Lawyers, there are comparatively few who can claim anything like a moderate title to distinction, & never was true merit better rewarded—& never was there a time, when men of solid acquirements, were more highly regarded, & more needed, than the present.

And tho' it is perfectly natural that I should feel an ardent attachment to the study of my profession, having always been about my father's office, when at home;[4] yet, aside from any feeling which arises from my own connection with it, there is certainly something in the study & practice of the Law, calculated to enlarge & liberalise & ennoble the Mind—which leads it to take a broad view, & learn & trace the history & progress of the relations of our own country with every other—Seek the causes of things—discover the origin & the reason of the changes which have taken place in Laws, Manners & customs; in Governments & nations—& enable a person who makes a proper use of his opportunities, to become familiarly acquainted with the human character, and from an intimate knowledge of the circumstances & wants of all classes of Society, to devise the most effectual means for promoting their happiness—which is the great end of all society—& the object for which society was formed. And when a Lawyer, to a thorough knowledge of Law, adds an acquaintance with science & literature, a knowledge of human nature, an amiable disposition and a desire to promote the happiness of his fellow men & to all this, adds an ability to redress the injured & avenge the wronged, to convince by his reasoning & charm by his eloquence, he mixes with society upon more than equal terms—and if after the anxieties of days & weeks amid the bustle of business, he can retire into the bosom of his family, that picture of heaven, & there meet the smiles & the benevolent feelings of its happy inmates, & be conscious of deserving them, he enjoys all the happiness tha[t] men can experience, "this side heaven."—He enjoys the esteem & confidence & the love of all classes of society, & his fame & fortune keep pace with his happiness.—I beg pardon for my long digression—

Will you write, if you can, by Mr. Coleman—and I should be very glad to know how your friends regarded our intercourse. If agreeable possibly I may visit you in a few weeks—I can now fix no time.

Whenever you have formed your opinion respecting my proposal, please to communicate it—Take your own time—& believe that whether communicated sooner or later, immediately or at a more future time, & whether you feel safe in reciprocating my attachment or not, I shall not cease to cherish that esteem for you which your virtues deserve: at the same time, I assure you that next to your happiness would be the pleasure of knowing that I was worthy of your lasting affection.—

I remain as ever Most affectionately Yours. Edward Dickinson—.

Remember me to your mother, brother & sister—I sent Wm. Mr. B. & C.s pamphlet respecting the "Round Hill" school, & now send him another that belongs with it.⁵ How is your sick brother? Has Wm. returned to college?—

If you can not write by Mr. C. will you send by some other conveyance, soon—

Excuse the length of this letter & I will promise not to send another of such an unmerciful prolixity—

1. Edward must be referring to the substance of their correspondence; the fact of their correspondence was hardly a secret.

2. The Northampton Law School (1823 to c. 1829) was also known as the Howe and Mills Law School, after its founders Samuel Howe and Elijah Hunt Mills. Mills, one of the most prominent lawyers in western Massachusetts, was a

congressman from 1815 to 1820 and a United States senator from 1820 to 1827. Howe was an associate justice of the newly established Court of Common Pleas in Northampton. In 1826, he was chosen by the legislature to fill a vacancy on the Amherst College board of trustees. Edward was deeply affected by Howe's untimely death in 1828 (see Letters 74 and 89).

3. Lyman Coleman graduated from Yale in 1817, where he was a tutor and divinity student when Edward was an undergraduate. During the intervening years (1817–20) he was principal of the Latin Grammar School in Hartford and was ordained at the Congregational Church in Belchertown in the fall of 1825. See also Letter 12, n. 5.

4. Samuel Fowler Dickinson was a successful lawyer who had already begun to neglect his practice. In a triumph of bad judgment, he sacrificed his personal welfare and that of his family for Amherst College. Samuel Fowler was one of the principal founders of the College, which admitted its first students in 1821. Edward attended Amherst during the first and third terms of his junior year in 1821–22 because of his father's inability to pay the bills at Yale. Edward's brother William, however, wrote him an impassioned letter cautioning against this venture. On 25 September 1821 he urged, "Now as you value your future interest Remain at N Haven do not follow till you know whether the 1st man has fallen into the ditch." See Dickinson Family Papers.

Edward was attending Amherst under duress, and in November 1821 he was one of two Amherst College students who, according to a protest letter written by President Zephaniah Swift Moore, "drank to excess . . . [and] behaved in a very indecent and riotous manner, and made great disturbance in and about the Institution [Amherst College], to the extreme annoyance of those residing in it, till one o'clock or later." See Frederick Tuckerman, *Amherst Academy: A New England School of the Past, 1814–1861* (Amherst: Printed for the Trustees, 1929), p. 71. Moore's letter was addressed to the officials of Amherst Academy, since a number of Academy students precipitated the incident by inviting Edward and one Philander Grey to an "oyster supper."

5. The future historian George Bancroft founded the Round Hill School in Northampton in 1823, together with Joseph Green Cogswell. An experimental, college preparatory school for boys—gymnastics was required as part of the curriculum—it attracted considerable attention during the 1820s. Bancroft abandoned the venture in 1830.

9
Edward to Emily Norcross
18 June 1826

Northampton, Sunday Morning, June 18, 1826.

My Dear Emily,

The fact of my writing letters on Sunday will be sufficiently explained by telling you that the purpose of study during the week renders it somewhat inconvenient for me to devote any other time to it, and I do not know that the most scrupulously conscientious can call the practice improper—tho' I should choose a different time, myself.

Mr. Coleman informed me last week, when here at an ecclesiastical meeting, that he should pass through Monson, to-morrow, on his way to Hartford, & you know too much of my disregard of ceremony, to make an apology for a second letter, while the first remains unanswered, necessary. For I conclude it is not *convenient* for *you* to write; and presume from your silence, that it will not be unacceptable to recieve & read epistles, even tho' they should not observe all the punctilio of a formal correspondence. I write, because I wish to write.

The last letter which I expected Mr. C. to carry, it seems, was intrusted to the care of a third person, under cover of a communication to Miss Flint [Flynt], but I presume you have recd. it—In it, I conversed, (if so I may call it,) freely on the subject of our proposed connection, & expressed my views & feelings in relation to it—as it is a subject, which, of all others, deserves the most considerate & candid & deliberate meditation.

The institution of marriage, as it is one of the first ever established, so it is one of the highest importance & most solemn interest—It is one in which our happiness most intimately depends—It was designed by the Deity that the sexes should be united—The enjoyment of each depends much on an association of persons of similar tastes & dispositions—of similar views & feelings—and it is not puerile or improper, that on a subject on which I hope we understand each other, we should be perfectly plain & use the utmost freedom of remark.

I have not attempted to conceal from you, my wish in relation to forming a more intimate friendship with you—I have not hesitated to propose the formation of a permanent relation—and I have frankly avowed my intention & communicated to you my mind. I have become convinced of your merits, & have endeavoured to refer you to sources, from which you might derive any information in relation to my character, which so short a personal acquaintance, might render perfectly proper you should have, if you wished it—and it adds much to your prudence, that you have not given me any definite decision till you could have sufficient time to know with whom you were treating.

You owed it as a duty to yourself & to your friends to act understandingly, and it is a trait of character which always gives dignity & respect to every person who possesses it; & the more so, from its being comparatively rare.

I think some of passing thro' Monson in the course of two or three weeks, & it is not impossible but I may be at Springfield, on the 26th, at the celebration of the Festival of St. John[1]—I. C. Bates Esq. of

Northampton is to deliver an address on the occasion, & from his well known talent at writing fine orations, something excellent may be expected of him, at that time.[2] If convenient for me to take my tour at that time, I may go that way, & from there to Monson, etc.

Will not many of your people be at Springfield, then? Will not Mrs. E. Norcross—and can you not go as well as not? If I go, I should be pleased to meet you there. Will you send me word whether you shall, or not?

I have not, as yet, formed any settled determination, as to a place for establishing myself in business—and my tour, whenever I take it, will be with a view of assisting me to form an opinion where I can settle with the greatest prospect of finding good society & a sufficiency of professional business. I have occasional foretastes of the pleasures of practice, in appearing before a Justice of the Peace in behalf of some poor criminal who wants his cause pleaded, gratis!

I have had an invitation from Am. College to deliver an Oration, in that place on the evening "4th of July"—but owing to the late notice, & the shortness of the time for preparation, (being only a fortnight,), I have not yet determined whether to accept the invitation or not. Rev. Mr. Fiske, one of the Professors, was first appointed with me for his substitute, & his health is such that he can not perform.[3]—If I undertake, I shall not be at Springfield, at the time above mentioned. (I did not discover this *breach* in my paper till I came to it.—You must excuse it.)—[4]

Mr. Coleman offered very kindly, to convey any letters from me to you, under cover of letters to Miss Flint—& proposed to talk with her about taking any thing from you to me, through the medium of letters from her to him—You can have the most perfect confidence in Mr. C.—& if Maria consents to it, & you are not unwilling to entrust your communications with her, it would open a convenient mode of conveyance. Mr. C. proposed the plan & said he should mention it to Maria: & no one but those two, need know any thing of the letters that pass between us. You can improve this suggestion, or not, as you please. I propose it merely on your account. Please to write to me, as soon as convenient, after you recieve this—Remember me to your Mother, & family, & Mrs. E. Norcross—How is your brother, who has been ill—& how is William—When do you expect him home?

Mr. C. will call on you, & you will find him a good, sensible, amiable & sociable man—You can not but like him. I congratulate Maria on the prospect of so good a husband—& Mr. C. on the certainty of so good a wife. My prayers for their happiness will follow them.—

Recieve, again, the assurance of my lasting affection. My most cordial wishes for your continued & increasing happiness—& may the choicest blessings rest upon you—and if I am worthy of your affection, nothing could afford me more pleasure than to be the lawful promoter of your lasting enjoyment. The clock strikes *ten*. I must prepare for meeting.

I am ever Yours,
Edward Dickinson

1. The reference is to the Festival of the Nativity of Saint John the Baptist.

2. Isaac Chapman Bates (1780–1845), a Whig lawyer and well-known orator who was active in Massachusetts politics, served in the United States House of Representatives for three terms beginning in 1827. He was elected to fill a vacancy in the Senate in 1842.

3. There were two Reverend Fiskes in Amherst in 1826, but Edward is referring to Nathan Welby, the professor of Greek language and literature, and professor of belles lettres, who was an expert on the battles of the American Revolution. Nathan Welby Fiske is perhaps best remembered today as the father of the poet, short-story writer, and novelist Helen (Fiske) Hunt Jackson. Helen Hunt Jackson was a friend of the poet Emily Dickinson's later years and hoped to be her literary executrix. See *Letters of Emily Dickinson*, vols. 2 and 3, passim.

4. There is a small crease in Edward's paper at this point that appears to have been caused by the manufacturer.

Edward apparently postponed his trip to Springfield because he had not heard from Emily. Springfield is about seventeen miles west of Monson and he hoped to meet her there. He also decided against accepting the invitation he had received to deliver a Fourth of July oration at Amherst. This is one of his more fragmented letters.

10
Edward to Emily Norcross
26 June 1826

Amherst June 26, 1826
"Festival of St. John."

My Dear Emily,

I came here on Saturday afternoon [24 June], & finding that the celebration of "St. John's Festival" was postponed till today [Monday], I was induced to remain for the purpose of hearing the address of our friend Rev. Mr. Colton.[1]

And by him I improve the opportunity of adding another, to the two letters which I have already written to you, since hearing any thing directly from you.

I had intended to be at Springfield to-day, where, if it had been fair, I hoped to meet you—and I then should have gone to Monson & Brimfield. My intention now is to take that course after the "4th of July"—probably the day after, when I should be happy to have another interview with you, if agreeable.

I wrote you in my last by Mr. C. that I had recd. an appointment to deliver an Oration at Amherst, at the approaching anniversary of Independence, but owing to the shortness of the notice & my pressure of study, I concluded to decline the acceptance of the invitation.

Great preparation for the celebration [of 4 July] is making at Northampton, I shall return there this afternoon, or to-morrow.

How is your health, & that of all your friends? How do you enjoy yourself this summer, & what is there doing in M. [Monson] to animate & cheer the people. Have you seen Mr. Stimpson & Lady of late? Parson Coleman, you have probably seen—and no doubt you are as well pleased with him as I am.

Will you write me by the mail of Thursday, if convenient, if you have not already written? I want to hear from you. Mr. Colton passed last night with us, & will return to-day.

I need not renew the assurance of my highest & lasting affection, & tell you that I remain as ever, *Yours*, truly. In the greatest haste. Have no more time, now.

E. Dickinson

P.S. We have just had a most excellent address from Mr. Colton, and it is but justice to say that it is not inferior to any thing of the kind that I ever heard. Undoubtedly a copy will be requested for the press, & I hope he will be disposed to grant one.

He said to me that Mr. Coleman did not go to Monson as he expected, on Monday week, but was to preach at Wilbraham yesterday & go to M. on Sabbath Evening, & if he did, he is of course weather-bound, & will be obliged to remain stationary, till the storm, which is here almost a tempest, abates. However, his confinement, I presume, is a pleasant one—& would need no artificial means to make him contented with his lot. Success to him!

May peace, prosperity, & happiness, together with all the rest of the blessings of heaven rest upon you & your friends.

Again Yours Affectionately,
E. Dickinson

1. The Reverend Simeon M. Colton was headmaster of Monson Academy and delivered the lectures in chemistry Emily and Edward attended together in Janu-

ary 1826 when they first met. He graduated from Yale in about 1806 and was a native of Longmeadow. The Academy flourished under his management.

Although Emily still had not responded to his proposal, on 5 July Edward visited Monson. In the following letter, he continued to pressure her to respond to his proposal, while also urging her to "Take your own time & your own way."

11
Edward to Emily Norcross
11 July 1826

Northampton July 11. 1826

My Dear Emily,

I send you some pamphlets which I presume it will give you pleasure to read—and I send them *now*, that you may finish them & return them by our friend Mr. Coleman, who informed me that he should visit Monson on Monday next.[1]

An opportunity to rest has restored my spirits, & removed my cold, which, in the absence of all other arguments, would be sufficient to prove that the mind's residence is in the *brain*—and in truth I must say to you that I do not recollect a week, in which I have been so completely destitute of sociability as I was, during the last—and lest you should impute it to my *indifference*, I owe it to you, to acknowledge that I never experienced so much pleasure in your society as at our last interview, and to say freely, as I have more than once before said, that my attachment to you has increased with my acquaintance.

And were I conscious of *meriting* a *reciprocation* of my *regard*, I should request you, as soon as prudence would permit, to communicate the result of your examination & enquiries, in such a manner, as should seem most likely to be conducive to your happiness—

Take your own time & your own way, & whatever will most promote *your* happiness, will in the same degree contribute to *mine*.

I was gratified to hear before I left Monson, that your brother was better—

I heard also from my Mother when I reached home, & found her health much improved by her ride to the Springs—hope her stay there will restore her entirely.[2]

Remember me most affectionately to your kind Mother & Sister—& present my compliments to Mr. & Mrs. Erasmus Norcross—

I shall probably write by Mr. C. on Monday. Wm. I believe, will return from New Haven next week—

If convenient, let me hear from you by Mr. C.

Mr. Bancroft's Oration on the "*4th*" *inst.* is to be published, & when it is so, I shall send *Wm.* a copy—[3]

Accept again the assurance of my lasting affection—and believe me truly, *Yours.*

Edward

P.S. I include a Note to you in this wrapper, lest some one might be disposed to untie the books & read the contents of the "billet"—[4]

July 11. 1826—   Edward

1. These pamphlets are no longer extant and cannot be identified. Edward's letter was written on a Tuesday so that he was giving Emily six days to read them. There is no indication that she did so.

2. This is one of Edward's rare references to his mother, Lucretia Gunn Dickinson (1775–1840).

3. *An Oration Delivered on the Fourth of July* was published by Shepard and Company, Northampton, in 1826. See Russel B. Nye, *George Bancroft: Brahmin Rebel* (New York: Knopf, 1944), p. 327.

4. By "wrapper" Edward probably means wrapping paper or package. There is nothing unusual about the appearance of this letter.

Inspired by the almost simultaneous deaths of John Adams and Thomas Jefferson, Edward expressed his determination to "follow their example, and to reach the summit of the Temple of fame" through "untiring industry, unyeilding courage, and a steady perseverance." Invoking the examples of "Pres. Monroe, Daniel Webster and the host of brilliant characters whose talents & exertions & resolution & determination to be great, have raised them to the highest honors in the State," he also expressed a fervent interest in female education—without, however, mentioning any specific role models for women to emulate.

12
Edward to Emily Norcross
12 July 1826

Northampton, Wednesday Eve, July 12. 1826.

My Dear Emily,

Oppressed with excessive heat, and fatigued with more than ordinary application to study, since my return, I gladly relax from the severity of business, and devote the evening hour, which my fellows are spending in cool retreats, to my friend; and rejoice at an opportunity of holding even a short & hasty *paper interview* with one for whom I feel so peculiar an interest, and to whom it always gives me pleasure to write.

The news-papers from all directions are dressed in mourning. The tidings of the decease of the Ex-Presidents, Adams & Jefferson, meet you at every turn, & salute your ears from all quarters.[1] The time of their death—the coincidence of the events—and the circumstances attending each, form a most remarkable occurence; and the thousand hurried associations which press upon the mind, and the vast field at once opened to the eye of imagination, while they impress the mind with the most varied emotions of solemnity, and draw from us the most humble resignation to the afflicting dispensations of a wise Providence, can not fail, at the same time, to fill us with wonder & admiration at the wisdom & benevolence & omnipotence of that Being whose "mysteries are unsearchable, & his ways past finding out."[2]

The pride, the glory, & the ornament of our country—the first among the authors of our independence—the framers & signers of the Constitution of our happy form of government—and the instruments of procuring those invaluable blessings which distinguish us from every other nation under heaven—the men to whom we owe our freedom of thought—freedom of speech & freedom of opinion—to whose exertions we are indebted for our emancipation from the shackles of British oppression, & to whom, under Providence, we ought to render the homage of grateful friends, and whose names should dwell upon our tongues, and the glory of whose achievements should form the theme of Eulogy to our posterity—two of these men are no more! Temples & churches—Senate chambers and the Halls of Legislation are hung in black! The public officers of the General & State governments—the municipal authorities of our cities, and all public bodies adopt some badge expressive of their sorrow at the loss to the country of two such distinguished men—Men, whose energy & courage in times which called for all the fortitude & unearthly bravery of the most daring spirits, hesitated not to come forward in the face of danger & of death, to nerve the warrior's arm—encourage the trembling citizen, and lead on to glory and independence—Men, safe in council, eloquent in debate, & of invincible valor—whose intrepidity in times of national distress gained for them the confidence of a vastly extended & mighty population—and whose virtue, & greatness & patriotism has secured for them the most lasting monument of their worth—the gratitude and respect & veneration of their country!— Their names are associated with *Liberty*, and while that is the *rallying word* of Americans, their names will be engraved on every heart, and their memory be cherished with the fondest recollection.

With such bright examples before us, how great are the incitements to virtue. How glorious to contemplate such shining patterns of all that is great & good. How enviable their fame! To be the authors of happiness to millions—and constantly increasing millions of people! This affords a spectacle at which even fancy wonders—Ambition bows before it! And all the powers of the mind yeild their voluntary homage!

Men are astonished at the powers of their own minds, and are lost in the contemplation of the grand and vast & incomprehensible designs of that Infinite Mind, which pervades the Universe, and takes in at a glance the past, present, & future.

How ennobling, how elevating & how enrapturing the thought, that these were *men*—that they were members of our own species—that they belonged to earth—and that the same Divine Essence which animated their bosoms, shines with brighter or fainter lustre in each one of us! Happy the idea, that by exertion, a pure and virtuous life—a determination to do valiantly for our country, and to promote the happiness of our fellow men, a man of good natural talents may accomplish purposes seemingly impossible, and enterprises the most difficult may be successfully terminated. And scarcely any sentiment has more truth and manly beauty in it, than that of the Poet, that,

"What man *has done*, man *can do*."[3] Enough of this.—
Peace to the souls of these departed *Worthies*—and may their usefulness on earth, afford them a sure passport to the unalloyed happiness of heaven!—

After contemplating such characters, I am always, more than at other times, impressed with the power which men can acquire by a judicious cultivation of the qualities which they possess and equally astonished that by far the greater majority can content themselves with making so moderate exertions, & so slight & ineffectual attempts to arrive at excellence in any thing they undertake. How men can be satisfied to see others outstrip them—and by mere force of application & diligence attain the highest honors of the state, and the greatest fame which can be acquired, without resolutely determining to follow their example, and to reach the summit of the Temple of fame, if untiring industry, unyeilding courage, and a steady perseverance can place them there—I see not—

But how few are there among the vast multitude, who take a rational view of life—who look at things as they are—and consider the object for which we were placed in this state of existence—and the number is equally small, who dare come forward and independently assert the rights of man, and dissemminate correct views of the dignity of human nature—

This is not according to my views of the subject, a scene of amusement—it is not a place for men to meet & sport, & part, & die—but a vast theatre for vigor and action—a place for exertion—a field in which to perform his part well, a man must exert all the powers of his mind & body—take advantage of circumstances and in all he does, have a direct reference to the good of his fellow-men. Such men, in the true spirit of dignity & manliness, exclaim with the Poet,

> "Honor & shame from no condition rise,
> "Act well your part, there all the honor lies."[4]

Are examples necessary? We have only to look at Pres. Monroe, Daniel Webster and the host of brilliant characters whose talents & exertions & resolution & determination to be great, have raised them to the highest honors in the State.

Nor are your sex to be disregarded—Their sphere indeed is wholly different—but not on that account, the less important—Females hold an exalted rank in the scale of being—and tho' their merits have not been duly appreciated, yet I hope to see the time when schools will be established & Institutions erected in which all the peculiar branchs of education appropriate to women shall be regularly taught—and their minds suffered to exhibit their powers. And while virtue is worthy of respect, so long will a Lady of an amiable disposition, a benevolent heart, a good mind, good sense improved by reading & reflection & manners refined by an acquaintance with good society, and possessing a good knowledge of domestic economy, recieve the unreserved respect & esteem & affection of every virtuous & noble minded man of our sex, & the union of such persons can not fail to ensure their happiness.

My paper is filled, and I have so unconsciously covered the sheet with what I merely intended to mention in a few lines, that I have no room for several things that I meant to say. And although I have tired your patience already you must excuse me for inclosing a Post-script—Will you not?—

I need not tell you again, that the pleasure with which I should call you *mine*, is only equalled by that which I experience in saying that I am *Yours*.

The clock tells me that I must retire.

"Good night."—Edward—

P.S. I expect Mr. Coleman to call on me to-morrow Evening and take this letter—He passed through this place on his way to his father's at Pittsfield, on Monday morning in fine spirits—Never did a man feel happier—and never did one deserve to be more so. My prayers for his success will follow him, and the knowledge of his happy situation will afford me much pleasure.[5]

1. John Adams and Thomas Jefferson both died on 4 July.

2. Rom. 11:33, slightly misquoted.

3. This saying recurs in Letter 23. Probably Edward is condensing line 606 from book 6 of Edward Young's *The Complaint, or, Night Thoughts on Life, Death, and Immortality,* "And all may do what has by man been done." He quotes *Night Thoughts* in Letters 23, 29, 36, 48, 64, 69, and 95.

4. Pope's *An Essay on Man,* epistle 4, lines 193–94. Edward also quoted these lines while delivering a speech in the United States House of Representatives during his term in Congress in 1854. He argued in favor of military rather than civilian control of armories such as the one at Springfield, on the grounds that under civilian control the armories would be excessively subjected to political power and patronage. See Bingham, *Emily Dickinson's Home,* pp. 554–55; and Leyda, *The Years and Hours of Emily Dickinson,* 1:305–8.

5. Coleman (1796–1882) did well in later life and is the subject of a lengthy entry in the *Dictionary of American Biography* (1934). He is described as an educator and writer of theological works. The entry concludes, "For some years the oldest active college professor in the United States, he was a man of commanding presence, courteous demeanor, warm sympathies, and strong convictions. Firmly grounded in the old faith, he was nevertheless hospitable to new ideas in theology" (p. 294). In the winter term of 1845–46, the poet Emily Dickinson was a member of his German class at Amherst Academy, of which he was the principal. As she explained in a letter to her friend Abiah Root, "I don't go to school this winter [because of ill health] except to a recitation in German. Mr Coleman has a very large class, and Father thought I might never have another opportunity to study it. It takes about an hour & a half to recite" (Leyda, 1:98). Edward, however, is referring primarily to Coleman's success as the suitor of Emily Norcross's cousin.

13
Edward to Emily Norcross
13 July 1826

Post-script-July 13th—Thursday Eve—[1]

Mr. Coleman has just called on me & offered to take letters—as he told me he would. I have been very busily occupied, & can now only find time to say a very few words. Much of what I intended to say in my P.S. must, after all, be omitted till another time.

I am unusually crowded with business—copying Law Lectures—assisting Messrs. Mills & Ashmun in preparing their cases for the next Supreme court[2]—and having several books before me which it is almost indispensable that I should read before I am admitted to practice.

I have not yet made any determination as to a place to establish myself in business, but think more of Amherst & Brimfield than of all the others concerning which I have made enquiry.[3] I expect to devote myself exclusively to my profession—and enter it with a full conviction that it is the most laborious, fatiguing profession, and requires constant & persevering exertions to gain that reputation which every man of a true ambition can not but desire—

Wearisome days & nights attend the industrious Lawyer's path—and if his exertions are crowned with success, his pleasures are proportionally great—and his happiness of a kind truly enviable—such a man can rejoice in the consciousness of having toiled for the good of others, & spent his strength in endeavouring to promote the happiness of his fellow men.[4]

I think of you much, & often, & my increased acquaintance only strengthens my desire to form with you the most solemn of earthly connections—that of marriage—I speak plainly—& speak my feelings, for I do not wish to conceal my object in my visits & intercourse with you—and this, I presume, you long ago, fully understood—[5]

Am I wrong in believing that our attachment is *mutual*?

I am perfectly satisfied in relation to your character & your virtues—and were you as well satisfied that our union would promote our mutual happiness, I would most cheerfully offer you my heart & hand—*Will you accept them?*—

My time compels my to stop—

Will you write by Mr. C.—Have your father & brother returned? How is your brother's health? Don't *William* return from College, next week?[6]

Has your mother enquired any thing in relation to the object of our interviews?—Should you think proper, I will address a letter to your father & mother on the subject, at a proper time, including it unsealed to you, that you might read it & deliver it or not as you pleased.

We ought first to make up our *own minds*—then consult them—or if you please, consult them *first*—[7]

I write always in much haste—& you know perfectly, my feelings—Excuse all imperfections—Consider the matter & not the manner—

Remember me again most cordially to your Mother, Sister, & Mr.

and Mrs. E. N—and receive for yourself my warmest affection—I have no apology to make for writing so much.

Edward

1. This letter is written on a separate sheet of paper and is essentially self-contained, although Edward calls it a "Post-script." Despite the absence of the usual "Affectionate Friend" or "My Dear Emily" salutation, it seems best to count this as a separate letter.

2. John Hooker Ashmun was a lawyer who assisted Howe and Mills in conducting the law school. Subsequently, Ashmun became a law professor at Harvard. Estimates of the school's enrollment vary from ten to forty. The names of most of Edward's fellow students are no longer available, but it is known that Franklin Pierce arrived in Northampton to begin his studies in the spring of 1826. Edward never mentions him, although Edward's term in Congress coincided with the Pierce presidency.

3. Brimfield is southeast of Amherst and perhaps five miles northwest of Monson.

4. In this paragraph (as in other letters), Edward concentrates on motivating himself in his professional labors by lecturing Emily about the strenuous life of a successful lawyer. Evidently, there was a pronounced element of monomania in his character, as there was in his father's.

5. Edward's emphasis on the solemnity of marriage perhaps reflects the tension he felt about their relationship at this time.

6. As usual, Edward refers to Hiram as "your brother" and calls William by name. Clearly, he felt closer to William and had more contact with him.

Joel Norcross did a certain amount of traveling for his business, which included extensive real estate and manufacturing investments as well as farming. He became a county commissioner in 1828, an office that he held until sometime in 1835. During the years that Samuel Fowler Dickinson was approaching bankruptcy, Joel Norcross's prosperity was increasing.

7. There is no indication that Edward ever consulted his parents about Emily, whom they had never met. Emily had already told him that she intended to make up her own mind about his proposal, but Edward does not sound persuaded. Not having heard from her, he had apparently begun to suspect that she wanted her parents' approval of their impending engagement. Hence his offer to write to them, which she eventually accepted.

It was now almost three months since Edward had received a letter from Emily, two months since he had formally proposed to her, and one month since his visit to Monson. Interestingly, Edward tried to adopt the terms of Emily's discourse which had equated silence with informality and language with what he now called "punctilio." Nevertheless, he quite sensibly observed that "it would give me much satisfaction to receive a plain statement of your sentiments in relation to my intercourse with you." Interestingly, too, this letter contains Edward's most extensive pronouncement on women writers: because they transgress the boundaries of sexual decorum, they are unsuitable as marriage partners. The paragraph in which he describes spending an evening with the novelist Catharine Maria Sedgwick—she has an "interesting countenance" but "rather masculine" features—contains one of his rare misspellings, together with an unintentional word repetition.

14
Edward to Emily Norcross
3 August 1826

Northampton. Thursday Morning. Aug. 3. 1826.

My Dear Emily,

The morning is beautiful—the weather cool—and I shall devote a few moments which remain before the mail closes to write you a *third* letter, while my preceding ones remain unanswered. And tho' you know that your letters are always interesting to me; and also, that it would give me much satisfaction to receive a plain statement of your sentiments in relation to my intercourse with you, yet I will not insist on punctilio, but presume that your reasons for not writing are good, and proceed with the correspondence, on my part, with my usual informality.

The time is so short, & so much before me to be done to-day, that I can say but little. Your brother William, I suppose, is now at home. I have expected a visit from him; and, also expected, from what Mr. Allen told me, when last at Monson, to have seen a party of young people from there, to visit Mount Holyoke, before this time.[1] There was a party from Palmer, about two weeks ago, on the same excursion—They visited Southampton Mines, & returned by the way of Springfield. I was in Springfield a fortnight this day week, & saw some of William's classmates, on their return from College. Col. Russell informed me that he had the day before, been to Monson to carry your Father & brother home, and that H's health was apparently improved.[2]

I was told, too, that Mr. Hayden & Miss Eaton were married the day before, & in consequence of the wedding-party being expected to pass thro' Springfield, on their way to Enfield, waited till a late hour in the afternoon, before I returned to Northampton to see them—but did not have that pleasure. I certainly wish them much happiness in their connection.[3]

I passed Tuesday Evening of this week, in company with Miss Sedgwick, the Authoress of "Redwood" & "New England Tale", at a party at Judge Lyman's.[4] She has an interesting countenance—an appearance of much thought, & rather masculine feautures. And I feel happy at having an opportunity of seeing a female who has done so much to give our works of taste so pure and delicate a character—and a conscious pride that women of our own country & our our [sic] own State, too, are emulating not only the females, but the men of England & France & Germany & Italy in works of literature—& we are warranted in presuming that, if they had opportunities equal to their talents, they would not be inferior to our own sex in improving in the sciences. Tho' I should be sorry to see another Madame de Stael—especially if any one wished to make a partner of her for life. Different qualities are more desirable in a female who enters into domestic relations—and you have already had my opinions on that Subject—More when we meet.

I sent you, the week after I left Monson, some pamphlets, to read— If you have perused them, will you have the goodness to return them, by the Stage, directed Me at Northampton, as they *were borrowed*. They were directed to your brother *William*.

My time has almost elapsed—and I have only enough left to say, that my attachment to you remains undiminished. You know my desire in relation to our future connection—I have made a repeated avowal of the interest I feel in you—and should be glad to know your sentiments—and it can not be necessary for me to repeat the assurance of the pleasure it would give me *to know that I was worthy of your unreserved confidence and affection*. Let me hear from you as soon as you receive this—How do you all do. Remember me respectfully to your Father & Mother, & Wm & Lavinia—& E. N. Esq. & Wife. I can not tell now when I shall see you. Perhaps in a few days, perhaps not, for some weeks. It will depend wholly on my business. Imperfect as this letter is, you will attribute it to my haste—The mail will close immediately—"Good Morning." Believe that I remain, as ever, Your most affectionate friend Edward Dickinson

1. Possibly the Plin Allen who in 1830 married Elvira Norcross, another of Emily Norcross's cousins.

2. Colonel Russell is unidentified and not mentioned again. He was probably a colonel in the Massachusetts Militia. In 1824 Edward himself became a "commissioned Ensign in the third regiment of Infantry in the first Brigade, & fourth division of the Militia of this Commonwealth." Edward uses the word "carry" to mean take, transport, or drive.

3. Edward was horrified when Hayden, otherwise unidentified, failed in business. See Letter 86. Emily also refers to the couple in Letter 15. Apparently they were conspicuous spenders.

4. Catharine Maria Sedgwick (1789–1867) published *A New-England Tale; or, Sketches of New-England Character and Manners* in 1822, and *Redwood: A Tale* in 1824. According to Nina Baym, "No other [American] woman writing in the 1820s and 1830s achieved Sedgwick's stature or rivaled her accomplishment." See *Woman's Fiction: A Guide to Novels by and about Women in America, 1820– 1870* (Ithaca: Cornell University Press, 1978), p. 63. This study also provides a stimulating analysis of Sedgwick's novels, in which "women display heroic traits within the limits of nineteenth-century social possibility," pp. 53–63. Edward sent Emily a copy of Sedgwick's historical romance *Hope Leslie* in July 1827, shortly after it was published. See Letter 46.

Judge Joseph Lyman was a popular host who also entertained Horace Greeley and Ralph Waldo Emerson. See *The Northampton Book: Chapters from 300 Years in the Life of a New England Town, 1654–1954* (Northampton: Tercentenary History Committee, 1954), p. 368. His property was purchased by the newly chartered Smith College in 1871 and became part of the campus.

Writing for the first time in three months, Emily accepted Edward's proposal, conditional on her father's approval. However, she gave no indication as to which direction her father was leaning. Nor did she explain why she herself had not asked for Joel Norcross's "advise and consent," at least informally. Perhaps she was waiting for her father to broach the subject. Perhaps she was providing herself with a convenient avenue of escape. Conventionally, courting couples arrived at a private understanding before seeking the consent of the bride's father. Ordinarily, such consent was granted. Emily's relations with her father both before and after her marriage appear to have been distant but cordial, though on at least one occasion she was intimidated by the thought that he might examine a letter that she had sent to her sister Lavinia from boarding school. In a number of letters, Edward had assured Emily that her happiness was his paramount consideration even if it led her to reject him. So too, in response to Edward's suggestion that he write to her father, Emily stated, "It would certainly be agreable to me still you must consult your own fealings rather than mine." At best, this was a lukewarm assent; but Edward, if not with his "usual informality" (L14), then with his usual "perseverance" (all of his letters), now had the opening he needed.

Her diffidence notwithstanding, Emily had expressed her desire to marry a man whom she did not know well, despite their seven months' correspondence and Edward's four visits to Monson. Such an undertaking required courage (or foolhardiness) on her part, and it is

not surprising that she sounds somewhat confused about her feelings,
a word she transcribed variously in her letters as "fealings," "fellings,"
and "feelings." Writing for the first time in three months, she con-
cluded, "I think you will not doubt that this letter was written in haste
I will therfore make no appologies."

15
Emily Norcross to Edward
8 August 1826

Monson August 8th

Dear Edward

I experienced much happiness in the perusal of your letter on friday
morning last [4 August] for which I feal myself greatly indebted to
you. Your kindness in this particular is not unnoticed by me as I have
been fearful you might suppose from my poor returns I have not
delayed all this while without much thought in relation to the subject
that has occasioned us many pleasent interviews and in which I have
realised much pleasure. Did I not rely with perfect confidence in what
you have expressed to me I should not take the liberty to include your
happiness with my own but at present I feal privileg[ed] to do it Those
pamphlets were not recieved untill after Mr Coleman returned I know
not where they were detained but it appears that I did not get them as
soon as you expected for this reason you will not be surprised that you
did not recieve them by him. I read them immediately after they were
recieved ever since I have been wishing to convey them to you but as
no opportunity appears except by mail I shall delay no longer but
comply with your request

I think you must be convinced ere this that your intercourse with
me is mutual although I have not explained to you my views as I have
wished but I will improve this opportunity to acknowledge my warm
and increasing attachment to you and that your proposals are what I
would wish to comply with, but without the advise and consent of my
father I cannot consistantly do it. As I regard his fealings very much
should I meet his approbation I will then assure you of my confidence
and affection. Let it be as it may [?] my attachment to you will not
easily be removed

I am sensible that it is unpleasant for you to introduce the subject.
You observed that you would write to papa if I wished it would cer-
tainly be agreable to me still you must consult your own fealings
rather than mine. Uncle E Norcross and wife favour me with frequent
calls they often speak of you and wish to be remembered when I write.
Since the return of my brother he accompanied with his wife com-

menced a short excurtion for pleasure in hopes that his health might be still more benefited as his former one had thus affected him but to our disappointment they had proceeded no father [farther] than Ware house point after an abscence of two days when papa was sent for. He had the night previous a severe attack of bleeding from the lungs which gave us quite an alarm he however reached home more comfortably than we anticipated and since then has appared improveing quite fast he walks and rides often and appears quite cheerful at present yet we consider his situation critical.

I now have the pleasure of William['s] society which I value very much. Mr Hayden and lady past us in great stile. Her fortune is predicted by almost evry one that saw the young gentleman and his associates. I could say much of them would time permit as the mail will soon close I will trouble you with no more at present. I remain yours. Emily Norcross

I think you will not doubt that this letter was written in haste I will therfore make no appologies

Edward chose not to write to Joel Norcross before receiving further encouragement from Emily. Nor was he in any haste to answer her letter, which he had probably received on the 9th.

16
Edward to Emily Norcross
23 August 1826

> Amherst, Wednesday Eve, 12. o. clock.
> Aug. 23. 1826.

My Dear Emily,

Altho' it is so late an hour, as I have an opportunity to send directly to you in the morning by Rev. Mr. Ely, I can not let it pass without saying a few words.[1]

Yesterday, afternoon, I was admitted to the Bar, and another fellow student, Wm. Locke [?], with me. We were admitted a day earlier than the usual time, on account of my wishing to attend the Commencement to-day.

I can not decide where it is best for me to establish myself in business; as soon as I conclude, I shall inform you of my determination.

Our Commencement was decidedly the best that we ever had.—The Style of the compositions & the manner of speaking was altogether superior to that of last year. Elvira & Julia & a Miss Ely were here— & Miss Ely is with us tonight.[2]

E. [Elvira] & J. [Julia] have gone to Northampton this evening, and are going to visit Mount Holyoke in the morning & return to Monson to-morrow. I expect to meet them at Northampton in the morning.

Your brother & Mr. Lyon & wife have not yet visited Northampton, as I expected. When are they coming?[3]

I shall leave N. H. [Northampton] this week, & make it my home here, till I conclude whether to remain here or not. Mr. Coleman took tea with us, with Wm. Dwight & his Sisters of Belchertown.[4]—and Mr. C's marriage is to be, as you probably know, on the 19.th Sept. I have recd an invitation to attend, & if convenient for me to visit M. [Monson] at that time, I should be extremely happy to be present at the ceremony, tho' it is uncertain whether I shall be able to be there—as our Military Reviews are expected to commence on the next day.[5]

Have you had any conversation with Wm. respecting the Subject on which we conversed, at our last interview? Has he said any thing to your father in relation to our intercourse, & do you know whether he approves, or disapproves of our meetings?[6]—I feel some solicitude to ascertain his feelings, and to know in what light he views my attentions to you.

I certainly regard his feelings very much, and should wish to have his countenance in our proceedings. I should be sorry to do any thing unpleasant to him, or to any others of your family—I wish to have a most perfect understanding with them all upon the subject. My mind remains unchanged and my attachment, as I have so often said before, only increases & strengthens by a more intimate acquaintance and my esteem for your virtues is of a character which can not diminish so long as those virtues are cherished. And I am thus plain, because I wish to be—and because I know you want me to say nothing but what I feel.

The object of our intercourse is a rational—an important one. The connection which will result, if you comply with my proposals, is for life—and we ought to enter upon it with much consideration, & much reflection. It is a Subject which interests me much. And if your happiness can be promoted with mine, I should feel the highest pleasure in making any exertion to increase & Secure it; A young man, you know, has to become known in his profession by degrees—and must *deserve* business, before he can obtain it, generally. Yet no man ought to rest satisfied short of the utmost exertion within his power—The more talents a man has, the more industrious he ought to be, and every man is under obligation to apply the whole powers of his mind & body, to the attainment of that learning and consequent fame & fortune, which every man ought to aim at. Nothing, scarcely, is too great for man to accomplish. And there is hardly a plan which he can not execute. Still, to gain celebrity, a man must be untiring—and his soul should be absorbed in the contemplation of those models of perfection who have been to the world such shining examples of what talents, united with industry, can accomplish. And it is no discouragement to the man of real resolution & determination of character that there are difficulties to contend with & obstacles to remove in his way to eminence. Competition is the life business—and the only way for a man to succeed, is to *do well*, & attend closely to the duties of his profession.

I join most cordially in the sentiment expressed in your last letter, of in [*sic*] including your happiness with my own—and hope to be so happy as to be united to you in that solemn connection—in marriage, which, our Maker designed to promote the mutual happiness of both sexes. It is an institution of divine origin—and the whole world bears witness that a union of persons of proper feelings & dispositions is the direct road to rational & substantial enjoyment. And I can not but repeat, that there is nothing in which virtuous minds receive so much satisfaction as in domestic life—and nothing can add so much to a man's happiness as to have a refuge from the agitations with which a life of business will necessarily be sometimes attended.

Whatever advances your happiness will in the same degree promote mine—and to contribute in any manner to it, I need not say, would be always a source of pure gratification. Go on in the ways of virtue—and by the exercise of all that is amiable & estimable, may you be fitted to enjoy all the happiness which mankind can experience, & be happy in the full assurance of blissful immortality. You must know that my eyes grow dim. & I must stop. Will you write me, in a short time—Give my respects to your father & all the family & E. N. Esq. & wife & Maria. *I am yours.* E. Dickinson

"Good night"—I return to Northampton in the morning—Edward[7]

1. Alfred Ely, minister of the Monson Congregational Church, was a close friend of Joel Norcross's. A member of the Board of Trustees of Amherst College, he was probably in Amherst to attend commencement. According to W. S. Tyler, "He was one of those men whom we always expected to see at our anniversaries, and other public occasions, and whose presence and countenance always gave us new courage; for we felt confident that God would sustain an Institution for which such men would honestly and ardently labor and pray." See *History of Amherst College During Its First Half Century, 1821–1871* (Springfield, Mass.: C. W. Bryan, 1873), p. 372.

2. Elvira and Julia Norcross were Emily's cousins. Miss Ely is presumably a relative of the Reverend Alfred Ely.

3. Mr. Lyon may be Horatio Lyon, a Monson businessman. That Edward ex-

pects these visitors, who were not mentioned in Emily's letter, suggests that oral messages were occasionally exchanged by the couple and delivered by mutual friends such as Coleman.

4. William Dwight is unidentified. Coleman lived in Belchertown.

5. As stated previously, Edward was a member of the Massachusetts Militia and participated from time to time in military exercises.

6. "He approves" refers to Joel Norcross rather than William.

7. A pointing hand precedes " 'Good night.' "

17
Edward to Emily Norcross
29 August 1826

Amherst August 29. 1826.

My Dear Emily,

My particular object in writing this morning is to say to you, that my present plan is to make a journey to Southbridge, & Brimfield, in the course of the present week, & shall probably go to-morrow morning—and shall intend to make *Monson* in my way, if possible and if perfectly agreeable, should be happy to add another to our already frequent interviews.[1]

I am now sitting at the writing-table in my father's office, and with what business naturally presents itself, & balancing between opposite advantages & disadvantages, have spent my time since Saturday Evening last. This week, I intend to make a final determination with respect to my place of settlement—and altho' the subject is one of so much importance to me & my friend, I am sometimes mortified at my own delay.[2] But, as I am under no particular necessity of being hasty, I can not but content myself with the belief, that my course is the most judicious one.

I think much of the subject of our intercourse—and feel no little solicitude to know in what light my visits are regarded by your father & mother—& others whose opinions you so highly value. And I need not repeat what I have so often said, that you owe it to your own happiness & your regard for your friends, to exercise all that candor & prudence, & make up your mind with a full knowledge of my character—& standing & prospects in life, which a person ought to exercise in relation to a matter of so much importance. Every thing connected with my history is known, & can be ascertained. Your friends can easily learn what I have been—what I am—& what is my prospect of success. And I have only time to say again, that to merit your affection would render me happy, and to be able to call you mine would not fail to produce in me the most substantial satisfaction. The stage has arrived & I must close. More when we meet. Please to receive my warmest affection & the assurance of my lasting attachment. My respects to your father, family etc.

Yours, Edward

1. Edward exaggerates in speaking of their "already frequent interviews." After their meeting in early January, he had visited Monson only three times—in March, May, and July.

2. "My friend" is Emily.

Edward visited Monson from 30 August to 2 September. On 5 September, he wrote Joel Norcross the following letter. Speaking of his esteem for Emily and attachment to her, he judiciously explained, "So far as I know, that esteem has been, in a measure, at least reciprocated." Joel Norcross did not answer the letter.

18
Edward to Joel Norcross
5 September 1826

Amherst, September 5, 1826.

My Dear Sir,

Although I have been known to you but a few months, and you can therefore, have but little personal acquaintance with me or my character, still you will permit me to address you on a subject, which though it is of a delicate nature, is of much interest & of mutual importance to your family & myself.

It can not be necessary that I should make use of any formality or ceremony: I will plainly say, that my business at Monson, during the past winter, led to my introduction to your family, & since my first acquaintance with your daughter Emily, I have felt a partiality for her, inspired by the virtues which I discovered her to possess, and my intercourse with her while at Monson produced an esteem which did not cease with our separation. I addressed her on the subject, a short time after my return to Northampton—and the correspondence which has since existed between us, & the interviews we have since had, have contributed to increase & strengthen my esteem & attachment for her; so far as I know, that esteem has been, in a measure, at least reciprocated. I have made proposals to her, to form with me, at some proper future time, a union for life. We have conversed freely & familiarly on the subject, and have thought it improper to proceed further in the business, without consulting you—and with the consent of Emily, I now refer the matter to your consideration, not doubting that your candor and prudence will induce you to approve or disapprove of our intercourse, as you may think most for the interest & happiness of all concerned.

I have made references, in my letters to Emily, to Gentlemen, from whom any information concerning me can be obtained.

And while I wish not to conceal the fact of my ardent attachment to her, & my admiration of her virtues, and of my sincere wish to become her legal guardian & protector, I can only say to you, as I have more than once expressed to her, that if, upon enquiry, or otherwise, you are satisfied that there is any thing in my character which will tend to render her or her friends unhappy,—or if, under all the circumstances of the case there is not a reasonable prospect of my success in my profession—& of my ability to promote her happiness, it would certainly be your duty to yourself, to Emily, and your family, to advise that our intercourse should cease.

But, on the other hand, should my proposal meet the approbation of yourself & Mrs. Norcross, as I sincerely hope it may, it would be a source of lasting enjoyment to me, and should I be permitted to realize the consummation of my wishes, no exertions will be wanting on my part, to secure the happiness of Emily, & to promote & increase, so far as honorable exertion is any assurance of it, that of all her friends, & connexions.

Will you communicate your opinion to Emily, or me, in any manner you may deem proper.

Please to accept for yourself & family the assurance of my warm regard, & believe that I remain,

> With the highest esteem & respect,
> Your sincere friend
> Edward Dickinson

After careful deliberation, Edward had decided to open his office in Amherst, although not in partnership with his father. Despite the press of his business, begun that day, he also hoped to attend the commencement at Yale with Emily. Meanwhile, he was anxiously awaiting a response from her father.

19
Edward to Emily Norcross
7 September 1826

Amherst, September 7. 1826

My Dear Emily,

Having a direct opportunity to send to Monson by a man who makes one of a party who passed us to the North on Monday morning last, and who returns with a Lady who did not accompany him when he went up, (from which I naturally infer that he has been married,) I improve it to say to you, that I reached home the night I left Monson, at 12. o'clock; and after much conversation with my friends, & Gentlemen in whose opinions I place much confidence, *I have, this morning, decided to open my office in Amherst, and shall raise my sign & commence my business this afternoon.*

My conclusion to commence practice immediately, will render it uncertain whether it will be convenient for me to attend Commencement at New Haven, as I have always intended. Tho' there is nothing to make it certain that I shall not. I presume you will go, & if I attend, I should be extremely happy to meet you there. If I go, I shall take the Stage at Northampton, Sunday Evening, or at Springfield on Monday morning. Should you & your father leave S. [Springfield] at that time, it is not impossible that I may meet you on the way.

I shall go if convenient—or rather, if it is not very inconvenient. Olive & Maria returned, the other day, before I left Monson, tho' I did not call upon them.[1]

I sent a letter to your father, by the mail of Tuesday, respecting the subject on which we have had so much conversation, and which has caused us so many pleasant interviews—I sincerely hope that he & your Mother will approve of my proposals to you, & that we shall be permitted to consummate that union which is the purest desire of my heart—and from which I should devoutly hope the happiness of us both might be secured & increased.

I feel anxious to hear from Wm. & your brother Hiram—How is their health—& has Wm. returned to New Haven?—

Is your father at Springfield, this week, as you expected—and has he recd. my letter?—Never did I experience precisely such sensations as when writing it—addressing a Gentleman with whom my acquaintance had been but short & on a Subject entirely new. How I did it, I hardly know—and how it will read I am at a still greater loss to determine.

I shall not cease to feel great anxiety till I have some intimation of the result—and that it may be such as will be the means of promoting the lasting happiness of each of us, I shall most ardently pray. Let me hear from you, as soon as convenient—present my warmest regards to your father's family, Your brother & his wife, & Mr. E. Norcross & wife—and any others you please; and be assured that I remain, as ever, with sentiments of lasting affection & attachment—

Yours, most cordially,
Edward

More if I had time—

I shall enquire the name of the bearer of this before I send it—

Before sealing this, I concluded to include Mr. Colton, as the most safe way of conveyance.[2] E——

1. Olive is Emily's cousin Olivia Flynt.

2. Presumably Simeon Colton delivered the letter to Emily, although Edward's records indicate that the bearer was "Mr. Field." If the bearer was Field, I do not understand Edward's use of the word "include."

Emily and Edward met in Springfield on 15 September. They were both on their way to attend the commencement at Yale and traveled to New Haven together. Returning from New Haven, Edward discovered an invitation to attend the wedding of his close friend Lyman Coleman to Emily's cousin Maria Flynt. However, because he was to participate in a military review at Deerfield, he was unable to attend; Edward's life was already highly scheduled.

20
Edward to Emily Norcross
19 September 1826

Amherst, Tuesday Morning, Sept. 19, 1826.

My Dear Emily,

While I am every moment expecting a man to call, who is to take this letter enclosed in one to Rev. Mr. Coleman, I leave my preparation for the Reviews just long enough to say, that I returned from Springfield about the middle of the afternoon on Friday, & found my friends all well.

I found a letter from Mr. Coleman, inviting me to attend his wedding on Thursday morning, & accompany him & his Lady, with you, to Springfield. And I regret exceedingly that it will not be in my power to comply with the invitation. But circumstances render it *impossible.* I start for Deerfield, this afternoon, where I expect to meet the Gover-

nor & his aide-de-camp—the Adjutant General, & the Maj. Genl—
my brother aid-de-camp.[1]

I shall be engaged in the parade, in martial exercises, while you are
quietly witnessing one of the most solemn, yet one of the most inter-
esting scenes which can take place. My heart will be with you—& I
shall pledge you all, at half past 8. o'clock A.M.—Remember me most
heartily to the Bride & Bridegroom—their several friends—& all
present at the ceremony.[2] Make my compliments to your Father &
Mother & William & Lavinia, your brother Hiram & his wife, E.
Norcross Esq & Lady—etc. Let me hear from you, soon—and in the
greatest imaginable haste, recieve my unfeigned attachment & affec-
tion. More, soon.

Most cordially *Yours*.
Edward Dickinson

1. Levi Lincoln was the Governor of Massachusetts. The other officials are un-
identified.

2. Note the informality of the wedding festivities from a modern perspective.
The handwritten invitation was extended within a week or so of the wedding
date, and the ceremony was apparently to occur in the bride's home at eight-
thirty in the morning on a Thursday. As was sometimes the custom, Edward and
Emily were invited to accompany the newlyweds on their journey home; honey-
moons were still comparatively rare. According to Ellen K. Rothman, the growing
elaboration of wedding rituals in the nineteenth century constituted a response to
the gradual dispersion of close-knit rural communities, in which the bride and
bridegroom usually set up housekeeping close to their original families. See
Hands and Hearts, chap. 2.

Perhaps Emily had imbibed some of her "prudence" from her father.
In any event, Joel Norcross still had not answered Edward's letter, nor
had Emily written to describe the Colemans' wedding, which she had
attended. Perhaps too Joel Norcross was hoping to see more of Ed-
ward in person before agreeing to his daughter's engagement, espe-
cially since Emily herself was inhibited about expressing herself to her
father.

21
Edward to Emily Norcross
30 September 1826

Amherst. Saturday Morning. September 30. 1826.

My Dear Emily,

Having heard nothing directly from you since I left you at Springfield, & presuming that you have good reasons for not writing, I shall again devote the very few moments that remain before the mail closes, (which is at 9. o'clock) to converse with you. And after expressing my regret that I was unable to be present at Mr. C's wedding, and to experience the pleasure of supporting him during the ceremony, & accompanying him & his Lady, with you, to Springfield I will say, that if my business is such that I can leave my office some day next week, my intention is to visit you, if agreeable—probably on Tuesday— perhaps not quite so soon.

I have had no intimation relative to the reception and consideration of my letter to your father, and feel desirous to know the result. Have you had any conversation with him upon the subject?—Will it not be proper that we should have a plain & full understanding with both your parents, when I next see you—or will it be more agreeable for you to converse with them alone? You fully know my wishes, & I think I can say that I know something of your feelings, & can not but believe that my attachment to you is in a good degree, reciprocal. I want to say much, but have no time to say it.—I had a pleasant time at the reviews, last week, have attended the Supreme Court at Northampton, this week—Spent Thursday Evening very pleasantly at a party at Mr. Mills'—Met Mr. Warland & daughters, the old Gentleman & two Ladies that accompanied us from Springfield to New Haven—Saw Mr. Lathrop, whom you met at Monson[1]—& heard much about Mr. C's wedding—and am now seated in my office, with a prospect of being able to pursue my business without further interruption. My father's family are all well. How do yours all do? Remember me to all your friends, excuse the haste in which I am *almost always obliged* to write, & believe me sincere in offering you my *heart and hand*. I must close, and remain *ever Yours affectionately*,

Edward

1. For Mr. Mills, see Letter 8, n. 2. Mr. Warland is unidentified, as is Mr. Lathrop.

On 5 and 6 October, Edward visited Monson but it was not one of his more successful trips, in part because Emily had not expressed herself "fully upon the subject" of her feelings; her parents were also non-commital. Nevertheless, toward the end of October Edward began to assume that they were engaged, that her parents did not object to their marriage, and to press for a wedding date.

In this letter as in many others, Edward's ideas about the ideal woman seem formulaic and naive, yet his interest in women's education was genuine: "Females have been much neglected, & their powers much undervalued." Later, he saw to it that his daughters had some of the best educational opportunities available to women at the time, though the poet also remarked that he distrusted her intelligence. Women were to be directed toward "the pursuit of proper studies," but men defined the limits of propriety, or sought to.

22
Edward to Emily Norcross
22 October 1826

Amherst. Sunday Evening. Oct. 22. 1826.

My Dear Emily,

Owing to serious indisposition after my return from Monson, occasioned by the severe cold with which I was then afflicted, & which made me much more unwell than I was willing to confess myself, and the great increase of my business & my cares which the absence of my father on a journey for the last week, had produced, I have not been able, till this Evening to write to you[1]—and it now gives me the purest satisfaction to "hold communion" with a friend in whom I feel so great an interest, & for whom I am happy to cherish so ardent an attachment. I have expected a letter from you for a week past, and hoped to have a more full account of your parents' views in relation to the subject of our intercourse, but after the length to which our correspondence has proceeded, is it not fair for me to infer that our wishes in relation to the subject of a permanent connection, are the same, and am I not right in my conclusion, that your family are not disposed to interfere with our arrangements in relation to it.

Viewing the subject, as I always have, in a candid & rational light, and as one which ought to be treated with the most perfect plainness and frankness, I have without reserve, made known my desire, and tendered my proposals, leaving it with you to accept or not, as you might judge most conducive to your happiness. And tho' you have not expressed yourself fully upon the subject, I should be unwilling to think that I did not understand you. I shall, therefore, say something as to the time when it would be proper to consummate our union. We are both young, & on that account, need not be in haste. In addition to that, you may not have had sufficient opportunity to become acquainted with my character, & my prospects in life—and it would certainly be prudent for you to wait till I have had some trial of my chance of success in my profession, for it would be farthest from my heart to wish to persuade you to leave your present happy situation, without a fair prospect that it would not be diminished by the proposed change, however much I might desire it. All young men commencing business, have a character to form for *themselves*. And tho' the opportunities of different individuals have been various, & their experience in business very unequal, and some idea can almost always be formed of a man's business talents, yet a man's success must depend on *himself*, and it is the safest to wait till the result is seen. A few months! perhaps.

The subject of marriage, tho' a delicate one, has claims upon the consideration of every individual. It was the obvious intention of the Deity that the sexes should be united—their happiness, when a union takes place under proper circumstances, and between persons in whom there is a proper similarity of tastes and dispositions, is much increased—it adds to the respect which each enjoys individually—makes life more agreeable from a consciousness of better answering the object of existence—increases their enjoyment by the ability of one to communicate happiness to the other, & diminishes the weight of misfortunes & relieves the sorrows of each, by the sympathy which is ever extended by one "kindred spirit" to another. There is something peculiarly grateful in the idea of enjoying the society of a friend in whom you can at all times place the most implicit confidence, with whom you can share your pleasures & your pains, who will rejoice at your success, and animate & encourage you in honorable pursuits—who by constancy & faithfulness, can add to the joys of prosperity, & cheer and support you in time of adversity—who can render your home a peaceful & contented and happy place—where all the joys of domestic life are fully realised—and where all the virtues take up their abode.

And when two persons are thus united—when those who are calculated by their dispositions, & their education to render each other happy thus form a connection, their home is the centre of all that is tranquil & delightful.—More depends on a *determination* to be contented, & to gather happiness from everything that takes place, than we are apt to imagine. It is easy to see obstacles in the way of enjoyment, if we *expect* to see them—but almost all of them are easily removed by a little resolution and the exercise of a little patience. With a becoming fortitude, hardly any difficulty will occur, which can not be overcome.

Females have been much neglected, & their powers much undervalued—and while we all ought to rejoice that exertions are now making [being made] to give them that place which they are capable of holding, & bestowing upon them that attention which can not fail to call into exercise the powers that have been too long suffered to remain dormant for want of proper notice, we ought to be careful to direct them to the pursuit of proper studies—those which will fit them to grace the Stations in which they may be placed and which will prepare them, more especially, to discharge the duties of domestic life in such a manner as to promote the enjoyment of those who must be the most immediately interested in their good management, is it not [?][2] and who would be proportionally affected by improper or unskillful superintendants. I have before said to you that good sense, improved by reading & observation, and an acquaintance with the world, an amiable disposition, & a thorough knowledge of domestic economy, and a desire to render all about her happy, constituted the excellence of the female character. A virtuous woman is indeed a "pearl of great price"[3]—and he who is so happy as to find her, needs nothing but a correct deportment and an industrious attention to his business to ensure him all the enjoyment which is allotted to men in this life. To gain the affection of a virtuous & faithful & constant woman, is more than a martial conquest—and the reciprocal feeling produced by such a triumph is beautifully expressed in a couplet inserted in my College Album, by a Classmate, now deceased,

> "Thrice happy they! whose friendly hearts can burn"
> "With purest flame, & meet a kind return."[4]

Wishing you to enjoy all the happiness which can flow from the full exercise of your virtues, I must depend on hearing from you soon, and knowing all that can interest me—and in the mean time, remember me cordially to all your father's family, & believe that *I am ever devotedly Yours—*

Edward

I shall write again, soon, & send some books to Mr. Coleman for you—perhaps this week. Let me hear from you, as soon as you recieve this, and be assured that it would afford me the most substantial satisfaction to know that I was worthy of your lasting affection, and that I might, ere long become your constant companion.

E——

We are to have a Newspaper commenced here, the first week in December next, to be called "The New England Examiner".[5] My business, thus far, has fully answered my expectations. I have had several cases, & a goodly number of clients.—We are all well.

P.S. I was at Belchertown on Wednesday of last week—called on Mr. Coleman & found him, & Mrs C & Olive in good spirits & appearing to enjoy them[selves] perfectly. They expect to visit Monson this week. Don't fail to write me by them if you have not already written. I shall expect a letter every mail. Will your father expect to have any further communication from me on the subject of our intercourse? Greet all friends in my name. *Edward*
How is your brother Hiram?

1. Samuel Fowler Dickinson was "frequently employed as the agent and advocate of the town in litigated questions" (Tyler, *History of Amherst College*, p. 119) and was elected to the Massachusetts legislature in 1827. But I have not been able to discover his specific reasons for traveling at this time.
2. A tear around the seal accounts for the obscure reading.
3. Matt. 13:46.
4. Edward's college album contains this quotation inscribed by Anthony W. Butler of Jefferson, Mississippi, but the original author is, alas, unidentified. Among the poets included in Edward's [Common] "Place-Book" are Shakespeare, Beaumont and Fletcher, Burns, Byron, Cowper, Thomas Moore, Scott, Thomson, and Young. The only identifiable American poet is James Gates Percival (1795–1856), who was all the rage in 1823. The album is among the Dickinson Family Papers at Houghton Library.
5. Edward subsequently wrote a series of essays for this newspaper, which was called the *New-England Inquirer*.

By Connecticut Valley standards where evangelical Christianity was the norm, Edward was not particularly religious. Although he attended church regularly and clashed with his daughter Emily when she refused to do so, he waited until 1850 to make a formal profession of faith. At that time the minister chastized him by saying, " 'You want to come to Christ as a lawyer—*but you must come to him as a* poor sinner—*get down on your knees & let me pray for you, & then pray for yourself' " (Sewall,* Life of Emily Dickinson, *1:66). But in October 1826 the sudden death of a young man "of an amiable & benevolent disposition, of agreeable deportment, and one who was esteemed and beloved by all who knew him" turned his thoughts to immortality, "which the imagination, in its utmost stretch, can not concieve—and the very idea of which involves us in wonder & astonishment."*

Yet Edward was no mystic. Just as he believed that "virtue & a virtuous conduct cannot fail to procure for us all that is desirable in this life," so too he reasoned that "the practice of the christian virtues will insure us an entrance into that kingdom where we shall forever enjoy ineffable felicity, & where our capacities for enjoyment will be unceasingly enlarged."

23
Edward to Emily Norcross
29 October 1826

Amherst. Sunday Afternoon. Oct. 29. 1826.

My Dear Emily,

I write with feelings of solemnity. To us here, this has been a day of gloom. Never have I known any event produce a more solemn effect than one which we have this day witnessed. Last evening, William Penniman, a member of the Sophomore Class in College, died![1] He was a son of Col. P. of New Braintree. His parents, sisters and one brother were here at the time. This morning, they returned. At half past nine, a funeral service was attended at the house of Mrs. Merrill, where he died, and his remains, attended by four of his Classmates, were carried to his father's.[2] He had formerly been a member of our Academy,[3] and was a young man of an amiable & benevolent disposition, of agreeable deportment, and one who was esteemed and beloved by all who knew him. And the circumstances attending his death were peculiarly affecting. He was sick but little more than a week. Being taken with a cold, he neglected to apply for medical advice, till a fever had fastened so firmly upon him that it could not be removed. The family is one of the most respectable in the place—lived perfectly happily—and seemed to be bound up in each other's prosperity & success. And though entirely unconnected with them, I have scarcely ever had my sympathy more excited. To see so amiable and agreeable a young man, just entering on his second year in College—beloved by his Instructers, his Classmates & his fellow students, and enjoying the smiles of a happy family, who anticipated much from him in future life—whose bosom beat high with all the noble feelings of the soul, and who looked forward with the fondest hopes & the brightest prospects—To see the fond hopes of parents in a moment blasted—and all the tenderest ties severed. To see youth, & goodness, & talents and every thing that can adorn & beautify life so suddenly cut off & laid in the grave, can not but draw the generous tears from the eye of the most disinterested or philosophical. We ought to be affected by the death of any one; but when so many circumstances combine to render the departure of a friend peculiarly afflicting, we should do injustice to the best feelings of our nature, if we did not pay a proper tribute of respect to his memory. His funeral is to take place on Tuesday—and the most of his Classmates, & many other Students will attend. Such affecting instances of sudden death can not but remind us of our own mortality—and though I am not much accustomed to moralise in my epistles, you will excuse the feeling which prompts me to do it on the present occasion. To one who reflects on the past, and who does not close his eyes upon what is daily occurring, it is impossible that the thought of death should not at some time come over his mind, & produce a solemn contemplation of what is inevitably certain, and lead the mind to think on that scene which we are all assured must sooner or later happen. While such thoughts occupy the mind, the common concerns—the common business of life, seems of small consequence—the mind for a moment, forgets its ambitious projects—the most brilliant schemes, for a time, cease to dazzle—fame, fortune honor & power, lose their charms, & the soul retires into itself, & holds converse with itself upon subjects which concern, not merely our interest for a month or a year, or a *life*, but for a length of duration which no human intellect can measure—which the imagination, in its utmost stretch, can not concieve—and the very idea of which involves us in wonder & astonishment.

With an interest so vast, in view, how proper, & how rational it is, that we should meditate seriously upon the state of being to which we are destined, and upon the kind of preparation necessary to ensure our unending happiness. To become truly an heir to such an inheritance, is worthy of the most serious consideration—and the reward of all who pursue the path of piety & virtue, is indeed large & glorious!—But I must end my moral.

Emily—We seldom realise the importance of the stations we occupy—seldom do we feel the weight of responsibility which rests upon us. Placed, as we are, in the midst of so vast a theatre of action, & surrounded with innumerable objects calculated to interest & animate us—& urged by a thousand motives to apply the whole powers of our minds to the accomplishment of some object which will promote the happiness of our fellow men, and knowing, as we do, the object [for] which men were sent into the world, we can hardly resist the temptation to form a resolution that we will devote our lives to the improvement of our species, & in attempts to lead them into the paths of happiness. Much may, indeed, be done, by example merely.

A virtuous life, correct deportment, & an universal benevolence will do much towards answering the great end of existence. All that is wanting to make any man what he *would be*, is a *determination* to become such, united with a prudent & judicious use of the necessary means. "All that man *has done*, man *can do*,"[4] is a maxim that will cheer a man in all his attempts at excellence, and support him in all times when his success appears doubtful. The pleasure of a man must depend very much on his attention to his business. The more *active* a man is, the more *happy* he will be. "Man was made for action"

> "Action's his sphere, & for that sphere designed,"
> "Eternal pleasures open on his mind."[5]

Examples of the truth of this sentiment are abundant.

We have only to look at our own country to find the names of hundreds who by their own native talents, & their unbending *resolution*, have raised themselves to the highest stations in the government—men, who, from a close attention to business, and an untiring industry, and a determination to overcome all obstacles in the way to fame & fortune, have placed themselves in situations, the most enviable, the most honorable & the most happy. With such examples before us, there is nothing to fear. Industry, frugality, application, honesty, & integrity: in short, virtue & a virtuous conduct cannot fail to procure for us all that is desirable in this life, and the practice of the christian virtues will insure us an entrance into that kingdom where we shall forever enjoy ineffable felicity, & where our capacities for enjoyment will be unceasingly enlarged.

That we may both possess, & continue to cultivate those virtues which will render us happy in ourselves, a comfort & blessing to our friends, ornaments in Society, the means of improvement and usefulness to all with whom we may be in any way connected—and that our course may be such as to gain the respect & esteem & confidence of all—that we may be conscious of the dignity of our natures—& our lives be marked by all the rewards of hono*ror*able [*sic*] intention & virtuous action—and at last be so happy as to be amongst the number of those who shall forever enjoy those pure, & exalted & unalloyed pleasures which can only exist in the immediate presence of the Eternal! will be my constant and most ardent prayer.

My father returned on Saturday Evening from a journey of a fortnight to the State of N. York. My sister Mary went as far as Pittsfield with him.

A Sister of Rev. Mr. Coleman returned with them to pass the winter with her brother at Belchertown. We shall carry her down on Tuesday.

Remember me particularly to your father, mother, brother & Sister—Your brother H. & wife—Esq. N. & Lady—& Capt. Flynt's family.[6] I expect a letter from you *daily*. Recieve the expression of my highest esteem, & believe me *Yours indeed*—Edward

There is now a stage from Amherst to Belchertown three times a week, and any thing you send to Mr. C. will reach me directly. I send you Winter Evening Tales by the Misses Porters.[7] The first & last stories you will find interesting. *Miss Mackay*, in the first, is truly a prodigy of female courage & fortitude, & Col. Ferguson is no less distinguished for [those?] high & manly & noble traits of character which [excite universal?] admiration.[8]—E——I send it, to Mr. Coleman for you.

P.S. I send you also the *"Scottish Chiefs."*[9] I borrowed the "Tales" mentioned before—Can you read them and send them to me in the course of two or three weeks? My Law business is quite respectable for a young Lawyer. I have several cases on hand for this week, & the next, and am encouraged to hope that I shall get a handsome support, at least—even in these dull times for business—Heaven's blessings rest upon you forever. E——

1. William Penniman is listed in the *Amherst College Biographical Record of the Graduates and Nongraduates, Centennial Edition, 1821–1921*, ed. Robert B. Fletcher and Malcolm O. Young (Amherst: Trustees of Amherst College, 1939), as a nongraduate of the class of 1829.

2. "Mrs. Merrill" boarded many Amherst College students.

3. Amherst Academy.

4. This maxim is also quoted in Letter 12.

5. These lines are also quoted in Letters 36 and 64. See Letter 36, n. 3.

6. Exceptionally, Edward refers to William Otis as "your . . . brother," and to Hiram as "Your brother H." Captain Rufus Flynt was Joel Norcross's brother-in-law and the father of Olivia Flynt and Maria [Flynt] Coleman.

7. *Tales Round a Winter Hearth*, by the English novelists Jane Porter (1776–1850) and her sister Anna Maria (1780–1832), was published in 1826. Jane was the better known writer. See also Letter 30, n. 1.

8. A tear in the paper around the seal accounts for the obscured words.

9. *The Scottish Chiefs* by Jane Porter was published in 1810. She had been raised in Edinburgh and was a childhood friend of Sir Walter Scott. Written in London, the novel was translated into Russian and German and was probably her best-known work.

Edward's boldness was rewarded by the following letter, in which Emily more or less agreed to the engagement he had proposed. Although she stated that "my feelings are in unison with yours," she was even more concerned with her father's feelings. Apparently he had never told her that he approved of the match but did indicate that he favored an engagement of some length. Edward may have found it

*difficult to distinguish Joel Norcross's reticence from Emily's, as I do.
In any event, Edward was not confident of the success of his suit until
he visited Monson in mid-November.*

24
Emily Norcross to Edward
30 October 1826

Monson Monday Evening

I regret very much dear Edward that I have not been able to answer
your letter which I recieved last week untill the present evening in
which you observed you had been expecting to hear from me for a
week past I am sensible it is what you had reason to expect yet I have
not willingly disappointed you. There are many things to prevent my
writing of which you are not acquainted but from what I have ex-
pressed, you cannot suppose me unmindful [?] of you that has oca-
sioned my delay as I have endeavoured to convince you of the reverse.
You remarked that you were quite ill after your return. I imagine our
social evening was not a proper remedy for your disease yet I enjoyed
it to well to speak unfavourably of it, but I would again consult your
own good rather than my happiness, with respect to our present sub-
ject it is one which I have regarded with tender interest yet I am
sensible that I have never exercised that freedom which I presume you
have desired me to still it has given me much pleasure to discover in
you so much frankness. My father has said but very little to me since
our last interview yet I think myself acquainted with his views and you
may rightly conclude that my feelings are in unison with yours I am
happy to learn that you are not disposed to be in haste the reasons you
have advanced correspond perfectly with my fathers views relative to
this particular point and his counsil you would ever wish me to recieve
would you not. I desire to say more to you but the late hour of this
evening will soon prevent me I have this evening called at Uncle E
Norcross after I returned recieved a visit from our favorite physician
who met you at our house one afternoon, and am now pleasantly
engaged in converse with you, while all around are quietly at rest.

Cousin Maria returned with Olivia quite unexpected yet I was
happy indeed to see them but regreted that Mr Coleman did not
accompany them. They observed that you called on them the morning
before. I have the pleasure of saying to you that brother Hiram still
continues better. He past two days of last week at Brimfield for the
purpose of attending a court of which Mr Mills was present. I am
quite unwilling to send you this hasty written letter but still more

unwilling that the mail should leave tomorrow without some communication from me but may I not safely entrust it with you.

I remain as ever yours.

Emily

Engaged at last after his stay in Monson from 16 to 18 November, Edward was far from jubilant. He was embarrassed that the horse he borrowed for the trip had died, outraged by the success of the Turks in the Greek civil war ("The Eden of creation is turned into a field of carnage & bloodshed"), and anxious about his ability to support a wife. There is also some indication that his physical separation from Emily was troubling him. Characteristically, he sought to suppress his erotic longings: "It is now between 11. & 12. o'clock—all around me are still, & you are probably quietly at rest—Yet, as ours must be a communion of spirits, what matters it whether our bodies are in one situation or another." Even Thanksgiving disturbed him, as he described "hundreds who live without so much as the necessities of life *the remainder of the year, collect their all, & forget their cares & troubles & miseries in one grand rioting—thus perverting an anniversary established for better ends, into a day of revelling & feasting & mirth." Endeavoring to cultivate the "real spirit of thankfulness," Edward signed himself "Yours forever." Clearly, he was angry and upset.*

25
Edward to Emily Norcross
27 November 1826

Amherst. Monday Evening. Nov. 27. 1826.

My Dear Emily,

Two of the Greeks are going to Monson to participate with you in the pleasures of Thanksgiving, and I am unwilling to lose so favorable an opportunity of writing to you.[1] The day after my return, my fears in relation to my horse were confirmed by the news of his death—and as much as I regret that so noble an animal should die in my care, and as much as I pity the owner, it is still a consolation to know that no blame is imputed to me by any one—All consider it as an accident, & we have got up a subscription for the owner, & shall be able to do something handsome towards making up his loss. It is past, & no doubt "all for the best;" and to mourn can do no good.

It is now between 11. & 12. o'clock—all around me are still, & you are probably quietly at rest—Yet, as ours must be a communion of spirits, what matters it whether our bodies are in one situation or another. I enjoyed our last interview extremely—and the mutual interchange of feeling to which it gave rise has contributed very much to my happiness. To be assured of what I before but hesitatingly believed, and to know that my attachment was mutual, and my proposals for forming the most interesting of all earthly connections, accepted, gave me the most sober & rational satisfaction. And nothing now could add to the pleasure with which I shall anticipate the consummation of our mutual wishes, but a conviction that I was worthy of your affection & confidence. How [?] I feel sensible, at the same time that I propose to you to leave your present happy situation, that you run a great risk—that you hazard your happiness—your all—and in confiding to me the protection of your person, & the guardianship of your peace & enjoyment, & the preservation of all that is dear to you, you show a spirit of dignified confidence & elevated trust in my integrity & honor, which are worthy of a more meritorious subject. And after making the utmost exertions in my power to deserve your virtuous esteem, I can only pray that your confidence may not prove to have been misplaced.

I am like the majority of young men who recieve an education & engage in a profession: I rely upon my exertions for success. My education is my inheritence—& my prospects of patronage depend on my diligence, industry, faithfulness, correctness in business & maintaining a character worthy of the confidence & respect of my acquaintance.

And with the illustrious examples around us, who have struggled to honorable eminence by their own resolute determination to be great, no man ought to be discouraged—but, on the contrary, there is every possible inducement to untiring effort, & the surest prospect that real merit will recieve its due, & that integrity & ability will recieve their reward. No man has a right to be disspirited—his duty to himself, his friends, his country, & his God, demand the exertion of his highest powers—and no one has a right to place himself in a situation in which he can not act with energy & decision & independence. And a man who is so fortunate as to possess this stern decision of character can not fail to press his way through opposition & difficulties, and reach the object of his highest reasonable ambition. Men are unconscious of the power which they possess—And when compelled by circumstances to make a desperate effort, the greatest difficulties vanish—the mightiest obstacles are removed—and the most powerful opposition disappears—and the path which, at first view, appears to lead over mountains and precipices, as you proceed, becomes smooth & plain & beautiful.

Look at the examples of our own country, South America & (I wish I could add with equal confidence,) *Greece*—There is no nation on the face of the globe that is attended with so many interesting associations. Where once flourished the arts & sciences in the highest perfection—the birth-place of the most celebrated poets, the most distinguished orators & the most learned philosophers—the seat of refinement—the pattern of taste & the dwelling place of beauty & elegance—& the abode of the gods & goddesses—& in short, the very name of Greece fills the mind with the idea of all that is beautiful & elegant—with all that can charm & please & animate—and the imagination delights to revel amid her rosy bowers, her groves & caves & grottoes—to wander amid her classic retreats—to view the place where Homer sung—where Plato taught—& the eloquence of Demosthenes charmed & persuaded & convinced & delighted.— And, would to heaven! there were but one side to the picture. But alas! how changed. The Eden of creation is turned into a field of carnage & bloodshed. The Paradise of the world is converted into a "den of thieves & robbers." Where once flourished the olive & the vine, now grow the thistle & the bramble—where once stood the temples of science & the altars of religion, now stand the Turkish Mosques—No longer do the inhabitants of that once happy land listen with delight to the strains of the choicest music—no longer do they hear the triumphs celebrated in the most beautiful poetry—their poets & their orators are no more—their galleries of paintings, the works of the most distinguished artists, no longer delight the eye, or gratify the taste, the sweetest music is exchanged for the harsh notes of war— their refinement, for barbarism—their hospitality, for cruelty—And could the spirits of those sainted heroes who fell fighting for their country in the days of her former glory, rise & behold the land of their fathers laid waste—their children murdered—their wives & daughters doomed to a fate *worse than death*—and their land in the possession of savages & barbarians—how would they shriek! & call on that Almighty Being [who] controuls the destinies of nations, & in whose hands are all worlds, to ride forth in the chariot of his might & kill & exterminate & annihilate these murderers—how would they imprecate the vengeance of Heaven on the heads of these butchers—these blood-thirsty tyrants—these enemies of the human race—and how earnestly would they "call on the rocks & mountains & caves of the earth to fall on them & cover them"[2] from the sight of such horrors! Would to Heaven! that all the powers of darkness might be let loose upon these ungodly savages, and that they might be permitted to drag them to the bottomless pit, where they might forever be compelled to drink the lowest dregs of the vials of the wrath of the Almighty! And if the prayers of all Christendom can be of any avail, they ought to ascend day & night for these unhappy & wretched people.

Please to express my grateful obligations to your brother Wm. for his kindness in carrying me home,[3] & remember me affectionately to your father's family & all your friends—& let me hear from you by the Greeks who will return on Monday.

Thanksgiving draws near—and the bustle & preparation which always precedes this annual feast, are every where visible—and hundreds who live without so much as the *necessities of life* the remainder of the year, collect their all, & forget their cares & troubles & miseries in one grand rioting—thus perverting an anniversary established for better ends, into a day of revelling & feasting & mirth.—

But should it be kept properly, hardly any thing could have a better effect upon the mind—and could that real spirit of thankfulness be exercised, which the constant reception of good demands, we should all become better, & be better prepared for the duties of life. I wish you much happiness & enjoyment in every thing, & shall ever rejoice to know that you are always prepared for a Thanksgiving—and in whatever amusements you engage, remember one who joins most cordially in every thing which can promote your happiness, and believe that whatever affects you, will interest me in the same way—and be assured that it will always afford me the highest pleasure to feel that our wishes—our object, our interests, & our happiness, & ourselves are *one & the same.*—Once more, let me repeat the assurance of my warmest affection, & sincerely subscribe myself, *Yours forever. Edward*

1. There were Greek refugees in both Amherst and Monson. In Letter 27 Emily refers to "the Greeks who reside with you," that is, in the Dickinson household.

2. Probably Heb. 11:38, expanded and slightly misquoted.

3. After Edward's borrowed horse sickened in Monson, William drove him back to Amherst.

Emily's letter is preceded by a short letter from her brother William to Edward, thanking him for the use of "goods and chattels" (presumably a humorous allusion to reading materials) and returning them. Both letters are written on the same sheet of paper.

26
Emily Norcross to Edward
2 December 1826

Sat.

Dear Edward

I fear you will think me quite inexcuseable unless I say one word to you. My engagements through the week have been so urgent that you must excuse me yet I have much to say and will write soon.

yours Emily.

Emily was quick to identify with Edward's physical misfortune—the incident with the horse—and sensed that, when he had written Letter 25, he was feeling sorry for himself. Although she apologized for the inadequacy of her letter, in fact she sounds more than usually responsive to him. Ignoring his anger which had not been explicitly directed against her in any case, she remarked, "Have you not often heard the observation that the bitter useually accompanies the sweet, but it may not always prove true, at least may one overpower the other."

27
Emily Norcross to Edward
15 December 1826

Friday Evening

May I hope dear Edward that you do not think me insensible how much I am indebted to you, as I am unwilling to suppose that you think more of recieveing letters from me than I do of answering yours. I have designed writing evry evening of this week but have not succeeded untill the present in my endeavours and it is attended with some inconvenience that I leave my Mother this evening as she is quite indisposed, but for the pleasure of conversing with you a short time I lay aside inconvenienties [?] as you may suppose I often admit them to prevent me from executeing my purposes I was happy to hear of your safe arrival home and that your misfortune was supposed no fault of yours. I imagine I thought more of it than any one else except yourself which is perfectly natural, but have you not often heard the observation that the bitter useually accompanies the sweet, but it may not always prove true, at least may one overpower the other We had an interesting visit from the Greeks who reside with you Constantine was very polite indeed to call with your letter as soon as he came in town, which was quite unexpected but I can assure you that it was read with much pleasure. I presume you have expected to recieve the book you left with me before this but I know of no particular opportunity that I can send it to you but if you wish I will send it by the stage.[1] With respect to our last interview it is not necessary for me to say that I enjoyed it for I presume you were convinced of it. And now dear E I must leave you but with the pleasent anticipation that we shall meet again. This letter appears quite to short but I have been obliged to write in haste and may believe that you will accept the few lines I have written from your sincere Emily

1. The book cannot be identified. Perhaps Edward left another historical novel, by a woman writer.

28
Edward to Emily Norcross
18 December 1826

Amherst, Monday Eve, 12. o'clock, Dec. 18. 1826.
My Dear Emily,

This has been an uncommonly busy day with me. I have had no leisure till now, when the last man has just left my office: and I should not address you so soon after the reception of your letter, (which came to hand this afternoon,) were it not to inform you, that in consequence of my father's expectation of leaving home the fore part of next week, to spend some weeks in Albany, on business before the legislature of N. York, it will be inconvenient for me to visit you for several weeks, unless I can go this week—and business is such that I must probably call on *Saturday*, in which case, I shall calculate to return on Monday Morning. If your Mother is no better, or it is otherwise inconvenient for you to see me at that time, will you inform me by the returning mail, & I will postpone it till my father's return.[1] *Possibly* I may go on *Thursday*—tho' probably not. You need not omit *writing* on that account.

I shall say but a few words—as I anticipate the pleasure of meeting you so soon. My health and spirits are good—my business equal to my expectations—and my hope that I shall succeed is not, as yet, in the least weakened. And while engaged in my business, & enjoying the pleasures of active life, it can not be necessary for me to say to you, that the anticipation of ere long being permitted to share those pleasures with one so dear to me, adds much to my happiness in the performance of all the duties which devolve upon me. My constant prayers will ascend for your health & your happiness, & the preservation & perfection of all the virtues which adorn & dignify & elevate the female character. And now I must leave you, My Dear E. let me join with you "in the pleasant anticipation that we shall meet again", & soon.[2] In the mean time, having presented my warmest respects to all your friends & my interest in their prosperity, recieve again the oft repeated assurance that there is no friend to whom your happiness is dearer than to Your Edward.

1. Edward visited Monson on Saturday and Sunday (23 and 24 December) as he intended to do.
2. Edward is quoting Emily's letter.

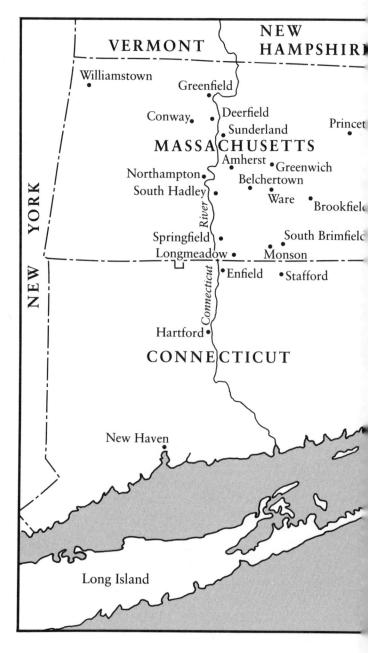

Map of the southern part of New England, taken from Timothy Dwight's Travels in New England and New York *(New Haven, 1821).*

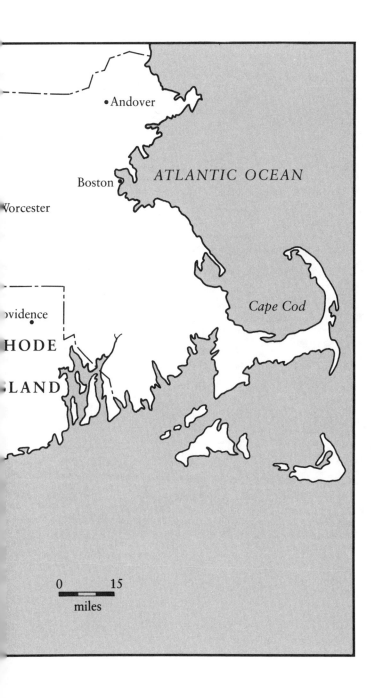

Andover

ATLANTIC OCEAN

Boston

Worcester

Cape Cod

Providence

RHODE

ISLAND

0   15
miles

*Edward Dickinson's first letter to Emily Norcross, 8 February 1826.
By permission of the Houghton Library, Harvard University.*

The first page of Emily Norcross's letter to Edward, 30 October 1826, in which she more or less accepted his proposal of marriage. By permission of the Houghton Library, Harvard University.

Betsy Fay Norcross and Joel Norcross in portraits by an unidentified painter, about 1820. By permission of Amherst College.

Lucretia Gunn Dickinson and Samuel Fowler Dickinson in silhouettes by William King, about 1828.

Emily Norcross Dickinson and Edward Dickinson in silhouettes, about 1828.

Emily Norcross Dickinson and Edward Dickinson in 1840, painted by Otis A. Bullard. By permission of the Houghton Library, Harvard University.

The Dickinson children: Emily, Austin, and Lavinia, painted by Otis A. Bullard in 1840. By permission of the Houghton Library, Harvard University.

The house on North Pleasant Street where the Dickinsons lived from 1840 to 1855, photographed in about 1870. By permission of the Todd-Bingham Picture Collection, Yale University Library.

Emily Dickinson in 1848, the only known photograph of the poet, taken at Mount Holyoke when she was seventeen. Amherst College Library. By permission of the Trustees of Amherst College.

*Austin Dickinson in 1850, photographed at the time of his
graduation from Amherst College. Amherst College Archives.
By permission of the Trustees of Amherst College.*

Lavinia Dickinson in 1852. By permission of the Jones Library, Amherst.

Edward Dickinson, in a photograph variously dated 1853, 1860, 1874. By permission of the Houghton Library, Harvard University.

*The Dickinson homestead, built by Samuel Fowler Dickinson in
1813 and photographed at some much later time. The bedroom
where the poet did most of her work is to the upper left. By
permission of the Houghton Library, Harvard University.*

II

LETTERS 29–68

[1827]

"My Mother is yet quite low"

"You have not done right in refusing so many invitations to visit Amherst"

This rather impersonal and low-spirited New Year's greeting was writ-
ten on Edward's twenty-fourth birthday. Given that he and Emily had
become engaged in the year just ended, his emphasis on neglected
opportunities is disquieting. I take it that Edward was feeling unap-
preciated and was attempting to transform his self-pity to socially
useful ends. To some extent Edward also saw himself as the redeemer
of mankind, which perhaps explains the as yet unconverted state of
his soul. Nevertheless, there are indications that he aspired to social as
well as religious grace: "An uniformly benevolent disposition—agree-
able deportment & winning manners tend to produce a kindred feel-
ing in all who associate with the happy possessor of these good quali-
ties. They give a charm & a grace to every word & action—and they
shew [show] a respect for society which indicates a generous and
liberal & noble soul—and seldom fail to command the esteem and
respect & confidence of all who witness their exercise." But Edward
was too solemn to master fully the social graces, and the poet alludes
to his social awkwardness repeatedly in her early letters.

29
Edward to Emily Norcross
1 January 1827

Amherst, Monday Evening, January 1.st 1827.

My Dear Emily,

While I most heartily wish you many "*a happy new year*," and
respond to the sentiment of the Poet, that

> " 'Tis greatly wise to talk with our past hours,
> " And ask them what report they bore to Heaven;
> " And how they might have borne more welcome news."[1]

I know you will unite with me in saying that if there is any period of
our existence when it is peculiarly proper for us to review our past
lives, it is at the close of one year, & the commencement of another.
We can not reflect on the past without emotions of the most varied
character. We can all recollect the scenes thro' which we have passed
—the pleasures, pains, cares, solicitudes, & anxieties which we have
experienced—In glancing from the beginning to the end of the year
that is now gone, a thousand interesting associations rush upon the
mind, & it is hurried from one scene, and one transaction to another,
giving us merely time to drop a tear at the remembrance of the suf-
ferings of some of our fellow men, and to feel a momentary glow of
pleasure at the happiness which multitudes have procured for them-
selves. Our hearts should overflow with gratitude, that while so many

millions of our fellow beings have been laid in the grave, and their day of probation forever past, we are still preserved—that we enjoy the blessings of health, and the pleasures of friendship—that while famine has raged, & pestilence prevailed in other countries, we have been well provided for—our friends have all been spared to us—and that we now enjoy all the comforts which can be rationally desired.

What have we done that we could wish otherwise—how could we have concluded to become more useful to society—what more could we have done to promote the happiness of our friends—what could have been omitted—could we have relieved the distressed—comforted the afflicted, soothed the troubled—calmed the agitated, extended our charity to the needy & destitute, or in any way, have done more good?

Have we neglected opportunities for the improvement of our minds, or our hearts? Have we profited by all the means of moral & religious instruction which we have enjoyed? And, in short, are there not many things in which we may improve, in the year to come? Can we not spend our time more profitably? Can we not render ourselves more useful? Can we not do more towards promoting the happiness of all around us—of meliorating the condition of the wretched—Can we not recollect some things which we should do differently in future— Have we been as prudent—as industrious, as resolute, and as deter- mined to pursue the paths of rectitude & virtue, as we ought? Have we cultivated those excellencies of character which are calculated to increase our respectability and our influence among our friends and acquaintance? Have we improved in our dispositions, our tastes, our habits, & our characters? Are there not some things in which we can constantly improve, and be constantly preparing to add to each oth- er's happiness, as well as to that of all who come within the sphere of our influence. It is almost incalculable, how much good one person, who is properly disposed, may accomplish. There are a thousand little circumstances which add much to the amount of happiness or misery in the world. A kind word, or look may often produce a pleasing emotion in the object of it for days & weeks.

An uniformly benevolent disposition—agreeable deportment & win- ning manners tend to produce a kindred feeling in all who associate with the happy possessor of these good qualities. They give a charm & a grace to every word & action—and they shew [show] a respect for society which indicates a generous and liberal & noble soul—and seldom fail to command the esteem and respect & confidence of all who witness their exercise.

And now Dear E. let us ask ourselves one solemn question—Have we experienced that radical change in our hearts, in our tempers & dispositions, which renders us the subjects of the favor of our Maker?

I make no pretensions to any thing of the kind. But I am not at all times unmindful of the subject. It is one in which we are all interested. It is entirely a personal concern—and each one must stand or fall by himself. And odd as it may sound for me to lecture on morality, I feel that there are times in which persons sustaining the relations which we do to each other, and expecting to be companions for life, can with propriety open their whole hearts to each other, and converse familiarly upon subjects which concern our future interests, and endeavor to excite each other to prepare for that state of being to which we are all destined, & fit ourselves for the enjoyment of those pure & refined pleasures which are in store for those only who fear & love & obey the Deity. And tho' I am not a christian, myself, yet I should rejoice to know that *you* were of that happy class—and while I judge only from your want of making a profession of that character, that you do not consider yourself as of the number, I should hear that I was mistaken, with the most heartfelt satisfaction.[2] Every thing that can increase your happiness, will, in the same proportion, promote mine—and to be assured that after spending the comparatively short time that is allotted us here, in such a manner as to be able, at the close of our journey, to [look back?] upon lives well spent, and enjoy the consciousness of having done all in our power to add to the sum of human happiness, we should both be admitted to a participation of those joys which are only found at the right hand of our Judge, and forever increase in knowledge and happiness, would give me a satisfaction which all the richest earthly blessings could not equal. Let our prayers ascend, morning & evening, for each other, and may we be prepared for a happy life and a peaceful death!

It is growing late, & I will tax your patience no longer. I feel much anxiety for your health, and must caution you to avoid exposing yourself too much to the cold. Let me hear from you, soon. I fear you are not sensible how much a cold affects you—and I must again urge you to be careful. And in saying "good night", & extending the parting hand, I feel the pleasure which arises from the belief that there exists between us a bond of attachment and affection, which I trust nothing but the loss of a virtuous reputation or the life itself of one of us, will be able to sever. Believe that I remain as

Sincerely as ever
Your Affectionate Edward

I am 24. years old to-day. One year to-morrow morning since I first went to Monson. E——

P.S. It has snowed almost incessantly for two or three days past—and there are no signs of fair weather, as yet. You had better ride to A. [Amherst] with Wm. when the sleighing becomes good—some day this week or next. Do you think it would be improper? If so, don't you come. You know best about it. I should be happy to see you.

1. Edward Young, *Night Thoughts*, bk. 2, lines 376–78.

2. Emily Norcross Dickinson experienced the necessary conversion and joined the church in July 1831, but the poet subsequently described her mother as lacking an authentic religious sensibility.

This letter is written on an unusually small sheet of paper and was hand delivered, presumably by Lyman Coleman.

30
Edward to Emily Norcross
17 January 1827

Amherst Jan.y 17. 1827.

My Dear Emily,

I send you a copy of "Thaddeus of Warsaw", which I presume you will find very interesting.[1] I am going to Belchertown with Parson Washburn, this afternoon, & carry it for Mr. Coleman to send.[2] I expect daily, to hear from you, & shall write again, soon. Do you mean to visit me, with William? In haste,

Your devoted friend
Edward

1. *Thaddeus of Warsaw* by Jane Porter was published in 1803. Perhaps in the early 1850s, the poet Emily Dickinson read this romance of political exile and may have been the person who added "& Miss E. Dickinson" to Edward's copy, which was inscribed "E. Dickinson 1827." See Jack L. Capps, *Emily Dickinson's Reading, 1836–1886* (Cambridge, Mass.: Harvard University Press, 1966), p. 99.

2. The Reverend Royal Washburn was pastor of the First Congregational Church in Amherst from 1826 until his death in 1832.

31
Emily Norcross to Edward
24 January 1827

Monson Wednesday Evening

Dear Edward

Late as it is I cannot excuse myself without conversing awhile with you. I am sensible that I justly deserve to be censured by you for remaining silant so long. Yet it is not entirely my fault that you have not heard from me I wrote last week and directed my letter to a particular friend, but through mistake it was not sent out as I expected a furthur explanation I must defer for the present.[1] I have thought much of the subject of your letter dear Edward and my feelings were much interested in the sentiments you expressed and for your benevolent wishes for my present and future happiness I can but ardently desire you the same It gives me pleasure to discover that you are so familiar with the interesting subject of religion, and it is my earnest desire that we may individualy[?] experience its happy influence convinced as we are that it is required[?] in any situation in life to render us useful and truly happy. I visited cousin Maria a short time since accompanied by Eliza Cousin Olive and William I enjoyed the interview very much, found them agreably situated as you have often told me my happiness however would have been much augmented could I have persued my journey still further but circumstances would not admit of it, and I presume that you are not disappointed that I did not as you left it for my decision.[2] How do you like the cold weather dear Edward of which we are well supplied I trust better than I do. Yet I hope not to complain of it. I regret that I must again repeat that I have much that would give me pleasure to disclose to you, and have not time, but I am happy to learn that my example is not worthy of notice. I suspect you would like to be excused from this hasty letter ere this but believe me your devoted Emily

1. Emily may have expected a friend to hand deliver her letter to Edward. I am puzzled by the fact that she did not send it to Edward along with the new one, once the mistake had been discovered, and cannot help wondering whether the missing letter ever existed. As usual, Emily writes after a lengthy delay (in this case about six weeks) to say, in part, that due to circumstances beyond her control, she is unable to write a letter that would satisfy either of them. Her letter was sent by mail.

2. In his Letter 29 (1 January 1827), Edward wrote, "You had better ride to A. [Amherst] with Wm. when the sleighing becomes good—some day this week or next. Do you think it would be improper? If so, don't you come. You know best about it. I should be happy to see you." In Letter 30 (17 January 1827), he per-

sisted, "Do you mean to visit me, with William?" Emily's logic assumes that Edward would not have been disappointed by a free choice on her part. Note that she does not describe the circumstances that prevented her from visiting Amherst.

Buoyed up by a job offer away from Amherst, in the following letter Edward sounds less tense about his career and more confident about supporting a wife. Though for the moment he was content to remain in Amherst and described himself as "perfectly satisfied" with his professional situation, in Letter 36 he was still tempted by the prospect of a more extensive practice in a larger place.

32
Edward to Emily Norcross
1 February 1827

Amherst. Thursday Morning. February 1. 1827.
My Dear Emily,

I can not let this pleasant morning pass without saying a few words to you, though I shall have but very little time. I have intended to write two or three times before, but my business, which you know, must always be first attended to, has prevented. I have been unusually occupied for the last two or three weeks, and am happy to say to you that business is as good as I ought to desire in the commencement, and I can not but hope that a diligent attention to it will insure me a fair share of practice, and I am determined that as far as exertion can do it, nothing shall be wanting on my part to *deserve* the confidence of all that need assistance from a person of my profession.

I was at Belchertown, on Wednesday of the week after your visit at Mr. Coleman's with Rev. Mr. Washburn, and was sorry to learn that you had come so far on your way, & could not extend your ride a little farther, as we should all have been extremely glad to have seen you & the rest of your party.[1]

We have an abundance of snow, and the sleighing has been excellent for several weeks, and business, in consequence, has been very lively. I have not had an opportunity, as yet, however, of improving it much, as the absence of my father a great part of the time confined me closely to my office.[2] He is now at Albany, tho' he has been at home a fortnight since he first went. His business before the Legislature is not yet finished, but he will return in the course of the next week.

I hope soon to meet you again. My business will lead me to Belchertown, on Tuesday or Wednesday of next week, and if possible, I shall intend to go as far as Monson. Probably I shall go on Tuesday and shall either set out early enough to reach there in the forenoon, and return the same day, or defer it till afternoon, & be with you in the course of the evening, & return early the next morning. Would it not be agreeable to you to return with me & stay a day or two. It would give me much pleasure to have you. Think of it.

I have lately had an invitation to remove to Princeton in Worcester County, & settle.[3] The offers are very favorable, & the encouragement held out, better than any place within my knowledge presents. Had it been made before I was established, I can't say what my determination might have been respecting the acceptance of it, but since I have fixed upon a place, it will require strong inducements to convince me that it is best to remove. I am contented, & thus far, feel perfectly satisfied with my situation.

My time, as I said, in the beginning, is short, & almost spent, and I must defer almost all I should be glad to say, till I see you. With respect to the time of forming the union on which we have agreed, I should like to converse with you, and perhaps with your father & mother, definitely, at our next interview. It is now proper, don't you think it is, that we should know something in relation to it—and it would be very agreeable to me, to take all circumstances into consideration, and conclude upon some time, which they and ourselves shall think proper. You all understand my circumstances, and I presume know something of my prospects of success—and tho' as I have said more than once to you, it is your duty to yourself & your friends to wait till you see & are satisfied that, under all the circumstances relating to me, I have a reasonable belief that my exertions will procure me a respectable standing among the profession, & ensure me a handsome support, yet, as soon as it is proper, I should like to consummate a connection from which I anticipate so much happiness, and I need not assure you again that it will ever be my highest pleasure to promote your happiness, & render you all you desire to be, & all that your virtues will not fail to secure to you.

I must stop. Give my compliments to E. Norcross Esq. & Eliza—Olivia etc. and receive for your father's family my high esteem—while you need not that I should say any thing which can increase your conviction that I am, & shall ever continue to remain your affectionate and devoted Edward

How does Hiram do. Remember me to him & his wife. In haste. "Good Morning"

E——

1. Belchertown is approximately eight miles south of Amherst and twelve miles north of Monson.

2. Edward means that he has not been able to take advantage of the opportunity for sleighing because he has been working so hard.

3. Princeton is approximately thirty-five miles northeast of Amherst.

As he had proposed to do, Edward visited Monson on 6 and 7 February. He hoped to establish a time for his marriage to Emily by conferring with her parents, but Mrs. Norcross was ill and he was not able to discuss this weighty matter with them, although he did broach the subject to Emily. On the way home, Edward had another accident. Alert to the symbolism of his ill-fated journeys, Edward rejected its prophetic power. He was determined not to be victimized by "superstitious notions."

33
Edward to Emily Norcross
21 February 1827

Amherst, Wednesday Evening, Feb. y 21. 1827.

My Dear Emily,

I intended to have written to you by the last mail, but was prevented—and as this has been a comparatively leisure day, and I have had but a few calls, I have written an Essay for the N.E. Enquirer, read Morgan's "Illustrations of Masonry", and shall now devote a portion of the Evening to you.[1] I have felt anxious to hear from [about] your Mother's health, as well as yours, but conclude that she has recovered from the ill turn which confined her when I was last at Monson. Do you get relief from the complaint which has so long troubled you? and can you not find the cause of the disease, & remove it? I think much of you, and should rejoice to discover some specific which would restore you to perfect health. However, you must continue to exercise patience, & cheerfully submit to the allotments of Providence—It is undoubtedly right, & we must not repine.

I did not reach home till evening, on the day when I left you, in consequence of being obliged to go to Enfield after my eldest Sister, who was there on a visit.[2] I was prevented from returning through Ware, as I intended, by meeting with an accident—in getting my sleigh badly broken—It seems as if the fates had conspired against me, & were I a believer in superstitious notions, & did I regard, in the least, the signs which have terrified many a timid soul, the road to M. would be thronged with terrors, & my imagination could easily forebode the most dire calamities—beset the way with impending evils, & fill me with anxious fears, lest misfortune was waiting in some secret place to seize me—but I am happy that I am not troubled with imaginary evils.—I seldom give myself uneasiness till there is a rational ground for it, & the accidents which have happened to me while going to visit you, have no terror in them, nor do I consider them as any evidence that the Unseen Agency which directs all events, has chosen this method to manifest his displeasure, as many would construe it—I have reason to be thankful that I have escaped any personal injury, & shall not complain till some disaster, greater than any which I have yet experienced, befals me. How soon that may take place, I know not, but while I am ordinarily prudent & careful, they will not be attributable to negligence.

You may think it strange, that I say any thing, in the present letter in relation to the subject on which I wrote in my last, & about which we conversed, at our last interview—the time of our intended union for life. But my object in wishing to converse further upon it, is, to ascertain the opinion of your friends—and when that is known, to make my arrangements accordingly. I have repeatedly said, you know, that I have no disposition to be in haste—and I should wish to consult your feelings entirely. You know my opinion—& recollect my proposal, & if the latest time mentioned is more agreeable to you & thought more proper by your family, I shall most cheerfully acquiesce—But if they should be inclined to fix upon an earlier period, as proper, I should be prepared & make suitable provisions for it.—

I know it is what you can not converse about, freely & familiarly, & you know that I could not say so much in a letter, as I could to sit down with a view to enter into the whole matter, & give every separate consideration its due weight, & its proper influence in making [up our] decision. Our *mutual happiness* is my object, & whatever promotes that gratifies my wishes. You know that my education is my fortune—my inheritance, that I have recd. my Academical & Professional education, and now depend on that for my Support—and tho' I am stating what I have said before, & what you have no doubt, long ago learned from other sources, still I wish not to lead you blindfold— I wish nothing to be concealed in relation to my circumstances, or my character—I want you to know *exactly what I am*—and wish you to *take me for what I am* & nothing more. My object has always been to induce you to refer to such sources for information, as would enable you to form an opinion according to the truth—I wish you not to be deceived, or disappointed—and I trust you know enough of me to be satisfied that while your happiness is so dear to me, I should feel it a duty which you would owe to yourself & your friends, if you thought my prospects were not such as to justify our marriage, at present, to say it to me exactly as you thought it. & a regard to *my* pleasure ought not to have the least influence in the case. You are happy, as you are, & you ought not to change till you are convinced, beyond a reasonable doubt, that it will be [un]diminished. I say all this by way of caution, & to put you on your guard, lest you form mistaken notions of a character with which you have had so little opportunity of becoming acquainted. Still you may rest assured, that all I *can do, will be done*, and that I shall exert myself to the utmost to rise in my profession—and no exertions will be wanting to attain that rank which will insure respectability & happiness.

Our College Chapel is to be dedicated, one week from to-day—a large, assemblage is expected, and we should be glad to see Wm. & you here at that time, & any other of your friends that can come. I feel anxious to have you visit us, & wish if consistent, you would come up on Tuesday & pass a little time with us. If the sleighing continues, I shall expect you & calculate on seeing you.

And now, My Dear E. my time is short, and I must defer much that I should be glad to say, till I meet you, or write you again. And in the mean time may you continue to cultivate your virtues, and become qualified, in every respect, to adorn & dignify every station in which you may be called to act. We are all acting under the weight of great responsibilities—talents are committed to us to improve, & account for—and while every earthly inducement—the prospects of honor & fame, & the more quiet, tho' more pure enjoyment of domestic felicity, urges us to be active & untiring in all the duties of our respective spheres, higher & more noble motives ought to actuate us—We are placed in a world of vicissitude & change—surrounded by an endless variety of objects, & conversant, necessarily, with a vast diversity of characters—Temptations beset us on every side[3] The allurements of vice are constantly presented to us—The powers of evil, & the "enemies of all righteousness," are not wanting in their attempts to lead us from the paths of virtue. We are constantly assailed from some quarter, with some unexpected motive—some inducement to stray from the line of duty. But, we can not guard our lives & conduct too strictly. We can not watch over ourselves too closely. And while a regard to our own peace & happiness—a desire to extend the blessings of education, & to impart to all the destitute, the choicest comforts which we enjoy, ought to impel us to use our utmost exertions to promote the prosperity of all within the Sphere of our influence—we should not forget that we act under the eye of a Power, who knows all our thoughts, and before whom we shall one day, be summoned to appear. May you be amiable, virtuous & happy—enjoy all the blessings which earth can give—shed an heavenly influence upon the world—& be as blessed as the lot of humanity will admit—& while my prayers will ascend for you daily, may we be so happy as to pass thro' life in each others society, rendering each other happy & useful & honorable, & at the close of it, meet in a brighter world, where we shall part no more. Present my compliments to your father's family, Eliza, etc. & believe me ever Your devoted Edward

Does Hiram continue better? If anything should prevent you from coming to attend our Dedication, you will not fail to let me hear from you, soon. Is the Greek, who has been so long sick, alive?⁴ Good night.—

1. William Morgan's *Illustrations of Masonry* was published in 1826, shortly after he disappeared under mysterious circumstances. There was speculation that he had been murdered by the Masons for having exposed their secret practices.

Edward wrote five essays on "Female Education" in the *New-England Inquirer*, which were published on 22 December 1826, 5 January 1827, 26 January 1827, 23 February 1827, and 20 April 1827. All of these essays were published under the pseudonym "Coelebs" (a bachelor) and were loosely modeled after the periodical essay style of the *Spectator*. Presumably Edward is referring to the essay of 23 February, in which he expostulated,

> How does it affect us—what ideas does it produce in our minds, to receive an epistle from a valued friend, with half the words mis-spelled—in which capitals and small letters have changed positions—where a plural noun is followed by a singular verb—where periods and commas are inserted promiscuously, without regard to sound or sense, or what, perhaps, is still worse, omitted altogether, and which nothing but the good sense of the reader would enable him to understand? These are, in fact, the fundamentals of all education, and no female ought to hazard her reputation or happiness, by remaining ignorant of these things which, more than all others, stamp upon the character, the impress of cultivation, or fix upon it the stain of radical deficiency.

Samuel Fowler Dickinson owned a copy of Mrs. Hannah More's novel *Coelebs in Search of a Wife: Comprehending Observations on Domestic Habits and Manners, Religion and Morals,* from which Edward derived his nom de plume. Samuel Fowler's two-volume edition was published in Boston in 1810 and was the fifth American edition. Byron satirizes the bachelor-hero's calculating priggishness in *Don Juan* bk. 1, canto 16, line 4, when he alludes to " 'Coelebs' Wife' . . . in quest of lovers."

2. Edward's sister Lucretia Gunn Dickinson (1806–1885) married the Reverend Asa Bullard in 1832.

3. Edward's punctuation is obscured by a tear around the seal.

4. Edward is referring to a Greek student at Monson Academy who boarded with the headmaster, Simeon Colton. See Letter 34.

Edward's religious imagination was excited by the anticipated death of a promising Greek student, as it had been by the death of William Penniman several months earlier. His political imagination was equally excited by the Greek struggle for independence, with which, as an American, he was patriotically identified.

34
Edward to Emily Norcross
24 February 1827

Amherst. Saturday Morning. Feb. y 24. 1827.

My Dear Emily,

Pandias very politely called at my office, last evening to inform me that Nicholas and Constantine were going to Monson this morning, in consequence of a letter recd. yesterday, in which news was contained, that the Greek who has been so long sickening at Mr. Colton's could not probably live much longer, and tho' I wrote so lately, I can not let so good an opportunity pass without saying a few words.[1]

I have felt much interested in whatever related to these young men, or their unhappy country—and, while this news is what I *expected* to hear, yet *to know* that a person for whom so much had been done, who was so intelligent, and promising, & for whom the united prayers of thousands had ascended, & who had formed so brilliant anticipations of returning to the land of his nativity, to assist in giving direction to the energies of his countrymen—to animate & cheer & encourage them in the holiest of all causes, the struggle for liberty—and who was peculiarly calculated, from the unusually intelligent mind which he possessed, of [for] exerting a most commanding influence in the councils of his nation—I say, to *know*, that such a person must die! and that too, at a time, when his exertions were so much needed—when all the independent nations of the earth are sympathizing with his oppressed & enslaved countrymen—when the exertions of all christian nations are tending, by every possible means, to meliorate their condition & free them from their chains & their bondage, is truly melancholy. Yet all things are ordered by an unseen Agency, to whose dispensations it becomes us always to submit—and if this dear young man *must* go, let us offer our most devout supplications to the Power who is able to hear & to answer, that when he leaves those who are bound to him by the most interesting of *earthly* ties, he may be welcomed to the paradise of God! I have no more time, as Pandias is to call as he returns from breakfast, & I must go to mine. They will return on Monday. Let me hear from you then. I shall expect you on

Tuesday. You will not doubt, that my attachment to you remains un-diminished, & that I am forever Your Edward. Pandias has come. Good morning.

1. Pandias and Constantine Ralli both attended Amherst in 1826–27. They registered for college from Scio, Greece. Nicholas Pantoleon Petrocokino attended Amherst in 1825–28. He prepared for college at Monson Academy.

Mrs. Norcross was still unwell, Emily was needed at home, and she declined Edward's invitation to attend the dedication of the college chapel in Amherst. As usual, she felt pressed for writing time: "I wish I had time to disclose my fealings to you but I fear my Mother will ask for me I therfore dare not leave but a short time." In later years, the poet Emily Dickinson would refuse invitations from potential suitors because of the illness of her mother. In May 1850, for example, she wrote to her friend Abiah Root,

> *When I am not at work in the kitchen, I sit by the side of mother, provide for her little wants—and try to cheer, and encourage her. I ought to be glad, and grateful that I can do anything now, but I do feel so very lonely, and so anxious to have her cured. I hav'nt re-pined but once, and you shall know all the why. While I washed the dishes at noon in that little "sink-room" of our's, I heard a well-known rap, and a friend I love so dearly came and asked me to ride in the woods, the sweet-still woods, and I wanted to ex-ceedingly—I told him I could not go, and he said he was disap-pointed—he wanted me very much—then the tears came into my eyes, tho' I tried to choke them back, and he said I could, and should go, and it seemed to me unjust. Oh I struggled with great temptation, and it cost me much of denial, but I think in the end I conquered, not a glorious victory Abiah, where you hear the roll-ing drum, but a kind of helpless victory, where triumph would come of itself, faintest music, weary soldiers, nor a waving flag, nor a long-loud shout. I had read of Christ's temptations, and how they were like our own, only he did'nt sin; I wondered if one was like mine, and whether it made him angry—I couldnt make up my mind; do you think he ever did? [Letters of Emily Dickinson, 1:97–98]*

But in February 1827, Emily Norcross was in good health. And in response to Edward's symbolic description of his inauspicious journey

she remarked, "I am happy to learn that your courage yet remains un-
daunted."

35
Emily Norcross to Edward
25 February 1827

Sunday Evening

I will comply with your request dear E with pleasure yet I can afford
you but a line. My Mother is yet quite low but we trust that she is
gradually recovering. I little anticipated when you left that she would
so long be confined you will doubtless presume that my cares have
been numerous and my solicitude great. Yet I hope that it has not been
unprofitable to me. I regret that it is not in my power to visit you the
present week, and would you not think me ungratful [?] to leave my
friends when so much needed at home. Yet I hope at some future time
I shall be so much gratified as to visit you which I certainly desire. I
heard of your misfortune the day after you left me which I was not
willing to believe, but I am happy to learn that your courage yet
remains undaunted. My health is much better than when you left me
and I trust should we meet again I shall be able to render your visit
more agreable than your last. Yet all is uncertain. I wish I had time to
disclose my fealings to you but I fear my Mother will ask for me I
therfore dare not leave but a short time. Will you now excuse me, as I
hope to be able to write again soon and believe me yours

Emily

36
Edward to Emily Norcross
7 March 1827

Amherst, Wednesday Evening, March 7. 1827.

My Dear Emily,

I had begun to write to you, & finished a few lines, when Mr. Ely
called upon me—& expecting Mr. Coleman would call afterwards, I
had prepared a short letter to send by him—& Mr. Ely would take it
in the morning, from Belchertown. But as both have passed without
the message, I shall now devote a short time, tho' it is quite late, to
converse with you.[1] Mr. Hunt was this day, ordained, at the North
part of the town. I attended the ordination and carried Mrs. Coleman
& Miss Perkins. The exercises were all appropriate & interesting. Mr.
Ely preached the sermon.[2]

Your letter was recd. on Monday Evening of last week, and it was quite unexpected to me to hear that your mother had not recovered her health, tho' I was glad to hear that she was improved. I have felt much anxiety on your account, & feared that your comfort would be much lessened by the effect of your ill health. It is perfectly natural, you know, that I should feel interested in every thing that concerns you, and nothing certainly can afford me more pleasure than to know that you are in the enjoyment of that, without which all other blessings can not be duly appreciated.

I was sorry that you could not attend the Dedication of our College Chapel last week, & make us a visit, with your brother—but, under your circumstances, I think you did exactly right—We owe the first duties to our family friends—and there is no situation in which the excellencies of females are more conspicuously exhibited, than in attending upon the sick—in watching over the progress of a friend's disease—in comforting the afflicted, & administering to the relief of those who are in pain or distress. Here is room for the exercise of patience & fortitude, & here it is, that the milder & softer virtues are called into exercise—and we should be guilty of ingratitude to desert them in time of need. I hope, however, that it will be convenient for you, at some time, not far future, to visit us, & the place.

I need not tell you, My Dearest Emily, that the more I become acquainted with you, the more ardent is my attachment, and the more earnest my desire to consummate a connection upon which we have agreed, and which will make me your Guardian & protector—and while I feel conscious that I have most unreservedly given my heart and hand to you, it is a source of pure enjoyment to me to feel assured that my gift has been accepted & that I have recd. a full equivalent in the confidence which you have placed in me, and the frankness with which you have expressed the reciprocation of my affection: and could I feel equally conscious that I was *worthy* of such confidence, I should certainly desire that our union might take place whenever it should be thought safe, by you & your friends, to entrust your person and the preservation & promotion of your happiness to my care. I intend, if agreeable to you, to converse with your father on the subject, when we next meet. It is impossible for me to tell you now, when that will be. The Spring Courts are near, & my time will necessarily be much occupied with my business. It may be in a week, & it may not be less than three or four weeks. I shall try to inform you, unless I go unexpectedly.

My health is perfectly good, and business such, that I would not wish to change my residence, except for a larger place and a more extensive practice. It is six months to-day since I commenced business, and if my encouragement continues as good for the remainder of the year as it has already been, I shall have no reason to complain. I shall do all in my power to merit it, & if I fail of success, it will not be for want of exertion. It is hard for a person to make his own way, surrounded by hosts of competitors, all struggling to eminence, & all desirous of gaining fame & fortune. Still it ought not to discourage his efforts. The inducement to exertion is the greater, the more powerful is the opposition with which we have to contend. Men were not made to be borne along in a smooth current, & sail on a waveless ocean. He can not fold his arms & be wafted by gentle breezes, into the haven of power or influence or respectability or honor. He can not sit quietly at ease, & receive the title of an active man. He can not move without the exercise of volition. He can accomplish nothing without the use of the necessary means. He may have friends that will sustain him for a time, but when they cease to have influence, he sinks into forgetfulness. I hold it to be an established truth, that it is best for every man to acquire his own reputation, & establish a character for himself. He is then independent of foreign aid, and unmoved by foreign influence. It should be, & it is to every man that has any energy of character, a pleasure to exert himself. It is productive of real, substantial gratification to press thro' difficulties, & encounter obstacles which will call out all the latent energies of the mind, & make a man feel the power that rests within.—To be surrounded with cares & solicitude, and obliged to act with decision & resolution, places a man exactly in the situation in which he ought to be placed. And, while I heartily subscribe to the truth of the sentiment, that "Life's *cares* are *pleasures*", and quote another equally beautiful passage of the same favorite Poet, which I may have quoted before, perhaps, that

> "Man was made for action, & for that Sphere designed,
> "Eternal pleasures open on his mind"—³

I feel animated with the thought that there is open before us a field large enough for all our exertions, and we have only to enter the lists and exert our utmost skill [?], and use our utmost endeavours to gain the object of our desires. Courage and confidence are the two great qualities which men ought to call to their aid in the accomplishment of their purposes. And in no situation does a man appear to be a *man*, so clearly, as when engaged in some noble enterprise which demands all his ingenuity, his firmness, his resolution & perseverance & decisive energy. The stronger qualities are the glory of men: and while troubles surround him, & misfortunes attend him, he rises like the sun, & shines more brilliantly from having been obscured by mountains or clouds. Then it is, that he appears in his true dignity—and then, more than at all other times, he exhibits that godlike fortitude & magnanimity, which show him to be endowed with a Soul, which is no less than an emanation of the Divine Essence. I must now once more extend the parting hand & say "good night." Go on in the ways of virtue—& continue what you have been—You will not fail to make all your friends happy—remember me to them all, affectionately, & accept again the assurance that you enjoy the the [*sic*] undiminished confidence & devotion of Your Edward

Write soon.

1. Edward's letter was sent by mail.

2. The Reverend William W. Hunt was born in Belchertown on 7 September 1796, graduated from Williams College in 1820 and from Andover Theological Seminary in 1824, and was ordained as pastor of the North Congregational Church in Amherst on 7 March 1827, the date of Edward's letter. He held this position until his death in 1837. Carpenter and Morehouse describe him as an enthusiastic revivalist and ardent advocate of temperance and antislavery in *The History of the Town of Amherst, Massachusetts* (Amherst: Press of Carpenter and Morehouse, 1896), p. 225. Presumably "Miss Perkins" was a daughter of the Reverend Nathan Perkins, Jr., pastor of the Second Congregational Church in North Amherst.

3. Edward's favorite poet is the didactic and somewhat melancholy Edward Young (1683–1765). The first quotation is *Night Thoughts*, bk. 2, line 160 ("Life's cares are comforts"), slightly misquoted. The second quotation, which was also used in Letters 23 and 64, is in the style of *Night Thoughts* but cannot be identified with a particular passage. Rather, Edward seems to be summarizing the mood and argument of passages that appealed to him, such as the following:

> Life's cares are comforts; such by heaven design'd;
> He that has none, must make them, or be wretched.
> Cares are employments; and without employ
> The soul is on a rack; the rack of rest,
> To souls most adverse; action all their joy.
>
> [2.160–64]

37
Edward to Emily Norcross
1 April 1827

Amherst. Sunday Evening. 1/2 past 10. o'clock.
April 1.st 1827.

My Dear Emily,

Although it is five weeks this evening since the date of your last letter, in which you intimated that you might write again soon, and I have recd. no communication from you; and though I have expected to hear from you for a long time, still you know enough of me to believe that it makes no difference with my feelings towards you. I am willing to attribute it to the suggestion of my own, that I might visit you before this time. My business has been such that it was, to say the least, very inconvenient. Last week was Court week at Northampton—I was there till Friday. Saturday I had cases to attend to at home—and am to have one on Monday, which with a town meeting will occupy all my time. Tuesday, I shall go to Greenfield Court—& if I can finish my business, I shall return Wednesday, in season to reach Monson on Wednesday Evening—if not, I shall probably find it necessary to go on Thursday (Fast day,) as it will not be convenient for me to be absent at any other time, soon. Probably I shall meet you Wednesday Evening.

How is your health, & that of your Mother? Are the rest of the family well? Is William at home—how do you enjoy yourselves—have you any remarkable intelligence to communicate—any thing of an interesting character to relate?

I have many things to say, but shall defer them till I meet you. Will it not be proper for us to converse with your father & mother in relation to the time of our marriage? Have you ever heard their opinions on this subject? It is time for all to have something definitely fixed upon, you know. And every thing ought to have a fair & full understanding.

My health is good—business encouraging—& every thing about as I could reasonably wish, at the commencement of my practice. I hope to succeed, & be able to render you happy. I think much & often of you—and should be glad to have more frequent communications from Monson.

The time is short—& I must close. Remember me to your friends, & receive the offering of a heart sincerely devoted to one with whom I hope to pass my life—& believe that I experience much pleasure in calling myself, Your Edward

In much haste . . . —Good night—

Edward visited Monson on 4–6 April as projected and had a satisfying discussion with Joel Norcross about his plans for the future. Probably a tentative wedding date was established at this time. In the following letter, he continued to press Emily to come to Amherst and hoped that she would visit him during the first week in May, accompanied by her brother William.

38
Edward to Emily Norcross
21 April 1827

Amherst. Saturday Evening. April 21. 1827.

My Dear Emily,

The week has closed, & with it its business; and I am glad of leisure to converse awhile with my dearest friend. It rains hard, and next to a brilliant moon-light evening, I prefer the monotonous pit-pat of an April shower to enjoy the pleasure of social intercourse—and I can assure you, that to a person situated as I am, with very little time or opportunity for anything like amusement, an evening of leisure, undisturbed by the relations of wrongs committed & injuries suffered by my clients, & a freedom from the intrusions of those who make it their object to call upon a Lawyer in a very *friendly* way, & before they leave, contrive to state some supposable case by which they may draw out a little *gratuitous information & advice* on some subject in which they are immediately interested, is a luxury, indeed. Glad am I to hear it *pour down*, for while I am out of the reach of the storm, I am sure of a little retirement—an hour of "solitude, sweetened" by the employment in which I am engaged.

I have, this week, issued another No. of my *"Coelebs"* on Female Education: and think it will not take more than two more No.s to complete all that I shall say on the subject, at present. I shall then have drawn merely an *outline* of the duties of women, & leave *them* to fill up the picture. I know not why it is, but I have long desired to say something to that class of the community, and felt much interest in having them correctly instructed, & their tastes and judgments properly formed. A vast number of my acquaintance seem to entertain notions of things—ideas of living—so entirely contrary to my own, that I have long wished to have some disinterested person, who was an accurate observer of men & things, undertake to effect a reformation, but no one has volunteered, and I have ventured my own remarks, my incompetency to do the subject justice, notwithstanding. However I shall not say half that might with perfect propriety, be said, but conclude what I have undertaken, with the hope that some one will pursue it, and be successful in bringing about that change in manners & fashions which the circumstances of the country, generally, so loudly demand.[1]

I sent Wm. another No. of the "Casket"[2] and a Note, inviting him to come to A. with you next week, or about the 1st May—and from the situation of my business, should prefer the latter time, if equally agreeable to you & him, as it will be a week of more leisure than the other, with me. I expect my brother home from New York, too, about that time, & he would be glad to become acquainted with you.[3] I proposed your coming with your *brother*, because I presumed it would meet your feelings more agreeably than coming with *me*, at *this time*, tho' you know it would give me pleasure to go after you, myself. My friends would be very glad to see you, & I want you should see them & the place—I want to have you a little acquainted with the *looks* of the town, at least, before you come to reside here permanently.[4]

My brother William who had just gone to New York when I was last at M. went with a view of seeing the place & learning the prospect of business, as well as for the sake of travelling a little for his recreation, after keeping in a store more than 3. years, without going, except once, so far as Boston—He set out, prepared to stay or return, as he should think best, when he had seen what he could do, & how he was pleased. He is now in a store in "Broadway," where he is pleasantly situated, & where he can succeed well, if he chooses to stay; but writes to me, that, he thinks he shall conclude to return to Amherst, and go into business here—that we may assist each other in business, and gratify the wishes of our family & friends by settling ourselves in business, at home. I have never, as yet, had reason to regret my decision to establish myself here, and should Wm. determine to remain, also, I should feel still more encouraged, as I feel great confidence in his ability to succeed in his business.

Emily, The more I reflect upon the connection which we are about to form, the more solemn & important it appears to me. It will, at once, introduce us to a thousand new relations, & impose upon us duties of a new and untried character. We are, at once, laid under the strongest of earthly obligations to promote the comfort & happiness of each other—We are bound by ties of a nature so strong that nothing but Death can sunder them—We must pass thro' trials & sufferings which will demand all our sympathy and fortitude to bear—& be placed in situations, in which our benevolence & charity will have frequent exercise—We shall be called upon to extend relief to the destitute—administer consolation to the afflicted, and do good as occasion may require. But all this ought not to intimidate us. Let us not shrink from any responsibility, however great. Let us not fear to undertake any thing which our *duty* requires of us. Let us not hesitate to do what all the wise & prudent have done before us. Let us resolve to be contented, & determine to be happy. Let us rely upon our united exertions to promote our mutual happiness. And tho' I shall be indebted to my success in my profession for a support, still, will not industry, frugality, economy, prudence & a diligent attention to business, with an ordinary blessing, ensure ultimate success, & a *competence, at least*? Need any man of regular habits, who will devote himself entirely to his own business, fear gaining a respectable support? And if people will resolve to live within their income, & be contented till it increases, will they not enjoy themselves as well, and even better than they will, to roll in their chariots, & riot in luxuries & dainties? Is it not surer that persons of industrious & economical habits will succeed, than that those who commence with fortunes, & who know nothing of the manner in which they are made, will keep what they inherit? Is it not better, in every respect, for a man to make his own fortune, by his own good management? Will he not be more likely to retain it? And is not the exertion requisite to accomplish it directly calculated to make him a more regular, sober, correct, & useful man—will he not [be a] better member of society, & will he not, in the end, establish a more lasting reputation & gain more substantial confidence? That this will be the case, or rather, that it has been the case, in nine cases in ten, is true—and it is equally true that I shall try to make for myself, my own fortune—and I shall feel always willing to live within my income. It is not the object of living, to vie with our neighbors in extravagance, or to outstrip them in the expense of a family establishment. I like every thing plain & neat, & simple, & those families always appear to me to be the most happy where these are the characteristics of their style.[5]—I know the risk is great, on your part, but if ordinary success attend my exertions, I have confidence enough in myself to believe that I can do enough to render us both *comfortable*, at least.

I have felt much better since conversing with your father on the subject of our marriage, & need not say to you that I enjoyed our last interview, *very much*. I have accomplished, in thus conversing with him, what I have, for some months, desired to do, but never summoned sufficient resolution before. And it has afforded me satisfaction to have a full understanding on a subject in which we are all so much interested, & to tell exactly what my circumstances were, so that you can all know precisely on what my prospects of success are founded. Emily, you know that I shall be obliged to gain my own fortune, my own reputation. And feeling as I now do, I must say that I am fully convinced that it is best I should. I rejoice that I *must exert* myself, and feel a conscious glow of satisfaction thrill thro' my bosom, at the thought that I must press *my own way* thro' the multitudes of competitors for honorable eminence, & should I fail, at last, of reaching the point at which I aim, & which I shall bend the whole energies of my mind & soul to attain, I shall enjoy the consolation of having exerted myself to the utmost, & done all in my power to accomplish the great end of my existence. You see that I have only room to tell you That I am most devotedly & affectionately Your Edward—

P.S. Do you expect to go to N. York with Mrs. C.? I shall expect to hear from you as soon as you receive this. And if it is any more convenient for you to visit me, next week, than week after, you will certainly do it. We shall welcome you most cordially *whenever* you come. Give my respects to everybody that has any thing to do with you or me, more particularly your father's, brother's, & Uncle E.'s family—I am as unceremonious as ever.

How is your health, & that of your brother Hiram? Are all the rest well? My father's family are all well, & *did my Sisters know* I was writing, would wish to be remembered.[6]

There is quite an attention to religion in College—and it appears to be increasing. Dont you wish it would reach you & me?

Will you ask Wm. to enquire of Mr. Colton for me, whether he has had any return from Boston respecting the Naturalisation of the Greeks? Our S. [Supreme] Court sits soon, & I want to know whether any thing is to be done respecting it. Mr. Colton will understand it. I have heard, by the bye, that Mr. Colton was on a Committee to examine the College Students the first week in May. Is it so?
E——D——

1. The "Coelebs" essay on female education that appeared in the *New-England Inquirer* on 20 April was the last in the series. In it, Edward Dickinson expressed the opinion that "literature is not the department in which *women* ought to shine," while nevertheless exhorting those women who chose "to forego the pleasures of domestic happiness, for the sake of *literary fame*" to "bend all their energies to attain that object, and when we bid them farewell, on their departure from society, we shall most cheerfully give them a passport to the honors of literary distinction, and joyfully participate with them in the rewards which await their approach to the portals of the temple of Minerva."

The "Coelebs" essays generated three responses from women readers who expressed varying degrees of indignation about the "Coelebian" program and tone. In letters to the editor, they challenged the essayist's motives, his knowledge, and his style. On 16 February, for example, "A Lady" compared his sentiments to those of an "eastern Sultan or bashaw" before concluding, "If as he professes, he is resolved to die a martyr to our cause, not unlikely he will fall as thousands before him have done, who for the want of holier motives have passed into oblivion unknown, unpitied, unlamented." Edward may have abandoned the "Coelebs" series because of the controversy it generated; there is a sixth unpublished essay at Harvard.

Perhaps the most interesting question about this series is why Edward chose to write it. In the second paragraph of this 21 April letter to Emily Norcross, he himself appears puzzled by his motives: "I know not why it is, but I have long desired to say something to that class of the community [women], and felt much interest in having them correctly instructed, & their tastes and judgments properly formed." A contemporary view was the following:

> Coelebs, it seems, has been admitted into all the families where there are literary ladies, and has found them *two knowing*, or else the moral culture of the heart has not kept pace with intellectual improvement; for they are *universally* contentious in the societies of their husbands, disputatious with their friends, negligent of domestic comfort, wretched in their taste, and no botanists at all! How, Messrs. Editors, are we to be profitted by such trash?
>
> 16 February 1827
"A Lady"
New-England Inquirer

This letter raises the possibility that, before meeting Emily Norcross, Edward had a failed romance with a woman who was his intellectual equal or superior. More probably, his attitudes were conditioned by his interaction with his mother, whose letters sound extremely intelligent, if somewhat anxious and underpunctuated. As I suggested in the Introduction, she was a more complex personality than Dickinson family biographers have recognized, to the extent that they have considered her at all. Perhaps her temper outbursts reflected her dissatisfaction with an exclusively domestic life, a life over which she had very little control. In any event, Edward's ambivalence toward literary women persisted even after his marriage. The poet Emily Dickinson explained to Thomas Wentworth Higginson in April 1862, "He [her father] buys me many Books—but begs me not to read them—because he fears they joggle the Mind" (*Letters of Emily Dickinson*, 2:404).

2. *The Casket, or, Flowers of Literature, Wit and Sentiment*, was a monthly magazine published in Philadelphia from 1826 to 1830.

3. William Dickinson (1804–87) eventually became a wealthy manufacturer and banker in Worcester. Edward seems closer to him than to any of his other siblings except Mary (1809–52), who married Mark Haskell Newman in 1828. Edward hoped that she would remain in Amherst after her marriage. See Letter 83.

4. The conclusion of this paragraph emphasizes the fact that Emily had never been to Amherst.

5. Barton Levi St. Armand has recently cast doubt on Edward's ability to live within his means in later years, beginning in the 1850s. After scrutinizing Edward's financial records, St. Armand has concluded that he borrowed at least $13,600 and perhaps as much as $18,000 from the estate of his nieces, the Newman sisters, of which he was the trustee: "Even a shrewd and ambitious country lawyer could not make enough capital to buy one substantial estate in 1855 and

build another in 1857. Village gossip itself noted the squire's newfound pros-
perity. . . . As executor of the Newman trust, Edward Dickinson loaned himself a
sum substantial enough both to renovate his own home and to construct a new
one for his son (ostensibly for the use of the Newman sisters)." See "Appendix B,
Austin Dickinson as Connoisseur," *Emily Dickinson and Her Culture: The Soul's
Society* (New York: Cambridge University Press, 1984), p. 308. Edward died in-
testate in 1874. He may have paid the Newman sisters back, but St. Armand's
presentation of the rather indecipherable record of the case leans in the other di-
rection. Indeed, he suggests that Edward's fatal stroke may have been precipitated
by a guilty conscience.

6. Edward's phrase "My father's family" emphasizes his ambivalence toward
his mother. In addition to Lucretia and Mary, his sisters were Catharine (1814–
95) and Elisabeth (1823–86). Because of Elisabeth's age, he was probably refer-
ring to Lucretia, Mary, and Catharine.

*This letter raises the possibility that Joel Norcross was an overly pos-
sessive father. At a time when Edward was pressing Emily to visit him
in Amherst, her father preferred to take her to New York. Thus, the
sudden illness of her brother William was not the only reason she
found herself disappointing Edward once again. As for herself, she
slipped rather easily into the role of a woman who habitually disap-
pointed her fiancé.*

39
Emily Norcross to Edward
30 April 1827

Monson Monday Evening

My Dear Edward

I suspect you will think this another evidence of my punctuality, but
my engagements have been such since I heard from you that it has not
been in my power to answer your letter before this evening, but I
suppose you have nearly become habituated to simular disappoint-
ments. Much do I think of you dear Edward particularly when in the
sweet enjoyment of solitude, and sincerly desire that I could interrupt
you. You have given me many polite invivations [*sic*] to visit you but
for very obvious reasons I have yet been prevented and am still under
the unpleasant necessity of saying that I must again refuse, and I
presume you will not be surprised when I tell you why. Brother Wil-
liam was violently attacked with illness a week on saturday last of
which he has been very sick indeed, but it gives me pleasure to say
that he is now apparently better, but is yet confined to his room. Thus
you percieve that sickness is a close companion of ours. A season of

adversity has long hung over us, but doubtless it is not without wise intention. You inquired if I were going to New York. I did not think of it when you were at Monson, but since then my father has proposed it to me, and thinks it the best opportunity that I may ever enjoy and is desireous for me to improve it. As I have been strongly solicited by other friends I think it an inducement to comply presumeing that you will not object to it. Should brother continue to improve I shall probably leave the first of next week, to be abscent two or three weeks. Perhaps it would be gratifying to you to learn something more of my parents views relative to our marriage as they have conversed familiarly with me upon the subject, they do not wish to intrude upon our arrangements at all. Still they would prefer the time prolonged and will you not dear Edward think with me that it would be more than I could accomplish to prepare so soon. I wish I knew what you would say to this, but I must leave it by saying that it is yet undetermined untill I meet you again, which I trust will be soon after I return. Cousin Maria Coleman spent last week at home, much to the gratification of her friends. I regret that William has not been able to make the enquiries which you wished, his ill health is the only apology that I can make you.[1] I imagine you will be surprised to observe so much blank paper but you know that it is nothing new for me. I must leave you, dear Edward by saying that

[I] am yours Emily

1. In Letter 38, Edward had asked William "to enquire of Mr. Colton for me, whether he has had any return from Boston respecting the Naturalisation of the Greeks." At this time, Edward was also the secretary of a committee that had been organized in Amherst for the relief of suffering in Greece.

40
Edward to Emily Norcross
4 May 1827

Amherst. Friday Morning. May 4. 1827.

My Dear Emily,

I recd. your letter yesterday, and regret that your friends should so often be afflicted with sickness, but it becomes us, at all times, to submit with cheerfulness, to the allotments of Providence, and to believe, as you say, that the intention may be wise.

I expected you at Amherst, this week, and am extremely sorry that it should so happen that you could not come. I wanted to have you become acquainted with my friends, & see the place, and I wanted to show you the house in which we shall probably reside. It is in the centre of the village, adjoining the building in which I keep my office, and with some repairs, would be a very pleasant place—as it is in as good a situation as any one in the street. Should I purchase it, as I now think I possibly may, I shall repair it, this summer, and make it every way comfortable & pleasant, in and about it. I shall probably make no certain determination till I have consulted you, & acquainted your father respecting it. I can have it, any time I please, as my father has the control of it, and can either *hire*, or *buy*, as shall be thought best.[1]

You say you presume I shall have no objection to your visiting N. York—certainly not. I am glad you have concluded to go, notwithstanding an absence of two or three weeks will postpone an interview which I had intended to have with you before the time of your return; yet you can not believe me so selfish as to wish you to forego the pleasure which the present favorable opportunity of making the tour will not fail to produce, merely for the sake of the pleasure which I should derive from visiting you in the meantime. I think the ride will benefit your health, and the pleasure of travelling at the most beautiful season of the year will be great. It is always agreeable to visit new places, and to witness new scenes, and I have no doubt that the journey will be gratifying as well as beneficial to you. I expect to go to Springfield on Tuesday to attend the Supreme Court, & should you take the stage to Hartford, on that day & pass that way, I shall be glad to meet you there, Tuesday Evening. I shall expect to hear, from your Uncle E. whom I shall probably see, what your calculations are, if I do not see you at Springfield.

As to the time of our marriage, we will converse when we next meet, which I trust will be soon after your return: suffice it to say, now, that I shall consult your wishes & your convenience, and shall wish to do nothing that may interfere with either. We can determine when we meet.

I have attended Court, at Northampton, two days, this week, but have not been able to leave my business at home, conveniently, to attend longer.

I expect the mail, every moment, & can say but little more. I shall feel anxious to hear from you, while on your journey. My most sincere wishes for your pleasure will follow you—& that your health may be confirmed, that you may have a safe & pleasant tour, & return, pleased & profited, will be my ardent prayer. And shall endeavour to visit you, as soon as I hear of your return, if my business will permit. You need have no delicacy in writing to me from N. York, if agreeable to you to spend a little leisure in communicating your discoveries to your friend, for his edification.

My brother William has not yet returned from there, tho' I recd. a letter from him this morning, in which he says he shall probably be at A. [Amherst] in the course of the present week. I have a great desire to visit that city, myself, & don't intend another year shall pass over my head without the sight of it.[2]

Remember me to your father's family, & tell them that I shall rejoice to hear that they are all in good health: and rest assured, that wherever you are, I shall think much of you, & anticipate with pleasure, the time when I shall be united to you, for life, should Providence preserve us.

I should say more, but have no time. I can merely add, that

I am sincerely & devotedly Yours
Edward

1. Samuel Fowler was probably speculating in Amherst real estate.

2. Edward visited New York for the first time in May 1830. At that time he wrote to his wife, "I find every thing here, which I have seen, grand & magnificent,—and just what I like. I have walked round the city today till I have worn the skin off both my heels, and been obliged to change my boots for my shoes, & go with one of them slipshod—making a fine figure in this great Metropolis; but never mind—they are not so particular here as they are in little villages" (Leyda, *The Years and Hours of Emily Dickinson*, 1:14).

This letter indicates that Emily met Edward in Springfield on Tuesday 8 May, as he had proposed, on her way to New York with her father. He and Edward had a "plain talk" about the time of their marriage, but Edward already knew from Emily's last letter that both of her parents favored a long engagement. This letter also indicates that Edward's brother William was in Amherst on his way to New York and that Edward intended to have him hand deliver it, together with a letter introducing his brother to Emily. However, William may have changed his plans, because according to Edward's calendar the letters were not given to Emily until after her return. At first he wrote, "both the last sent by Mother to N. York." This entry was subsequently crossed out and followed by the note, "Afterwards given to Emily— Nov. 6. 1827." It is not clear to whose mother he is referring, how he planned to have William deliver the letters since he did not have Emily's New York address, or who finally gave the letters to her. Possibly Betsy Fay Norcross gave the letters to Emily on her return from New York and Edward changed the entry in his records on 6 November. In any event, the letter should be read in light of the fact that Emily did not receive it during her stay in New York and his diatribe against urban prostitution should be read in light of his erotic frustration.

41
Edward to Emily Norcross
27 May 1827

Amherst. Sunday, May 27. 1827.

My Dear Emily,

My brother Wm. who was in New York when you reached there, returned on Wednesday morning last, to prepare to commence business, having formed a partnership with a Gentleman in the City; and they are to begin business in Albany. My brother goes this evening, & as he will probably be in New York in the course of the present week to purchase goods, you might reasonably wonder, did I not improve so favorable an opportunity to write to you. I have heard nothing from you since we parted at Springfield, nor do I know in what part of the City you are; but I shall instruct my brother in such a manner, that he will probably find you. He will give you a *letter of Introduction* from me, which I presume will not be unpleasant to you, and if he can afford you any facilities for increasing your acquaintance with the City, or contribute, in any way, to your happiness, you need not fear *troubling* him, but feel as safe in his care as in mine.

I have thought much of writing to you before, but waited to hear *where* you were—and for information how to *direct* my letter—I have concluded that you do not intend to write, & I presume your reasons for it are good, or you would not omit what would afford me so much pleasure. However, I shall no longer deprive myself of the happiness which the holding sweet converse with my dearest friend never fails to produce.

I have been grateful, indeed, that the weather has been so favorable since you left home. Scarcely a day of cold, or rainy weather has occurred since your arrival in N.Y., and my enjoyment is much increased by the belief that you will be pleased with your visit, & that you will recover your health which has not been perfectly good, for some time past. I think much of you every day, and neither night nor morning passes without witnessing my most sincere and devout prayer to Heaven that you may realise all & more than you could reasonably anticipate from your journey, and that you may return in safety—improved in health, and pleased & gratified by the variety of scenes which you must have witnessed, & the new ideas which you can not but have acquired.

We are now, Dear E. passing, in all probability, the most interesting period of our lives. We are just entering upon the business—the realities of life—We are just coming before the world, as actors among the vast multitudes which people it—We are about forming the most interesting, the most solemn, & the most important of all earthly connections—We ought to improve all our time to the best advantage—We are bound to exert ourselves to the utmost to promote the happiness of each other, and that of all our fellow men around us. We are to become acquainted with the various classes of men, & the various ranks of society, with whom we must [?] associate. We shall be surrounded with temptations to vice—to depart from our duty—We shall be presented with all the allurements which the fancy can suggest—imagination will be busy in discovering means to influence us to leave the paths of virtue & innocence & rectitude. But let us guard our ways—let us resist the first approach of the tempter—Let us put on the shield of conscious virtue—let us look down every thing which may attempt to excite our passions, & thus lead us to ruin. Let us beware of the seducing arts of base men—let us watch against the intrigues of those whose flatteries serve only as a cloak to complete their direst purposes. The more I become acquainted with men, the more deep is my conviction that the human heart is capable of the most horrid plans, and that a base purpose will in some way, or at some time, find means for its accomplishment—I have been astonished to view the degradation & misery and absolute wretchedness to which some of the inhabitants of our most flourishing cities are reduced—I have shrunk from the deadly influence which the habits & practice of some of the lower classes can not but exert upon all who witness them. It is truly sickening to a person of any sensibility—to a person possessing any sense of right & wrong, to behold the enormities of which the heart is capable—to know, from actual observation, that, the minds of men, the very emanations of the Divine Essence itself should be suffered to busy itself in the filth—in the mire of all that is awful & revolting—to become monuments of the signal displeasure of that Being who created them for the most noble—the most exalted purposes! My heart fails me to paint the scenes of too common occurance in all our cities—the abodes of death, the places where innocence has no dwelling—where virtue never comes—where some of the once most lovely of the fair creation are forced to resort to hide their shame—rather the victims of the seducer's arts are forced to congregate, and where hundreds of unsuspecting females, who have lost their honor in an unguarded [?] moment, when perhaps they thought themselves safe, are found living in the most loathsome prostitution. Such cities swarm with men of fashion—men who, while their words are fair & their manners fascinating, are bent on no other purpose but the gratification of their unhallowed passions at the expense of all that is dear in life—Good Heaven! My blood boils at the idea of seeing & knowing that such unrighteous abodes are suffered to exist—Would to God! I had the power, I would march thro' the cities of the land, rooting out these monsters of vice—these "charnel houses"—these destroyers of the health, the reputation & the morals of our most promising youth of both sexes—I would overturn & overturn, till virtue was again placed upon the throne, & all these abominable vices forced to do her homage. But I have insensibly said more than I intended—There is another & a brighter side to the picture. There are, in cities vast numbers of the most intelligent, the most enlightened, & the most virtuous people. There are thousands of objects worthy of the attention & regard of every stranger. I think every person can pass a portion of their time as pleasantly & as profitably in such places, as in the country. The difference & the superiority of manners—the accomplishments of the most genteel portion of the citizens have a fine effect upon all who are in a situation to observe them. The world of new objects which are presented to the mind—the thousand changes which are constantly taking place in every thing about you, & the innumerable objects of curiosity to which the attention is daily directed, contribute much to the pleasure & the improvement of those who have been accustomed to the society & manners of the country. Here the powers of men are the most conspicuously exhibited—the many buildings—expensive establishments, splendid liveries, & costly retinues—Here we see the display of the ingenuity of men in the mechanic & fine arts—skill is exhibited in a vast variety of ways, & every branch of business is constantly receiving some new impulse by the new inventions, discoveries, & wonder-working power which is applied by the ingenuity of some fortunate American—Here are the high & the low—the pure & the impure, the virtuous & the vicious—& that too, in the greatest extremes—Here we may learn what to choose & what to avoid—& amidst the multitudes with whom we are continually coming in contact we can not but learn much of what I consider as the most important of all sciences, the knowledge of the *human character*. But my paper is nearly filled & I must come to an end.

Let me give you one word of advice, at parting. Do not expose your health, for any purpose, but take every possible means to preserve & confirm it, and form as many good acquaintances as you can. I shall feel anxious for you till I hear of your return, soon after which I hope to meet you. And if you can do it conveniently, I wish you would write me as soon as you receive this, let me know something about your situation & the time at which you expect to return.

And now, my dearest E—I must leave you, & let me feel assured that wherever we are—however employed, there can nothing injure us while we pursue the paths of honesty & integrity—while our lives are marked by a virtuous conduct—while we preserve the strictest sense of the obligation we are under to each other, & to the world, to add to the amount of happiness that already exists, we shall enjoy the consciousness of having attempted to discharge our duty. And while we call to mind the mutual promises which exist between us to be faithful & constant to each other during our lives, let us, in the sight of Heaven, resolve that while we are suffered to remain here, we will exert our mutual efforts to encourage virtue & discountenance vice— and let our ardent aspirations ascend to the throne of the Eternal, that our union may be blessed & happy. I can say no more—and I need not assure you that I shall ever remain most affectionately

Your Edward

I went to Belchertown with Brother Wm. yesterday afternoon—called at Mr. C.'s—found Mrs. Flynt there, & that Mr. C. & Olivia had gone to Boston—Mrs. F. came up on Friday last—& left all the folks at Monson well.

I had a plain talk with your father, at Springfield, relative to the time of our marriage. We shall decide when you return. Come soon, won't you?

Rev. D. Crosby, a classmate of mine in College came in town last evening from Albany, where he has been to get married. Did you not know a Miss *Sherman* who was staying at President Day's in New-Haven, while you was attending school there? She is now Mrs. Crosby—He is settled in Conway, about 16. miles from us. I shall see them this evening. They are going to Boston & Andover.[1]

We are all well—My father goes to Boston this week, as Representative, to be absent some weeks, & I shall be more than usually employed in his absence.[2] Make my compliments to Mrs. Carter—[3]

A Miss Montague who belongs to our village is going to N.Y. to pass the summer with her sister, Mrs. Post—& goes in company with my brother—You may see her—[4]

The "Mount Pleasant" school commences this week.[5]

1. The Reverend Daniel Crosby (1799–1843) was a member of the Yale class of 1823. An 1826 graduate of Andover Theological Seminary, he was ordained as pastor of the Congregational Church in Conway, Massachusetts, in January 1827. His wife and two children survived him.

2. Samuel Fowler served in the Massachusetts legislature from 1827 to 1829, as well as in 1805–1809, 1813, and 1816–18. In 1828, he ran for the United States Senate unsuccessfully. In June of that year, he placed a promotional notice in the local paper indicating his intention to open a law school, a scheme which also came to nothing. The concluding paragraph of his advertisement is almost confessional in tone. Otherwise, the similarity between his faith in hard work and Edward's is striking. More generally, the best discussion of Edward's need to assume his father's burdens is Cynthia Griffin Wolff's *Emily Dickinson* (New York: Knopf, 1986), chap. 1.

3. Mrs. Carter, who lived in Monson, is unidentified, unless she is the wife of the Dr. Carter mentioned in Letter 72.

4. There were many people in Amherst named Montague, but I have not been able to identify this "Miss Montague."

5. The Mount Pleasant Classical Institute was founded by Chauncey Colton and Francis Fellowes, both members of the Amherst College class of 1826. "The buildings of the institution, capacious in size and of greater architectural pretention than was customary at the time, were erected in 1826 and 1827" (Carpenter and Morehouse, *History of the Town of Amherst*, p. 271). A college preparatory high school for boys, the Mount Pleasant school's most famous graduate was Henry Ward Beecher.

Edward visited Monson on 13 and 14 June. His visit seems to have put him in a good humor. Letter 45 indicates that he and Emily took a long ride together to Stafford Springs, Connecticut, which is about twelve miles south of Monson.

42
Edward to Emily Norcross
27 June 1827

Amherst June 27, 1827.

My Dear Emily,

A man has just called who is going directly to Monson—and I have merely time to say that Brother William & Sister Mary expect to go to Stafford Springs to-morrow, if the weather will admit—& will probably make you a short call on their way through M. [Monson].

Why can not you & your brother find time to visit us, this week—I presume you would rather come with Wm. than to see me at M. so soon again. I will carry you back, after you have stayed a few days. We shall all be happy to see you, & I shall expect to see you, in the course of the week. Don't think me too urgent, in making this request. I hope your father & mother will not object.

The country is now beautiful—& the leisure which I shall probably have, for a very few days, will enable me to visit the places which you would be pleased to see, better than at any other time, for some months. Our courts will soon be near, & my time will then be wholly occupied, & render my absence very inconvenient. If my brother goes, I will be more particular by him.[1]

Strawberries are abundant here, & cherries & currants are nearly ripe. The whole vegetable kingdom now appears in its greatest beauty —and every thing contributes to the pleasure of a person who sees the "agency" which operates to produce such beauties.

The man waits & I must stop. We are all well—Give my respects to all your friends, & believe me, tho' in the greatest haste,

Yours entirely & devotedly,
Edward

1. Edward means that he will send a letter by William.

Exceptionally, Emily wrote to Edward on the same day he was also writing her. Because her letter was written in the evening, I have placed it after his.

43
Emily Norcross to Edward
27 June 1827

Monson Wednesday Evening

My Dear Edward

After passing the afternoon and eveing [*sic*] at my brothers with the sociable young ladies Miss Fannings I have retired to my chamber to improve the last moments that remain in conversing with you con-cludeing that you placed some reliance upon my last engagement.[1] I am unwilling to disappoint you. I have not had the pleasure of hearing from you since you left me but suppose that you were fortunate other-wise I should have heard. Uncle E and wife spent the evening with me after you left much to my gratification as I felt quite solitary after parting with you. S. Warriner visited Monson last week he passed an evening at our house and was quite urgent that brother and myself should accompany him and Cousin Olive to Stafford Springs but oweing to previous engagements of my own I was obliged to refuse no disappointment to me however as I had so recently been there. Also Mr Stimson and Lady have lately been home with the dear child I called on her saturday last found her quite miserable poor woman thought I [,] I had rather be a spectator but I presume she is reconciled to her situation or ought to be.[2] The spirit of independence begins to beat high with us as we anticipate quite a celebration but for my own part I shall rejoice to see it past yet it aught ever to be deemed an interesting anniversary. Two weeks this evening dear Edward I was participating [in] much happiness with you, our interviews are not easily forgotten by me, have you not thought of our ride Edward I presume you have it was very pleasant indeed to me. I have done but little else but visit and recieve company since you were hear but I trust that I am nearly through for the present. I expect the Miss Fannings at house tomorrow to spend the day with me, probably the last visit I shall recieve from them. Dear Edward I know not what you will say to this letter but if you can read it you may think yourself quite fortunate. I would like to say more to you but it is so late I must be excused. I wish very much to hear from you.

I remain your devoted Emily.

1. On 6 May 1830, William Otis Norcross married Mary Fanning, the daughter of a New York City merchant. They had six children. Perhaps before his marriage, he became a fruit farmer in Newark, New Jersey.

The phrase "my last engagement" probably refers to a promise to write Edward more frequently.

2. Apparently Mrs. Stimpson was in ill health following the birth of her child. Emily's fear of childbirth and its consequences emerges here.

Edward's calendar indicates that this letter was hand delivered by his brother William and sister Mary. With the exception of Edward's younger brother Samuel who attended Monson Academy, William and Mary were thus the first of Edward's relatives whom Emily was to meet. Indirectly, then, this letter underscores the fact that she had not yet met his parents—an oddity only partially explained by Edward's emotional distance from them.

44
Edward to Emily Norcross
28 June 1827

Amherst June 28. 1827.

My Dear Emily,

Since writing to you yesterday, I have been occupied every moment, & now a man sits in my office—but as my brother & sister are going through M. this morning, you will permit me to introduce my brother to you—and to say a word: for I have not time to do much more. They will probably return to-morrow, and you need not be informed that it would add much to my pleasure to have you accompany them—as, from the state of my business, unless it is convenient for you to come this week, I should prefer to have your visit deferred a few weeks, & I will go after you, myself. If you have a desire to be at home to attend the celebration of Independence, perhaps I might carry you in season to pass it at M. if agreeable—& you thought it best not to make a longer stay with us. We concluded *not* to celebrate the day—here.

How is your health? Does it remain good? Are your Mother & the rest of your friends well? How are the N.Y. Ladies? as *sociable* as ever?

I recd. a letter from Mr. Warriner last Saturday, giving me a very eloquent description of a ride from M. to "Stafford Springs—"

I yesterday saw Mr. S. under whose care you rode from Springfield to Hartford in your journey to N. York—He came out from Northampton as one of a wedding party—the marriage of a young Gentleman who studied with Doct. Hunt, to the Doctor's daughter.[1]

My brother is almost ready & I must again, My Dear E. say Good morning. More when we meet, which I hope will be soon. Till then, I am

Yours. Edward

Excuse the haste of this & yesterday's, and destroy both, when once read.

1. "Mr. S." is unidentified; there was a Doctor Ebenezer Hunt in Northampton at the time but he is otherwise unidentified, as are his daughter and her husband.

45
Edward to Emily Norcross
1 July 1827

Amherst. Sunday Evening. July 1. 1827.

My Dear Emily,

Your letter was recd. last evening, and I can assure you that it was read with much pleasure; and tho' I wrote twice during the last week, (neither of which, it seems you had recd. at the time you wrote,) and had considerable expectation of seeing you & your brother in Amherst, last evening, yet I can not pass the latter part of this evening so pleasantly as in conversing with a friend, whose company is always a source of the purest happiness to me, and to whom it always gives me great satisfaction to write.[1]

I had not time in either of my last letters to tell you that I reached home, in safety, about midnight on the evening after I parted with you, and you will smile to know, also, that I was overpowered, more than once, in the course of my dark & solitary ride, by a short *nap*, and when about two miles from home, was roused from one of my lethargic fits, by my horse's turning [?] up, & stopping before a man's door. No accident, however, happened to me, and I was very fortunate in reaching home, that evening, as it rained the next day, and in addition to that, I found some men waiting to do business with me which rendered my return very seasonable. I have thought much of our ride to Stafford Springs, and never enjoyed myself better, and I need not say to you that it is impossible for you to receive more happiness from our interviews than I do. I would have them more frequent, but you know that it is important to attend as closely as possible to business, the more so, as I have so many competitors.[2] My business requires a great part of my time, & the remainder I devote to study. I have no reason to complain as yet, of my success. Yesterday, I had seven justice cases, and am employed to go to Greenwich on Tuesday of this week, in three more.[3] So you see, it must take some of my time to prepare—and I am willing to devote my whole attention to my profession, with the exception of what my friends have a right to claim—and a little which I feel that I ought to spend in reading miscellaneous works, Newspapers Etc. just enough to keep up with the world around me, & save me the mortification of being ignorant of what *others* know.

William & Mary returned on Friday evening, after a pleasant ride—came home through Brimfield, Ware, & Enfield—& were much pleased with their short excursion—and my sister feels a benefit from the ride—and I was glad to hear that you were all well.

Emily, your *birth-day* returns on Tuesday [3 July][4]—and should this letter find you safely at the end of another year of your life, let me congratulate you that no disease has impaired your constitution, that your health has been preserved and improved—and that your friends have been all spared to rejoice with you—and let me unite with you in gratitude to the Being who has kept you & me, & who alone has brought you to another of the most interesting periods in a person's life—and I can only request you to refer to my letter of the 1st Jan.y last, *my* birth-day, for a more full expression of my feelings in relation to the subject—believing that your feelings are in unison with mine, & that any pleasure which I experience will produce a glow of sympathy in your bosom. The celebration of the Anniversary of Independence follows next, and I am happy to hear that there is patriotism enough in Monson to notice it in what I think, is the proper manner. I know it is always attended with much fatigue, & the parade & ceremony of such an occasion produce a weariness & a desire to have it over, and nothing but the *oration* is interesting to *one part of the people* (the Ladies.). Still so much has been done to pervert the true spirit which animated the men of '76—to whose heroism & unparallelled courage & valor we are indebted for all the high civil, literary & religious privileges which we now enjoy, that I rejoice to hear that something is doing. I do not approve of its being made the occasion of dissipation & revelry—nor do I ever desire to witness such revolting scenes as are too often exhibited on that sacred day⁵—but, My Dear Emily, I do feel sincerely, that if there is any patriotism left in the bosoms of the descendants of the Pilgrims—if there is a spark of that holy fire which animated those venerable men who achieved our Independence, & who gained for us our precious liberties, that it should be occasionally kindled into a flame, & that the breasts of all who possess a lively gratitude for past favors should be warmed with a desire to manifest a rational joy—& express their regard for the virtues of the pure love of country which once filled the bosoms of those who are now in their graves, & whose spirits have long since gone to receive their reward. I shall think of you, on that occasion, & shall be happy to pledge you in a social glass, *"for the sake of the heroes of '76"* at 2. o'clock P.M. Tell Mrs. E. Norcross that I shall depend on her wining us—Our *spirits* can meet, if we can not, you know.

The "Mount Pleasant" school has commenced under very favorable auspices—having something more than 30. scholars and tho' scarcely any of us had much *faith* in the success of the establishment, yet we shall all be glad to be agreeably disappointed, and shall rejoice to have it flourish. The Corporation of the College are improving the grounds about the buildings, & will prepare them so that they will appear quite handsome, by Commencement, which is 7. weeks from the next Wednesday—the 22. August.

And now, Dear Emily, let me say something about affairs a little more intimately connected with our anticipated union. I have thought much of the subject, and presume that you have—and tho' I always regarded the marriage relation as the most important of all connections, as I reflect upon it, the solemnity & sober reality of it is much magnified—and the interest which we must necessarily feel increases, as the time which separates us from the expected period for the ratification of our contract, gradually shortens. To feel & know that there is one to whom I can confide my most secret plans—with whom I can converse most unreservedly upon all subjects—and with whom I can most confidentially entrust what would otherwise remain hidden in my own bosom, certainly must produce a pleasure which can only be realized by those who have experienced the same feeling. "We can't expect perfection," but it is the duty of all to determine to be as happy as human nature will admit; and if persons set out to exert themselves to do all in their power to promote their *mutual* happiness, as well as that of all about them, they certainly will have an *approving conscience*, which is worth all the "wealth of the Indies, or the mines of Potosi"—and with an ordinary blessing, they will not fail, in most cases, to ensure a life of rational enjoyment.[6] If there is any object worthy of the highest exertions of the powers of man, it is the desire of securing domestic felicity. This accomplished, a man can buffet the storms & tempests which sometimes assail the most meritorious, who mix with the world, and are liable to the changes produced by the revolutions of the "wheel of fortune." A man can do almost any thing which he *determines to do*—the mind, says one, is omnipotent—and its energies when fully applied, can accomplish the most mighty undertakings.

Having given you, My Dearest Emily, my hand & heart, & recd. yours in return, how can I feel otherwise than resolved to use every means which God has placed in my power to render you happy—To be your protector—to enjoy your confidence, & to have you lean on me for support, gives me a consciousness of my ability to perform any reasonable task—and while, in the sight of Heaven, we have mutually pledged ourselves to be true to each other for life, let us join in invoking the blessing of the Creator upon us that we may live to become *one*—that we may realize even more that [than] we can reasonably anticipate—and that we may live to be useful members of society—be esteemed by all, & deserve the confidence & respect of all with whom we may become acquainted, & at last, be recd. together, to mansions of perfect blessedness. I am yours forever

Edward

I shall want to hear from you again, soon.—and should say much more to you now, if my paper was not already full. You will receive this on Independence morning—E——

Make my respects to all your father's family—E. N. Esq'.s & Capt. Flynt's etc. How do you all do? Is your mother in good health? My mother's health is rather poor.

Tutor Lathrop, who attended Mr. Coleman's wedding has gone to Norwich Vt. to assist in taking charge of a Military School.[7] We have a bible-class for men, which I attend. How does the new Lawyer flourish? Does he have any business?[8]

1. When he was in Monson on 13 and 14 June, Emily and Edward may have tentatively agreed that she would visit Amherst at the end of the month. This is a reasonable supposition because her letter of 27 June says nothing about a visit.

2. In addition to Edward's father who was no longer very actively engaged in his law practice, there were three other lawyers practicing in Amherst in 1827: Ithamar Conkey (1788–1862), Lucius Boltwood (1792–1872), and Osmyn Baker (1800–1875). Conkey was for many years a trustee of Amherst Academy and at the time of his death was the treasurer of that institution. Like Edward, Baker attended Yale and the Northampton Law School. Boltwood, a Williams graduate, read law with Samuel Fowler and became his law partner in 1817, though it is unclear how long the partnership lasted. He was active in the founding of Amherst College and is described by Richard B. Sewall as a man "of parts" (*Life of Emily Dickinson*, 2:335).

3. Greenwich, Massachusetts, was about twenty-three miles east of Amherst. The town no longer exists.

4. Emily was turning twenty-three.

5. As is indicated by Letter 25, Edward had strong feelings about how holidays should be celebrated. After his death, the poet commented on his aversion to the exchange of Christmas gifts. See *Letters of Emily Dickinson*, 2:531.

6. Dickinson's poem "A Mine there is no Man would own" links the images of "Potosi" and "Indies" to refer to inner worth. The interior or psychological mine which is contrasted with social wealth is consistent with Edward's emphasis on self-approbation. Her emphasis is more psychological than moral, however. See *Poems of Emily Dickinson*, 2:786.

7. "Tutor Lathrop" remains to be identified.

8. Edward is referring to Reuben A. Chapman, who became chief justice of the Massachusetts Supreme Court in 1868. In 1859, the poet was embarrassed when she fled from him because "Mr. Chapman is my friend, talks of my books with me, and I would not wound him" (*Letters of Emily Dickinson*, 2:348–49).

46
Edward to Emily Norcross
10 July 1827

Amherst, Tuesday Noon. July 10. 1827.

My Dear Emily,

I have just come across Mr. Field of Monson, and send you, by him "Hope Leslie," a new Novel, which I presume you will find interesting—as the characters are drawn in a striking light, and innocence & villainy strongly contrasted. Magawisca, the Indian girl is a noble character—possessing all the nobleness & magnanimity of the finest spirits—for she acts apparently from the most purely disinterested motives—Hope, possessing, as she does, the liveliness & vivacity, & playfulness of a favorite girl, can not fail to excite the most lively emotions, & draw out the most unequivocal feelings of regard—As to

Everell, you will find in him, whatever can attach a woman to her most confidential friend.[1]

I have some business at Springfield, Wilbraham & Ludlow, in a few days, & may possibly come around by M. whenever I go. It may be in a very few days, or not for a longer time. Just when I can leave home the most conveniently. My business is at present unusually good, & keeps me confined to my office, almost exclusively: but I am willing to devote myself to it—and am glad that I am obliged to do it—I must close. Give my respects to your father's family—Hiram's & Uncle E's—and believe me with undiminished affection

Your devoted Edward

Excuse the brevity & the haste.

How was the celebration of Independence?

I thought much of you—drank *your health* at 2. o'clock—dined with the Free-Masons—and attended a *tea-party* at 5. o'clock. P.M.—[2]

Will you write me—I want much to hear from you.

1. *Hope Leslie; or, Early Times in the Massachusetts* by Catharine Maria Sedgwick was published in 1827. See also Letter 14, n. 4. According to Mary Kelley, "The appearance of her third novel provided critics with further evidence that Sedgwick ranked with Washington Irving, James Fenimore Cooper, and William Cullen Bryant as a founder of American literature." See Mary Kelley, ed., *Hope Leslie* (New Brunswick: Rutgers University Press, 1987), p. xi. Mr. Field of Monson has not been identified.

2. Apparently Edward's reading of the anti-Masonic tract mentioned in Letter 33 had not alarmed him unduly.

47
Emily Norcross to Edward
14 July 1827

Monson Saturday Morning

My Dear Edward

It is something quite new for me to be engaged in writing in the morning but the circumstance of my writeing to you makes it appear quite consistant.[1] Last evening I was prevented by company which is the only one I have been home through the week. Do you not suspect that I am becomeing quite disipated at least I shall anticipate a lecture or two when we meet. How have you spent these moonlight evenings have they not been delightful yes, dear E but [of] your society I must be deprived. Often have I sit by my window when all was perfect stillness around me thinking of you I recieved your letter the morning of the celebration [of 4 July] as you exspected before this I had heard that you was comeing to join the festival and was somewhat disappointed in not seeing you.[2] We had quite an interesting day I think you would have been very much gratified I would give you a description of the ceremonies of the day if I had time but you must excuse me untill I see you. It did not occur to me that you would think of my birthday most certainly I have great reason for gratitude for the blessings and priviledges I have enjoyed. I was very happy indeed to recieve a call from your brother and sister. As the Miss Fannings which I presume you have not forgotten were visiting me at the time and they are such wild creatures I was fearful they would think we were quite to rude, but by the way is not your brother disposed to be a little roguish.[3] I recieved a call from Miss I Dwight yesterday her health is very poor I should think her situation was critical yet she appears quite thoughtless.[4] Mr Hayden and wife visited Monson the present week in great style also Mr. Eaton and a sister of Mr H to whom he is engaged perhaps you have seen them as they were going to amherst to call on a brother who is at school.

And now My dear Edward is it necessary for me to add that I wish to see you. I presume you are convinced of this truth but I do not wish you to come to interfere with your engagements at home. As saturday is a busy day you must not expect but a word from me. I recieved the books you sent by Mr Field I find them quite interesting.[5] I am unwilling to leave you quite so abruptly, but it is requsite that I should return to my engagements.

> From one whose affections can never
> be removed
> Emily

1. Presumably she means consistent with her other responsibilities, or convenient.

2. Again, it appears that some oral messages were exchanged by Emily and Edward through third parties.

3. William has not been characterized by Edward as "roguish"; Emily's observation reaffirms my sense that, under some circumstances, she had a good sense of humor.

4. "Miss I Dwight" remains to be identified. In Letter 58 Edward mentions a Miss Julia Dwight. Both women may be the sisters of William Dwight of Belchertown who were mentioned in Letter 16.

5. Edward apparently sent at least one other book in addition to *Hope Leslie*, but it cannot be identified. Emily's statement is a rare indication that she may have been reading some of the books he sent her.

In the course of transacting the business to which he had alluded in Letter 46, Edward visited Monson for the twelfth time on 17 July. "So full an expression of mutual regard" took place between Edward and Emily that he sounds more relaxed than usual, although he felt compelled to warn her against frivolous or even "dissipated" feminine "chit-chat." (With tongue in cheek, she had referred to herself as dissipated in Letter 47, adding, "I shall anticipate a lecture or two when we meet"; he now urged her quite seriously toward greater sobriety.)

48
Edward to Emily Norcross
22 July 1827

Amherst. Sunday Evening, July 22. 1827.

My Dear Emily,

It is a most cool and beautiful evening, and all the young people are enjoying their walks, while I am more pleasantly occupied in conversing with my absent friend—and you will not have reason to be surprised, after so full an expression of mutual regard as has taken place between us, that I should so soon devote a part of an evening to you—and tell you that I reached home the night after parting with you, at about 12. o'clock, in perfect safety, tho' very much fatigued.[1] My brother had taken your letter from the Post Office, & gave it to me on Wednesday morning [18 July]—and you need not be told that the perusal of it gave me much pleasure, tho' I had but just seen you, face to face. I suppose the Misses F. have now gone, and left you time for a little rest, and some sober reflection—and I can not avoid saying (tho' in the most confidential manner) that I think their society less improving than that of some other females of my acquaintance—and if they are correct patterns of city refinement, my opinion of the manners of our good *country women* will be much elevated. If, as you say, you *"have become dissipated"*, I hope you will now return to your accustomed sobriety—and, from my knowledge of your character, I presume a cessation of such continual chit-chat will be no small relief to you.

It happened very well for me that I returned as I did from Monson, as the next day was one of the most profitable business days that I have ever had—having full employment, & that too, of the most lucrative kind—and my brother had been obliged to do some, in my absence. And while my weary limbs & sleepy eyes would gladly have found repose, my duties forced me to put my bright side out, and to *seem* more than I really felt myself *to be*. Glad was I to hear the sounds of business cease on the succeeding evening, & to hear the clock strike *10.* that I might retire, & gain my usual rest—and as I dreamed of riding over hills & dales, and called to mind what I had so recently seen, & the incidents of the preceding day, I was lost to all sense of my own identity till the breakfast bell restored me to my consciousness.—

Just entering, as we are, My Dear Emily, upon the wide field of action—and just coming upon the stage to act on our own responsibility, and to stand or fall by our own merits, I feel much interest in having every thing which concerns either of us, managed in the most prudent, the most judicious & the most proper manner. We have no time to lose—We are born—we are in the world—and we must, at some time, leave it—and there is a vast field for exertion before us. We can not sit idly by, and see ourselves raised to fame & fortune—We can not roll in our chariots to glory & honor—We can not expect to arrive at any thing high, any thing praise-worthy, without the use of the necessary means. We must *resolve to do*, and the thing is done. For, as a Poet beautifully & emphatically expresses himself, "If nothing more than purpose in thy power",

The *purpose firm* is equal to the deed.[2]

And I do believe, Dear E, as I presume I have more than once before expressed to you, that almost every thing which a man *determines* to do can be accomplished—I believe the great secret of becoming eminent in any profession, or of gaining any desirable object, lies more in the *unconquerable will*, than in any other power—I know that the men of stern & immoveable resolution—and obstinate determination to press thro' all opposing difficulties, however great, are seldom driven from the accomplishment of their purpose. I know that every thing not absolutely requiring the aid of Omnipotence can be attained by a man who has respectable natural abilities, united with untiring industry & persistence, and it ought ever to be a source of the purest enjoyment to every man of enterprise, that there is enough to do—that there is room for him to exert himself, and that his nature is so constituted, that "cares are pleasures"[3]—and happiness proportioned to the exertion which is made to attain it. I envy not the man who can roll in his *gilded coach*. I desire not the pleasure which he feels, who riots in ill gotten wealth—who wastes his time to spend what has been collected by his successful ancestors—I do not wish to arrive at distinction thro' any passage but my own exertions. It is enough for a man to enjoy health, & to be privileged with a supply of business—It is the highest reward which a man gains for *himself*—It is more desirable to enjoy self-acquired honors, than to wear those which have descended to us—of infinitely more value to wear the *laurels* which *our own* hands have plucked, than to be decked with ornaments which the wealth of our friends may have enabled us to wear. I always feel an ardor & an enthusiasm when upon this subject which leads me to say, perhaps, too much. But excuse me—You know my feelings—You know that I am to make *myself* whatever I may become—and you know that I am contented with my lot—yea, much more—I am even happy in the idea that I am as I am—that I must depend on my own success for my support, and that of My Dearest E.—and I feel no fear—I harbour no dismal foreboding of ills to come—I cherish no apprehension of future bad fortune. I can only say, with the utmost reverence to that Power which created, & which constantly sustains you & me, that I am resolved to do my utmost, & leave the event [result] to heaven.[4]

And when I tell you, that I should rejoice that the time of our intended marriage could be fixed at a much earlier period than that which was last concluded on, I do but repeat what you have already heard me express—and what I would again urge, were it not that the argument of convenience might prevent my success. What should you have thought of Thanksgiving as the time, had we not determined otherwise?—

I must close. Preserve your health—& your sobriety. Don't expose yourself to cold—& take all possible care to retain the present full measure of spirits which you seem to enjoy. Write me, as soon as you can—tell me all about yourself—all about the family—all that is new or interesting in Monson, and remember me most particularly to your father's family—and tell Eliza that I lost nothing but my hat & whip (both of which I found) the last night's journey home.

And now, My Dearest Emily, receive my hand at parting & believe that I shall think much of the time when I anticipate the pleasure of a visit from you & your friends. For the present, Adieu! and it can scarcely be necessary for me to add that I remain yours with undiminished affection & attachment, and shall ever remain most devotedly

Your Edward

Excuse the haste & the consequently poor writing—

Can you read it?—

I send this to N. Hampton P. Office.

1. Edward did not stay overnight in Monson.

2. Edward Young, *Night Thoughts*, bk. 2, lines 89–90.

3. This maxim is also quoted in Letter 36.

4. In many of his letters, Edward emphasizes that his success depends entirely on himself. Presumably Samuel Fowler attempted to transfer some of the business he was unable to transact to Edward. Presumably, too, Edward was not competing with his father for clients, given the waning of his father's interest in the law. For a different reading of Samuel Fowler's influence on Edward, see Cynthia Griffin Wolff, *Emily Dickinson*, especially pp. 25–30. Wolff argues that Samuel Fowler was a financial millstone around Edward's neck even during the courtship years and consequently that Edward was obsessed with economic self-reliance.

This was a happy time for Emily as well. She was enjoying an active social life, despite her complaints about it, and even agreed to come to Amherst for commencement, albeit in her rather tentative way. Her comparative lightheartedness is reflected in the conclusion, "I must leave the apologies" (for another time).

49
Emily Norcross to Edward
3 August 1827

Monson Friday eve

My Dear Edward

Although I have been prevented from conversing with you untill a late hour yet I know that you have been exspecting to hear from me before this I do therefore esteem it a priviledge to deprive myself of repose for the purpose of being more pleasantly engaged. I was much relieved to learn of your safety home as I ever experience much anxiety about you when you leave me as you have formerly been quite a subject to misfortune. I regreted you leaveing me that evening more perhaps than you was conscious of yet I endeavoured to console myself with the reflection that it was for the best as you realy found it to be. Yes dear Edward the Miss Fanings [*sic*] have left us and I suppose you now think me quite at liberty. Most certainly I do find myself quite relieved. It is far from being a desireable life to me to visit and recieve company as much as I have practice[d] it for a number of weeks, and I know not what you will think of me when I tell you that I visited the Springs at Stafford the present week, with your honourable brother Chapman.¹ This is a specimen you will imagine of my steady habits as you please to call them but I did not go without company however and I presume were you familiar with the circumstances of my going you would not disapprove of it at all, but I will say to you that it was not agreable to me, but you know we must not look for our own gratification entirely when we think it for the best to do otherwise when I meet you I will give you a particular history of it do you exspect My dear E to see me at commencement will it not interfere with your engagments. If not perhaps I may come as I desire it very much, I have said nothing particular of it at home but I presume there will be no objections made if all are well.[2]

How is your health dear Edward when it is so excessively warm I trust you do not feal as languid as myself but the evenings I enjoy very much I could sit by my window all the night but your society I would like to complete my happiness but I suppose it is no new thing to desire what is not in our power to enjoy but I trust that I shall not always be obliged to say this there are many things I wish to say to you but I choose to defer them untill we meet. I must now bid you good Evening.

Yours Emily.

I must leave the apologies.

1. Emily refers to Reuben A. Chapman as "your honourable brother" because Chapman was a lawyer. In what follows, she quite sensibly anticipated a little jealousy on Edward's part. See also Letter 50.

2. Again we see that it is difficult for Emily to assert herself with her parents or to communicate effectively with them.

50
Edward to Emily Norcross
9 August 1827

Amherst, Thursday Eve, Aug. 9. 1827.

My Dear Emily,

Your letter was recd. on Tuesday, and perused with the pleasure which your communications to me always produce—and when you observe, that you "know not what I shall think of you, when you tell me that you have again visited Stafford Springs "in company" etc, I confess that I was, at first, somewhat surprised; but feeling, as I do, the utmost confidence in your prudence, & discretion, and knowing, as I think I do, that you are sincere in what you have said to me, I should do you & myself most manifest injustice to harbour, for a moment, the most remote suspicion of the purity of your motives, or the propriety of your conduct—and I feel perfectly safe in the assurance which a knowledge of your character produces, that "all is right"—however, you need not be surprised that I thought it a little strange that my "honorable brother," as you call him, should so soon have become *so very polite to you.*

I shall expect to see you at Commencement *most certainly*—and shall not be satisfied to receive a denial, at that time—neither shall I consent to have you return till you have passed a few days with us— You must not let your delicacy in relation to our intercourse deprive me of the pleasure which I have so often before anticipated from receiving a visit from you, and as often been disappointed. I shall expect to see you & *William*, & E. Norcross Esq and Lady, at our house, on Tuesday; Will Lavinia come—or Olivia F. We should be happy to see them with you. We do not calculate upon a very good Comt. as the class to graduate, is not, to say the least, above the ordinary stamp. There will be one address or more before the Literary faculties in College, on the afternoon of Tuesday, and prize-speaking on Tuesday Evening. You will be pleased with that, & you must try to reach Amherst as early as you conveniently can on Tuesday afternoon. I think the exercises of Tuesday Eve. much the pleasantest part of the whole—and I shall arrange my business at home so as to interfere as little as possible with my duties to my friends. You need not feel any fear of interrupting my business—and I entreat you not to suffer that to deter you from your expected visit. We all want to see you, and shall be more than disappointed if you don't come.

My brother William went to Albany on the first day of this month, and is now, I suppose, in N. York, purchasing his goods. His departure has somewhat the same effect upon the young people here, as that of the Misses F. has upon M.—and as he was rather inclined to *roguery*, when out of business, it is a source of pleasure to me and to all of us, that he has now engaged in business which will necessarily keep him regular. We have *settled* his "outrage upon the blacks" since his absence, by paying rather dearly for his frolic.—They are now all quiet.[1]

I have just recd. another letter from Mr. Warriner—He speaks freely of Monson, and says that he expects to visit there with his sister, about the 20th of this month! (Let this be confidential.)

Don't you imagine that he is rather blinded by that power which sometimes seizes men, suddenly, and holds them firmly? And do you not believe that he is making his arrangements for a regular seige upon our friend [Olivia Flynt]?

Our Clergyman, too, the Rev. Mr. Washburn, has not escaped the influence which acts upon the laiety—but has been induced, whether from advice or request, to enter into a contract with a Miss P—a daughter of our former Minister, who is no more than 8. or 10. years older than himself, and who has not enjoyed that state, after which age becomes uncertain & fluctuating, and memory fails to record the years as they pass swiftly by, longer than five or seven years! We all wish him "Good speed", and hope his brilliant anticipations will be more than realized.[2]

Mr. Coleman has been in town two or three times, of late, at meetings of the Trustees of the Academy etc., and I called at his house a week ago this evening, and found his "dearer half" like all other Clergymen's wives, much increased in matronly dignity, since I last saw her—and Mr. C. rather blushed when he says that "she will probably not visit us at present."[3]

The evenings now are most beautiful, and you scarcely need be told that they do not pass without many pleasant reflections about My Dearest Emily, and you can not have wished oftener than myself, that we could enjoy each other's society. How delightful after the business of the day is finished, to enjoy the intercourse with my friend, which always makes me happy. How long, Dear E. must we desire more frequent meetings, and be deprived of the privilege! I trust not always. I feel much interest in having the time arrive, when, with the blessing of Heaven, I can claim a right to protect & cherish you, & when we shall be bound by the Law of the land, as we already are, by that of a stronger power, to seek each other's happiness, & unite in our efforts to spread the blessings which we enjoy—to add to the happiness of our friends, and to promote, as far as in our power, the melioration of the condition of all about us.

The "Mt. Pleasant" school is quite flourishing—having 37. boys present, with a large number more engaged. They are about making considerable addition to the buildings which are already quite spacious, to make room for their pupils as fast as they apply for admission. Miss Colton officiates as Governess of the establishment, and is well spoken of by those who have become acquainted with her.[4]

I sent you a Sermon by Olivia, which will last till I see you, when I shall have a short moral *lecture* for you. The Sermon is written in good style, and the description of a woman who "builds her house" is admirably drawn, & wants but little of perfection.[5]

It is growing very late, & I must close. Go on in the ways of virtue—and "be all that you have been known to me"—and as we part, for the present, accept, My Dear Emily, my pledge of lasting attachment, and let us renew the mutual promises which exist between us to become *one for life*, and, before we separate this evening, implore the protection & blessing of our Maker. Remember me affectionately to all our friends, & believe me, as ever,

Your sincere Edward

We are all well. Let me hear from you. next week.

Chauncey Colton & Mr. Thayer tell me that they expect to pass thro'
M. the fore part of next week on their way to Stafford Springs.[6] If so,
you may possibly hear from me, by them, as they have been kind
enough to offer to carry any thing for me.

P.S. If you have finished reading "Hope Leslie" & the "Casket" all of
you, will you please bring them with you at Comt., as the Casket is
borrowed of one of the Senior Class, who is to leave, and several are
desirous of seeing the Novel. Don't bring them unless you have done
with them.

1. William Dickinson's " 'outrage upon the blacks' " was not reported in the
New-England Inquirer; it is not clear whom, if anybody, Edward is quoting, since
he habitually employs quotation marks for paraphrases. But in April 1828 the *In-
quirer* contained an article on "Free Blacks in Hampshire County" in which the
following facts emerged. In Amherst, there were ten or eleven such families, com-
posed of from fifty to sixty "souls." A large number of the adults were employed
in white families as domestic servants. The author observed, "Every white boy
knows well that he may teaze the black in the house of prayer, and throw stones
at him in the streets, and escape with impunity." The author argued in favor
of meliorating "the condition of our colored domestics and laborers" on the
grounds that such a melioration would purify the moral atmosphere of the com-
munity.

2. The Reverend Royal Washburn married Harriet Parsons, the daughter of the
Reverend David Parsons. Parsons was dismissed from his ministry in 1819, fol-
lowing a dispute with his congregation. He was about seventy at the time; his
daughter was probably middle-aged in 1827. Nevertheless, Edward is unusually
malicious about the age difference between the Washburns.

As his mother was to discover, Edward was not fond of aging women. When he
failed to invite her to live with him after her husband's death, she complained bit-
terly, "The Idea struck me very unpleasantly that other parents had suffered in
rearing their families [but] they must be set aside because they are old[;] it looks
to[o] much like heathenism." See the letters written by Lucretia Gunn Dickinson
pleading with Edward for help in Leyda, *The Years and Hours of Emily
Dickinson*, 1:56, 58.

3. Maria Flynt Coleman was pregnant. Her daughter Olivia was born in Octo-
ber.

4. Presumably "Miss Colton" was the sister of Chauncey.

5. This sermon cannot be identified, but Edward might have sent Daniel A.
Clark's *The Wise Builder, A Sermon Delivered to the Females of the First Parish
in Amherst, Massachusetts*, which was published in Boston in 1820.

6. In 1831, Martin Thayer became a proprietor of the Mount Pleasant Classi-
cal Institution. In 1827, he was one of the trustees of Amherst Academy.

Emily and her brother William were in Amherst on 20 August for the College commencement, but she probably did not stay overnight. It seems likely that she met Edward's parents at that time but neither she nor Edward comments on such a meeting in subsequent letters.

51
Edward to Emily Norcross
1 September 1827

Amherst, Saturday Morning, Sept. 1. 1827.

My Dear Emily,

I presume you will be surprised that I have not fulfilled my promise to visit or write to you, in the course of the present week—but when I tell you that an unexpected occurence in relation to brother William's business led me to start for Boston on Monday Morning, from which I returned on Thursday Evening, you will see that it was not consistent for me to perform either. I have an opportunity to send to Springfield, this morning, & shall say a few words, merely to tell you that I intend, if business is so that I can be spared, to visit you about the middle of next week—probably on Wednesday.[1] I have some business within a few miles of M. and shall take time to make you a call. I saw my friend, Wm. M. Towne, at Worcester, on Thursday, & he proposed to me to meet him and Miss Robinson, a *particular friend* of his, with you at Brookfield, to dine on Wednesday.[2] I agreed to write what I would do, on Monday Morning—& shall hear in reply, on Tuesday. Should you like to go? If so, I will make preparation for it.[3]

I visited Andover, while on my journey to Boston, & attended Commencement at Cambridge—found many old friends and acquaintances, & enjoyed myself finely.

How is your health, since your return from Amherst? Are you all well?—You have recd. a visit, I hear, from our friend W. [Warriner] of Springfield—who appears quite pleased with M. and does not hesitate to speak of his enjoyment, while there, in most enthusiastic terms. How does he succeed?—

The bearer of this to SPF [Springfield] is nearly ready—Will you not, therefore, excuse me—Make my regards to all your father's family—be assured that I will not write many more so dry letters—Expect to see me on Wednesday forenoon next, if the weather is pleasant—and believe that in offering, again, all I have to bestow, I am most sincerely

Your Edward

1. "Recd by Mr. Sweetser from Amherst & mailed by S. W. Jr." is penciled on the outside of this letter, which was hand delivered by Sweetser and then mailed from Springfield by Warriner. The postage was six cents.

2. William Moore Towne graduated from Amherst in 1825, studied and practiced law in Worcester, and in April 1829 married Frances Robinson of that city. It is possible that he also attended the Northampton Law School.

3. Emily did not respond to this suggestion in writing but may have been able to transmit an oral message. Brookfield, Massachusetts, is approximately fifteen miles northeast of Monson. I am unclear as to how much traveling Edward was proposing to do in a single day. For example, was he proposing that he and Emily would return to Monson Wednesday night after dining in Brookfield? This seems unlikely.

Edward visited Monson on Wednesday and Thursday, 5 and 6 September. What follows is one of Emily's most affectionate letters, as, for example, when she wrote, "[There is] nothing in the world I value so much as your society," or, "Could I but give you the parting kiss before we part." The visit—presumably without a side trip to Brookfield—must have been a success.

52
Emily Norcross to Edward
14 September 1827

Monson Friday Evening

Your request my dear Edward with my engagment has not been forgotten yet you may suppose that I have defered granting it untill the last moment.¹ I believe however you useually listen to my apologies I have been much engaged since you left me. This afternoon and evening I have been occupied with a company of young ladies which I was very happy to see, but do you not think my happiness much increased since they have left me, as I have retired to my favourite chamber to devoute [?] myself entirely to you, most certainly you cannot doubt the pleasure ever realised in conversing with one so dear to me. I was particularly anxious for you the morning you left me, judgeing from my own fellings [*sic*] I thought I could know something of yours was you not happy to find yourself at evening snug in your office without any thing to molest you. Undoubtedly, but my compassion would not extend so far but what I would have interrupted you with an eve[n]ing call had it been in my power, sufficient to have made a few enquiries. I suppose you met the wise man at Springfield no doubt he had many interesting communications reserved for you. May I hope that you heard them patiently. His honourable lady has returned from the Springs a short time since I have not yet had the pleasure of seeing her but have learnt that her health was much improved Mr. S I presume will feal quite interested in the recieving the information.[2] May he have wisdom sufficient to lead him to examine the foundation upon which he stands before he publishes his intention in visiting Monson, but it does not concern me at all I therefore relinquish the subject for the present. The management of my own affairs is enough for me without interfering with others. I suppose you have not forgotten that you invited me stron[g]ly to visit you again now my dear Edward you must excuse me, convinced as you are that [there is] nothing in the world I value so much as your society you cannot therefore doubt where I would wish to be do you not think the study of self denial will become quite familiar to us, but never mind time is gradualy passing, ere long I shall go to spend my days with you. I suspect you think this will be a serious one indeed but it will then be to late to retrace your steps. Is it decided that you come to Monson at the review I should be much pleased to see you, but do not flatter myself at all as I expect to be disappointed. My dear Edward I must leave you I fear you will not be able to read what I have written. Could I but give you the parting kiss before we part. .I did not think this word would sonud [sound] so foolish but you must excuse me when you reflect that it is from your affectionate Emily. It will give me much pleasure to hear from you

Pleasent dreames to you dear Edward.

1. By "engagment" Emily probably means her promise to write.
2. "The wise man" is *Solomon* Warriner, Jr. Emily is dubious about his prospects for success in his romance with her cousin Olivia Flynt. The word "feal" has been corrected from "fell."

53
Edward to Emily Norcross
21 September 1827

Amherst. Sept. 21. 1827.

My Dear Emily,

Nicholas has just called to inform me that I can send directly to Monson, this afternoon, and notwithstanding I have waited in expectation of hearing from you, every day for a week past, I can not let the opportunity pass without saying all that the few minutes which I have before Mr. Keep goes will allow.[1]

I reached home safely on the evening after I left you, and found two or three letters from brother Wm. who was then at Boston. He has since returned to Amherst, and is now a *partner* in the store under my office. He lives with us, and I hope the disappointments which he has experienced the past summer will do him good.[2]

Have you recovered your health? Are you now free from the unpleasant feelings which you sometimes experience? Have you been well since I saw you?[3] Do you enjoy yourself? How do all the family do? Give my love to them all.

I. Eaton & Miss Hayden are married—and have gone to St. Louis in Missouri—1500. miles! A soldier & his wife—with a small salary, in a strange place—without friends or relations, must feel solitary indeed—I wish them well.[4] Has Mr. Chapman visited Blandford, since I was in Monson. I understood, in Springfield, that he was engaged to Genl. Knox's daughter, as you knew before. Is he as gallant as ever?—[5]

The terms in the College, Academy & Mt. Pleasant have all just commenced, & the great increase in each makes the place appear quite lively, after a vacation of several weeks. When will it be the most convenient for you to come home with me & make us a family visit?[6] I may come after you in a few days. Most gladly would I come for you to make a *permanent stay, now,* but I suppose that can not *be—Can it?*[7]—I must stop—shall write as soon as the fore part of next week, again, and shall expect a letter, to-morrow, from you. Accept, My Dearest Emily, my heart, hand, & all I can call mine, and believe that in every vicissitude I shall ever remain your most affectionate & dedicated friend Edward

Have E. N. Esq. & party returned from their journey?—Give my respects to them

Will there be a review at Monson?—How is Hiram—

1. Emily wrote next on 24 September, but Edward did not receive her letter of 14 September until the day after his letter was written; that is, he received her letter on 22 September. By modern standards, the Monson-Amherst mail service was speedy; a week's delay was unusual. Normally, letters were received on the day after they were posted. There also appears to have been mail service on Sundays and national holidays such as the Fourth of July.

"Mr. Keep" may be the John Keep who was a member of the Amherst College class of 1829. He was born in Monson and prepared for college at Monson Academy. If the Keeps were still living in Monson in 1827, Edward might also be referring to John's father, Simeon.

2. William was having trouble establishing himself in business, his plan to set up shop in Albany having fallen through. He never attended college and had been working and living in Boston since he was fifteen. As I suggested earlier, he became a successful banker and manufacturer in Worcester.

3. Edward seems, rather consistently, to have been more concerned about Emily's health than she was herself.

4. "I. Eaton & Miss Hayden" were presumably related to the Mr. Hayden and Miss Eaton who are mentioned in Letters 14 and 15. Otherwise they are unidentified.

5. According to Edward, Chapman was a flirt. See also Letter 50.

6. When she was in Amherst on 20 August, Emily may not have stayed overnight. By "family visit," Edward probably means an overnight stay in the Samuel Fowler Dickinson household.

7. From his point of view, Edward had agreed to a wedding date, presumably in the spring of 1828, that was much too far in the future.

54
Emily Norcross to Edward
24 September 1827

Monson Monday Morning

My dear Edward

As Mr Colton has visited Monson and returns to amherst this morning I will say a few words to you by him.[1] I recieved your letter saturday evening, and do you not suppose that I was much disappointed to learn from it that you had not heard from me. As I wrote to you more than a week since I know not dear Edward the fate of my letter, but I know this, that it left Monson in our mail a week on Saturday last, but I can assure you that I have experienced no little anxiety about it but I cannot but flatter myself that it is in your safe hands before this. It would give me pleasure to answer all your enquiries but fear that I shall not have time this busy morning. The review is on tuseday next. I suppose there is no prospect of your being here I should be happy indeed to see you, but do not expect it, the enquiry is often made whether you are to be present. My health is very good indeed. Yet I was not sensible of recovering so rapidly as Miss Olivia after a visit from Mr. Warriner.[2] I have much to say but must defer it untill I write again. I must leave you yet it is ever with regret that dear friends are seperated you know.

from one entirely yours Emily

1. Mr. Colton is Chauncey rather than Simeon.

2. Emily's sense of humor surfaces again; Warriner was courting Olivia. In general, Emily sounds less fearful about sickness than does Edward. It is perhaps worth remarking that she had more experience with terminal illness than did Edward, all of whose siblings were living.

The excessive rationality of Edward's style is apparent in the following letter, in which he seeks to imagine their mutual future life. Like many of his other fantasies, this one has very little specific texture. Eschewing the confessional mode, he nevertheless portrays Emily as the friend "to whom I can confide, with the most perfect security, all my secrets, and who will feel it a pleasure to share my sorrows, as well as participate in my enjoyments." But Edward is also unable to imagine the ways in which he will respond to her affectional needs. Thus, although he remarks that "we have had time to become considerably acquainted with each other, and each of us have had opportunities for learning the characters of the other," his language continues to preclude intimacy.

55
Edward to Emily Norcross
24 September 1827

Amherst. Monday Evening. Sept. 24. 1827.
My Dear Emily,

Your letter which was written on Friday Evening Sept. 14. & mailed the next day, did not reach me till last Saturday night—and you will not be surprised that I thought it somewhat strange that I did not hear from you before—where it was detained, I know not; and although it is late, and I shall go to Northampton to-morrow morning to attend the Supreme Court, I can not deprive myself of the pleasure of conversing a short time with my dear friend—and you know the happiness which I experience when I can find a leisure hour, at the close of the day, to devote myself exclusively to you. It is not, My Dear Emily, the mere hour when I am writing, that you are in mind—it is not an occasional respect which warms my bosom, & produces a momentary glow of pleasure at the recollection of the many pleasant interviews which we have enjoyed—but a steady, settled feeling of the more pure esteem & affection which produces emotions of solid satisfaction in the assurance of having a friend, to whom I can confide, with the most perfect security, all my secrets, and who will feel it a pleasure to share my sorrows, as well as participate in my enjoyments. Such a person, My Dear Emily, I think I have in you—and you are too well convinced of my attachment for you to need any assurance that your happiness and my own are inseparable. I know not what is in store for us—We may be very happy—We may be the reverse—We may be fortunate—We may be unfortunate. We ought to form a cool and deliberate determination to do our best—to take the course which seems most likely to ensure our happiness, & pursue it with a due regard to the

Power which created & which governs all. It is no light thing, Emily, to form a connection of the kind which we are about to form. It is not a matter for any but the most serious, the most rational reflection. I doubt not that the subject has been duly considered by us both—and I feel that we have made up our minds after mature consideration. We certainly can not incur the censure of being hasty. We have had time to become considerably acquainted with each other, and each of us have had opportunities for learning the characters of the other. It would be very gratifying to me, if our union could take place sooner than we have agreed—What say you to it? Can it be done consistently? And do you suppose your friends will consent to it? Are not our own feelings in unison on the subject? But I defer it till we meet again.

Professor King who has been a missionary to Palestine for some years past has arrived in town, and last evening in the College Chapel, gave a short sketch of his journey in that interesting country.[1] His account was heard with the liveliest interest, and his description of scenes which he had not only witnessed, but passed through, was most striking, & exhibited the character & manners of the inhabit- ants in a light entirely new. I could spread over much of my sheet in giving you an account of it, but can not take time for it now. Suffice it to say, that to see & hear a man who had visited & stood upon almost all the places mentioned in the new testament—who had viewed all the places where our Saviour was born, brought up—educated & preached—and been on the very ground where the most solemn of all events took place—where the Redeemer of the human race was ex- ecuted by his enemies—I say to see & hear such a man would produce in the mind of every reflecting mind, emotions of no ordinary charac- ter. I thought much of you, & wished you could have been there—It would have been interesting to me, (altho' as I have before said, I make no pretensions to seriousness,) to have conversed with you freely upon a subject which so intimately concerns our future welfare; and little as my general appearance would indicate it, there are many hours in which the future is distinctly brought to mind—when the affairs of less consequence are laid aside, & the business of a state to come contemplated. Could we know, My Dearest Emily, that we should *together* inherit the mansions of bliss above—that we should have our portion assigned us with all those myriads of blessed spirits who surround the throne of the Eternal! Could we be assured that after lives of usefulness here, we might have a seat allotted us in the abodes of glory—how would our hearts palpitate with joy!—Do not think me a hypocrite—or accuse me of bigotry—There are times when it is honorable to our natures to indulge our thoughts, and meditate on things which we must see whether prepared or not. But I leave them for the present.

You say in your letter [52] that I "must excuse you from again visiting me at Amherst." Why so, Emily? I had calculated to go to Monson, on the day of the Review, or the evening preceding, and after attending it, to return with you—and if I go, as I now anticipate, I shall be much disappointed if you do not come with me. I hope you will think it best to comply with my wishes in relation to it, for you know that you have never made us a *visit*—which I think you ought to do. However you must decide. It is now quite probable that I shall attend the Review at Greenwich on Monday next, & go from there to Monson, Monday afternoon, tho' not certain. To-day I have had the pleasure of reviewing 3. companies—at the *request* of the officers who wished to practise before they met [?] where a mistake would be more noticed. The week after next, I shall be gone five days, beginning on Monday, and must have a hard siege.[2]

The Irishmen are to be tried at Northampton, this week, for *murder*. Will *either of the Monson Lawyers* be there?[3]

I was at Belchertown on Saturday—saw Mr. Coleman—his wife was well, he said, tho' I *did not call, as you may well suppose*.[4] And now, My Dear Emily, I must leave you, let me join with you in the wish that we could press the parting hand, & give the parting ——s [kisses] but while that is denied, let me hope that ere long we shall enjoy each other's society constantly, & experience the true happiness which kindred spirits (are not ours such?) are fitted to produce. My compliments to all—and till we meet (which I hope will be soon) let my paper tell that I remain, as ever, Your Affectionate

Edward

Good-night—"Pleasant dreams to you, Dear Emily."—

I mail this at Northampton P. office.

I expect my brother from Northampton to-morrow to go into Wm's store.[5] Don't be disappointed if I should not come to Monson to attend the review.

1. The Reverend Jonas King was appointed Professor of Oriental Literature at Amherst in 1821. His name appears in college catalogues from 1822 to 1828, but "except on a flying visit, he did not reside during that period nearer to Amherst than Athens, in Greece." See Edward Hitchcock, *Reminiscences of Amherst College: Historical, Scientific, Biographical, and Autobiographical* (Northampton: Bridgman and Childs, 1863), p. 37.

2. A notice in the *Inquirer* on 7 September signed by "A. Howland," major general of the Fourth Division of Massachusetts Militia and Edward Dickinson, "aid-de-camp," contained a schedule for the October reviews, which were to take place from the first through the twelfth. Commissioned as an ensign in 1824, by 1825 Edward had attained the rank of major. "I was afraid to go a grade higher, lest I should get too strong a thirst for military glory," he explained during his only long speech in Congress, in 1854. See Bingham, *Emily Dickinson's Home*, p. 544.

3. The Monson lawyers are Erasmus Norcross and Reuben A. Chapman. "The Irishmen" are unidentified.

4. Edward did not visit the Colemans at home because of Maria's pregnancy.

5. Samuel Fowler, Jr., appears to have completed or abandoned his studies at Monson Academy.

56
Edward to Emily Norcross
26 September 1827

Amherst, Wednesday Evening, Sept. 26. 1827.

My Dear Emily,

"As wave follows wave," so you may think my letters crowd, one upon another, in thick succession. I returned from Northampton this evening, & found a letter from you, which was forwarded by Mr. Colton on Monday last—and you have probably recd. mine before this, in which the subjects of yours are explained, & that, contrary to your expectations, it is not improbable that I may be at your review on Tuesday next.

It is Court week at N.H. [Northampton] you know, and the Irishmen expect their trials to-morrow—the company of militia in Springfield of which Mr. W. [Warriner] is an officer, is expected at N.H. tomorrow, also, when I shall probably obtain the latest information from our friends at M—I will say nothing by way of anticipation. My time will necessarily be occupied during the week at Court—and if I go on a reviewing tour next week, two days, I shall have the remainder at home—and go again, the week after, 5. days. After that the business for November Court will come on, and I must be confined to my office. Things begin to look a little more lively—and appear somewhat like business—there is always a dull time from August Court till October—a good time for recreation—

It is very late—and I can say but a few words—We are all well—and all want to see you. Will you not come with me on Tuesday next? The evenings are now beautiful, and the brilliant moonlight ought not to pass unenjoyed. I am happy to hear that your health is so good—&

hope it will remain so. Take care of yourself, won't you? Don't expose yourself to cold—the evenings, you know, are damp. My respects to all—tell me all that is interesting or new—and consent to become a resident in Amherst as soon as you can, for you know that your society always makes me happy. My prayers for your health & happiness—& tho' you are asleep—give me your hand—Good night—May heaven's blessings rest on you & your devoted Edward

Mr. Chapman passes the night with us, & will return to Monson in the morning.—
I know not the meaning of your present inclosed in your letter by Mr. C——[1]

1. The present Emily sent in Letter 54 that was hand delivered by Chauncey Colton cannot be identified.

Edward visited Monson on 1 and 2 October. He was ill when he reached home, but by 17 October he was fully recovered and determined to extract some concession from Emily. He wanted her to agree to advance the date of their marriage but knew that he was in a weak bargaining position. He also wanted her to visit him in Amherst but anticipated that she would be reluctant to do so. Thus, after rebuking her—"You have not done right in refusing so many invitations to visit Amherst, and you ought not to make any apology, why you can not come, at the present time. I believe you can arrange your affairs so as to be absent two or three days without any very serious inconvenience"—he added, "If you can not, I will consider that as a reasonable excuse, and visit you the sooner." Or if she was herself unable to visit him, he wanted her sister Lavinia, then fifteen, to come in her place. At the very least, he expected to see her brother William at the Cattle Show in Northampton. Despite Edward's emerging sense that Emily's behavior and perhaps that of her parents was unnecessarily rigid, his faith in her remained undaunted; he concluded the letter, "I saw you, in my last night's dream."

57
Edward to Emily Norcross
17 October 1827

Amherst, Wednesday Morning. Oct. 17. 1827.

My Dear Emily,

I have been prevented from writing to you till the present time, and I have but a little while now to converse with you, as the stage passes at 1/2 past 8. o'clock. It is two weeks this morning, since I left Monson, and I reached home about one o'clock—My cold was very severe—and continued a week. One day I was confined to the house. I did not attend but two reviews, last week, on account of my health, as well as on account of bad weather—went to Wendell on Thursday, and Greenfield on Friday, and had two pleasant days. On my return, found my father & brother William both unwell, and unable to attend to business, and was occupied with them till yesterday, when they recovered so far as to be out, and able to do something.[1] I am now retired, and happy that I have a little leisure to enjoy your society—to converse with you, in a familiar letter, and to experience, in some degree, the pleasure which an interview with my Dearest Emily always affords. The morning is beautiful, and, after so long a time of clouds & storms, the privilege of making you a short morning call by sunshine, is a precious one. I think much of you, Dear Emily, and regret that is so, that it is inconsistent for me to urge your coming to stay *permanently* with me, till the time set by your friends, and once assented to by us. But, if it must be so, we must be patient—time moves rapidly, and it may be best for us both, that we have so long an opportunity to acquire experience, and render our acquaintance with each other more perfect.

The "Cattle Show" at Northampton takes place on Wednesday of next week—when I expect to see Wm. here, and will give you one more invitation to come up with him. I expect him on Tuesday, and if you will come and stay till Thursday, you will gratify me, and my friends. You have not done right in refusing so many invitations to visit Amherst, and you ought not to make any apology, why you can not come, at the present time. I believe you can arrange your affairs so as to be absent two or three days without any very serious inconvenience. If you can not, I will consider that as a reasonable excuse, and visit you the sooner. I shall expect Wm. certainly, & if you do not think it best to accompany him, yourself, why not let Lavinia come? She would like to ride, and would be pleased with seeing the manufactures exhibited at Northampton—There are a great rarity of fine specimens of domestic industry & skill which it would be creditable to any Lady to imitate—and I consider it as an honor to any female to have her name publicly announced as having obtained a premium for her excellence in any branch of domestic economy, and think it quite an inducement for all who can, to attend, occasionally, such an exhibition. Tell Lavinia that I shall not leave you again without saying *"good bye"* to her—Remember me particularly to her.

Is your health good? Do you enjoy yourself well—are all your friends in good health?—Make my compliments to them all. And now, My Dearest Emily, I must leave you, in this hasty manner, as the mail will soon arrive—I have only time to say, be careful of your health, don't expose yourself to cold—think that you have not only your own individual happiness to regard, but that mine is increased or diminished with yours—our happiness is & ought to be inseparable—Preserve your health, then—continue in the paths of innocence and virtue and fidelity—continue to cultivate those graces which are the charm of your sex—and let our sincere desires for that pure character and unsullied reputation which are the pride of both sexes, incite us to avoid the appearance of evil—and let our conduct be marked by that correctness which shall insure us happiness, and may an approving conscience be our reward—Write me immediately—accept again the pledge which I have so often given you of my entire devotion to you, and believe that I shall ever remain most sincerely and entirely Your affectionate Edward

Good Morning. I saw you, in my last night's dream.

1. Curiously, Edward writes as though his mother played no part in nursing his father and brother back to health.

Psychologically, Edward was not a canny romantic strategist. Although he recognized that Emily was "practising upon [his] patience," he continued to assure her that nothing she failed to do could diminish his affection for her or alter his behavior. Thus he robbed her of a crucial incentive to comply with his wishes. He was afraid to risk her displeasure and much less confident of her affection for him than of his for her. He hoped, however, that she would choose to please him, especially after he explained, "My Mother & Sisters want much to see you, & I have told them that I expect you, and you must not say no. this time." But whether intentionally or not, Emily continued to humiliate him.

58
Edward to Emily Norcross
20 October 1827

Amherst. Saturday afternoon
Oct. 20. 1827.

My Dear Emily,

I have this moment seen Mr. Field who starts immediately for Monson, and says he will wait a few minutes for me, if I want to send. And you know that I never neglect an opportunity to write, if I can't say but a few words.

I am in perfect health, and expect to see you and William at our house on Tuesday of next week. My Mother & Sisters want much to see you, & I have told them that I expect you, and you must not say *no.* this time. I hear that our friend, the Parson [Coleman], has a daughter, a week or more, old, and that Miss Julia Dwight is married. I have heard nothing from you, since I was at Monson, and conclude you are all well—else I should have heard. You might find time, I should think, to write a short letter before many weeks more elapse. I suppose, however, you are now practising upon my patience—and I can assure you, that however much I want to hear from you & see you, that these long intervals will not diminish my attachment, or render you less dear to me, and you may feel the fullest confidence, that I shall forever remain most unreservedly, & entirely Yours—

Edward

Remember me to all the family etc—

I wrote to Wm. yesterday.

He will receive it, on Sunday Evening—[1]

I need not say, "*In haste*" E——

1. Edward's letter to William has not been found. Presumably he urged him to come to Amherst and to bring Emily with him.

This is one of Emily's most spirited and outrageous letters. Holding Edward to his promise in Letter 57, she asserted, "Did you not remark that if I declined visiting you that you should make it an apology [excuse] to visit me the sooner. I think much of the engagement [promise] may I hope that it will not escape your memory." Although Edward typically closed his letters by conveying his respects to her family, she says nothing about conveying her respects to his mother and sisters, who were hoping to see her and perhaps even to meet her. Nor does she suggest an alternate date for a visit to Amherst.

59
Emily Norcross to Edward
22 October 1827

Monson October 22
Monday evening

My Dear Edward

While I sit solitary in my chamber this evening how happy should I be could I welcome you here I think I should be quite social for a while I hope not troublesome however. It rains finely this evening I think the prospects rather uncertain for tomorrow yet we know not what the day will bring forth. I will observe the reception of your letters with pleasure Yet you must know it was painful for me to learn of your being ill after you left me, but I was quite aprehensive of it and was very solicitous for you untill relieved by your letter.

My dear Edward you have again urged me to visit, and what shall I say, had I given you the least encouragement I would not deny you but at present I think it will be inconsistant for William or me to gratify you I presume you are sensible that it is a busy season, and as my father has frequent calls away it is quite inconvenient for William to be abscent he leaves for Hartford wednesday I may accompany him my engagements are now somewhat pressing.[1] As I wish to accomplish all in my power before the cold winter which awaits us, not so much occupied however but what I can write a line to you before many weeks as you say. This is a close hint to me do you not hope I may improve by it. And now my dear E do you suppose that I would neglect you for the trial of your patience certainly not, you are to dear to me for this, but perhaps I have given you reasons to think so was you not pleased to have such interesting inteligence from Mr Coleman. I can hardly realise that Cousin Maria has become a mother. I conclude you will not feel so delicate in calling upon them in future. I understand Mr C is quite elated with the little stranger, no wonder at this do you think so I shall have much to say to you when we again meet which I can not write. Mr. Wheller [?] and wife passed a night at my brothers of last week I called on them the morning before they left yet I did not venture to ask for you but was quite happy to see them.[2] Did you not remark that if I declined visiting you that you should make it an apology to visit me the sooner. I think much of the engagement may I hope that it will not escape your memory. Yet I have ever said to you not to leave when inconvenient with your business I must now my dear Edward bid you Good Evening and may I hope that you will not be disposed to think hard of me.

Your sincere Emily.

1. The "he" in "he leaves for Hartford wednesday" may be either Joel Norcross or William.

2. "Mr. Wheller and wife" are associated by Emily with Amherst. They are unidentified even if, as seems likely, Emily has misspelled "Wheeler."

Edward's patience was wearing thin. Emily did not visit, Lavinia did not visit, and even William disappointed him by not attending the Northampton Cattle Show.

60
Edward to Emily Norcross
1 November 1827

Amherst. November 1. 1827.

My Dear Emily,

I have an opportunity, this morning, to send to Monson, and I take a few moments from my business, to write to you—as I intended to write, this evening for to-morrow's mail. Your letter was recd. on Thursday last, and read with much pleasure, and tho' I was at a loss to know the reason of your delaying, for so long a time, to give me any evidence that I retained a place in your remembrance, yet I was willing to be so charitable as to suppose that you always have good reasons for all you do, as well as for all you neglect to do—and I hope I shall not have occasion again to remain so long ignorant whether you are among the living or the dead. I shall, in future, expect a *definite promise.*[1]

I was disappointed in not seeing you & Wm. at Amherst last week, as I expected—I attended the "Cattle Show" at Northampton & was much pleased with the exhibition—particularly that of the manufactures. The Address was excellent & will probably be published.

My father is now on a journey to the State of N. York, to be absent two or three weeks, and I am necessarily more than usually confined. My own business, too, keeps me quite close to my office—tho' I hope to be able to get time enough to visit you next week, probably on Tuesday or Wednesday—as the courts are near at hand—and the week after next I must go to Greenfield—then to *N. Hampton* & shall be much occupied, as I have business at both. We have made new arrangements in relation to the continuance of our Newspaper, & shall improve it, soon.[2] I have much to say, but must defer it, till we meet. I am obliged to stop, as the bearer of this is about starting. Love to all—and assurance of entire devotion to yourself—

Edward

1. Edward means a definite promise to visit him.

2. "The size of the paper was to be increased about one-fifth and its appearance improved. . . . Under the new management, the *Inquirer* was edited by Prof. Samuel M. Worcester of Amherst College. The paper was enlarged by the addition of one column to each page, and the publication day was changed from Friday to Thursday. . . . The publication was continued about a year under its new management and then was given up" (Carpenter & Morehouse, *History of the Town of Amherst*, p. 341). An announcement of the paper's reorganization appeared in the issue of 16 November. The *Inquirer* had been purchased from the printing firm of J. S. & C. Adams by "a number of gentlemen, who have determined on carrying forward the publication on an improved and extended plan." Edward may have been one of these gentlemen. After the paper's demise, there was no newspaper in Amherst until 1839, but even then the Amherst *Gazette* was published for only a few months. In 1844, the more durable *Hampshire and Franklin Express* began publication.

In response to what appeared to be Emily's unaccountable reluctance to visit him and his family in Amherst, Edward visited Monson grudgingly on 6, 7, and 8 November. He returned home in a snowstorm and the trip was arduous. Deflecting his anger from Emily onto the elements, he describes soothing his irritated spirits by drinking "a few bottles of cordial" with some of his bachelor friends. Although not unprecedented, such revelry was out of character for Edward. Perhaps unconsciously, he was attempting to enlist Emily's sympathies by suggesting that even a man as stalwart as himself had a breaking point. This letter also contains an interesting fantasy of Emily as a recluse, which emerges as a defense against his feeling of neglect.

61
Edward to Emily Norcross
11 November 1827

Amherst, Sunday Evening 1/2 past 12. o'clock.
Nov. 11. 1827.

My Dear Emily,

I have been to South Hadley Canal this evening, to carry Sister Mary to begin her school, and left her at Esq. Bowdoin's, where she is to board[1]—and just returned, taken two cups of tea, and notwithstanding it is so very late, I will not sleep while I have an engagement unfulfilled, nor deprive myself of the pleasure of conversing a short time with you for the sake of a little more repose. I returned from Monson the other day, in perfect safety, having had the pleasure of walking my horse & breaking a path thro' the snow-drifts for the *short space of 15. miles*! and reaching Belchertown at 3. o'clock in the afternoon!!! Got home about dark, where I was hailed by old & young, as one who had emerged from a most tremendous snow-storm, and come off victorious in my contest with the elements. Fortunately for me, one or two other young men were caught in the same predicament with myself, and shared the amusement which this most unwelcome trick of the clouds afforded to all the Bachelors in the neighborhood. Suffice it to say, that a few bottles of cordial washed away the stain which our misfortune (as they call it,) brought upon us, and satisfied the claims, which a jury of Bachelors convened expressly for that purpose, formally & solemnly set out against us. The snow is not so deep here as at M. tho' it is quite comfortable sleighing.

I called at Mr. Coleman's, and learned that Maria was more comfortable, tho' I should judge from what I heard, that her situation was yet very critical. She takes cold very easily, and even the curtains of the bed can not be drawn, without affecting her sensibly and they find the utmost care necessary to guard against a more dangerous confinement. Are you not sorry for her? Her mother said that she has had a cough for several years, and is predisposed to colds—says, also, that the difficulty in her head troubles her—and I fear that she will be confined during the winter, if she is so fortunate as to escape even then.

Have you been [done] your missionary tour with Amanda?[2] I have felt much anxiety lest your zeal in the cause of benevolence should lead you to expose yourself too much to the severity of the weather— You must not suffer your missionary spirit to take the place of prudence—You must be careful of your health, first of all—I fear that that is not so firm as you wish to believe it is. I don't wish you to shut yourself up—and draw around the hearth with a cloak & shawl about your shoulders—and shiver at the sound of every blast—nor do I desire to have you neglect what you consider as your duty, merely because the weather is not quite so comfortable as you might wish— nor do I intend to say that you ought not to cultivate a reasonable degree of resolution, & perseverance—but merely give you to understand that my opinion of your health is such, that you ought to take some pains to prevent any exposure which may prove injurious, and while in the ardent pursuit of some favorite object, you do not forget yourself & your friends—[3]

I shall go to Greenfield Court on Tuesday or Wednesday, and be absent two or three days—and with what preparation I shall be obliged to make for some trials in which I am employed there, & at Northampton, next week, and other business which is now pressing, I shall be very much occupied, the two coming weeks—I have as much before me as it is possible for me to accomplish in all my time, and it is precisely what I like to be fully employed.

How is Lavinia's *cough*? Are you all well? When will you[r] father probably visit Amherst? Can't Lavinia accompany him. It is late, and I must stop. I will make no apology for what I have written—take it as it is. Write me by the Thursday's mail, as I requested—make my regards to all the family, & receive yourself, my warmest affection—and forget any of the silly expressions in this scroll, when you reflect that it is from Your devoted Edward[4]

I shall write again, the first leisure hour I can get in an evening. Good night.

Mary's school is to consist of a few small scholars, the children of the families who are not willing to send to the district school—she anticipates some pleasure from having more opportunity to read than she can get at home.

1. As Edward explains at the close of this letter, Mary was operating a small private elementary school. Esquire Bowdoin was probably the father of Elbridge Gridley Bowdoin, to whom the poet addressed her valentine poem of 1850. See *Poems of Emily Dickinson*, 1:1–2. Elbridge Gridley Bowdoin and his father William were both lawyers.

2. Emily may have been collecting money for a religious charity.

3. In this paragraph, Edward's concern about Emily's health begins to sound obsessive, especially when coupled with his fantasy of her reclusion. His concern about her health was undoubtedly exacerbated by Maria Coleman's difficult recovery after the birth of her first child.

4. Edward may have been thinking of his gay bachelor persona in the first paragraph as one of the "silly expressions in this scroll."

Although she answered his letter almost immediately, Emily glossed over its angry and distraught tone. Instead, she praised what she described as Edward's habitual tendency to "cheerfuly submit to the misfortune of the day," a tendency that she was also trying to encourage in herself. The most passionate moment in her letter occurs when she describes the approaching "seperation of a beloved husband and wife," owing to the serious illness of the wife: "The thought completely overcomes me." Possibly this exclamation was an oblique compliment to Edward, but it also reflects her sensitivity to the emotional risks of marriage. Her next thought, "My dear Edward will you now excuse me," perhaps suggests that she often disguised her fear of rejection by absenting herself—that she withdrew from intimate personal relationships or entered into them halfheartedly in order to spare herself the anticipated pain of rejection or abandonment.

62
Emily Norcross to Edward
15 November 1827

Monson Thursday Morn

My Dear Edward

Although it is somewhat difficult for me to write at this time, yet your perfect punctuality shall not pass unobserved but [I] will lay aside all duties for the sake of gratifying myself as well as my friend. I imagined much trouble about you as perhaps you might term it, but was greatly relieved by your kind letter which I anticipated. Your engagments are not easily forgotten by me yet you should not deprive yoursefl [yourself] of rest to accomplish them. I think your ride home must have been quite solitary. I could think of you my dear Edward which was the only favour I could bestow and this I fear would assist you but little through the tedious ride. I was quite unreconciled to your destiny, but had you defered your visit for pleasent days I know not when I should have seen you, but I suppose we aught to think that evry event is wisely ordered and cheerfuly submit to the misfortune of the day I have ever discovered this disposition in you, which has given me much pleasure. I conclude you are not at home now, as you spoke of being abscent two or three days. The weather is so very uncomfortable it give[s] me much anxiety for you, as I know you are obliged to expose yourself, but remember that I feel particularly interested for your health, and that you aught to do all in your power to preserve it I regret hearing of Cousin Maria: [?] continued illness as she is very dear indeed to me, but we must learn from this dear Edward that there is no happiness but what is mingled with sorrow. Mrs. Newton['s] situation is very distressing. I fear that we must soon witness the seperation of a beloved husband and wife. The reflection is meloncholy, yet we do forget that we are alike expose[d] to the same disappointment. The thought completely overcomes me. Mrs Ely of whose situation you have heard me speak in confidence requested prayer last Sabbath I know not what will be her fate.[1] My dear Edward will you now excuse me as I have been obliged to write in much haste do not keep this letter a moment after you have perused it. My health is perfectly good.

Yours Emily

1. Mrs. Newton is unidentified; Mrs. Ely may be the minister's wife.

63
Edward to Emily Norcross
26 and 27 November 1827

Amherst, Nov. 26. 1827.

My Dear Emily,

Your very agreeable letter was received on last Saturday week, according to agreement, and I am happy to have it in my power to acknowledge in grateful terms, the pleasure which this instance of "perfect punctuality" as you call it, produced.[1] I was at Greenfield Court, as you imagined, when your letter was written, and a most uncomfortable time it was. I left home in the rain on Tuesday morning, and returned on Friday. Last week, I was at Northampton Court till Friday afternoon, and had the pleasure of succeeding in my cases— much beyond what I had reason to expect, which you know, to a young man must be pleasant indeed. The woman of whom I spoke, as taken up [arrested or tried] for stealing, and for whom I was employed, escaped well, and went home with a light heart and a quiet conscience. In my other cases, I was equally fortunate.

I am now hesitating whether to go to Springfield to-morrow. Did I think you would be there, I should at once conclude to go. It is possible that I may, as it is, tho' not very probable. If I do I shall send you a Note from there by the mail of Wednesday Morning. (I am here interrupted & must stop.)

Tuesday morning.

A Mr. Cutler, who is going to Stafford after Iron-ware has just called at the store, and I have asked him to wait five minutes for me to write you a few lines.[2] I think I shall not go to Springfield to-day. I recd. a letter from Mr. Warriner last week, saying that he had been to M. again, and giving me an account of his visit—said he saw you & you was well—for this part, I was obliged to him. How does he succeed? Does Miss O. attend the Concert at Spf. [Springfield] this evening? I wish them all a pleasant time—I have written to Warriner, that I shall "take a cup of kindness for Auld Lang Syne" and sing that cheering song, with some of my friends here precisely at 10. o'clock this evening (Tuesday) and have invited him and all the Monson people who may be in Spf. to join me & take a glass of wine, with me, precisely at that time—Will you remember me, in the way the most agreeable to you, at that time—I shall give *you* a *special pledge*—let it be *mutual*—

My Sister Mary returned from South Hadley on Saturday last to keep Thanksgiving—She has a select school of about a dozen—& likes it very well—

Mr. Newman, of whom you once heard me speak, lost a Sister last Thursday, which prevented us seeing him on Saturday, as we anticipated. He is a fine young man, & was educated at Bowdoin College, in Maine.[3]

Will you write me by Mr. Cutler, who returns tomorrow—You can leave a letter at the Tavern—He will bring it safe.[4]

How do you do? are the family well? When will your father visit Amherst?

I can not tell when I shall visit you again—I will let your people know in season to prepare for *a storm*—Let the winds howl—let the storms beat—let my horses die!—let my sleighs break—let all the elements conspire against me. I can not, so long as my person is safe—I shall not be discouraged—I feel a full recompense in the pleasure which your society always gives to balance all—Let us continue virtuous & we shall be happy. I shall expect a letter from you to-morrow, certainly—I shall write again soon—Till then, believe me entirely Yours

Edward

1. When he was in Monson in early November, Edward must have extracted a promise from Emily to write at certain specified intervals.

2. Possibly Edward is referring to the George Cutler who was a local merchant. "The store" belonged to William Dickinson.

3. Mark Haskell Newman was Edward's future brother-in-law.

4. "The Tavern" was in Monson.

64
Edward to Emily Norcross
30 November 1827

Amherst. Friday Eve. Nov. 30. 1827.

My Dear Emily,

Mr. Underwood from Monson, has this evening called at my office, says he is going home to-morrow, & very politely offered to take any communication that I may wish to send to my friend.[1] I wrote a hasty letter on Tuesday & expected an answer yesterday, but the man by whom it would come has not yet returned.

Thanksgiving is over—and to-morrow will probably witness the return of men from their amusement & dissipation, to regular employment.

To-day has been a busy one with me. I have been engaged the whole day, in a most interesting, as well as important trial. A young man from Boston came here to attend the Academy to fit for College—The evening before Thanksgiving, he joined some of his companions in a "cup of kindness," and participated rather too bountifully in the "good cheer" which was provided—The effect upon him was perfectly astonishing. He wanted to fight every body he saw—and defied every one he met—and on Thanksgiving day, after the effect of the liquor was past, a partial *derangement* ensued—and last night, at 12. o'clock, he was taken out of bed by a Sheriff on a warrant for breaking open the grocery shop, under my office and stealing a quantity of money & Notes & other property amounting to $200. or $300—and he employed me as his counsel—We have spent almost the whole day on the trial, and it is one which excited a very great interest—the respectability of the young man, and the influence of his friends in Boston, drew together a great crowd of citizens and students—and I am happy to tell you, that after a laborious investigation, I succeeded in getting him *acquitted*—much to the joy of all who attended the trial, or who knew any thing of his character, tho' the evidence against him was "strong as proof of holy writ," and the chances against him were two to one—However, he has escaped, and you well know the pleasure which I must feel in having assisted in rescuing a young man of promise from the inevitable destruction which must have followed a conviction of so high an offence—and the advantage which it is to me to *succeed* in my causes.

The more opportunities I have to engage in the active duties of my profession, the more I become attached to it—and I would at any time, prefer the management of an interesting case, to the pleasure which *almost* any society could produce—(You can make the exception to this rule—) There is a satisfaction attending full and regular employment—in being placed in situations in which a person is obliged to exert himself—in which he must, of necessity, apply the whole powers of his mind—which is of a nature too high, and too exalted to be realized in the "haunts of pleasure," or in the "bowers of inglorious ease." Give me business—Let me labor with some definite object before me—Let me be obliged to accomplish some important and difficult task, and I enjoy myself. Rather would I be surrounded with clients—and deprived of all the pleasure which society brings, than drag along in the monotonous path of the ploding [?] and stupid,

> "Man was made for action"—
> "Action's his sphere, & for that sphere designed"
> "Eternal pleasures open on his mind."

An active life is my delight—I like the bustle of business—tho' the retirement of study is also very pleasant—but could I choose for myself, I would confine myself to study one third of the time—spend a reasonable portion in the domestic circle—*in the bosom of my family* —and the residue in the most arduous and responsible duties of professional life. Time must determine, whether my wishes will be gratified.

My Dear Emily, how have you spent the Thanksgiving? Have you enjoyed it? I have thought very much of you, & *more* than *often* wished that I could enjoy your society here. Why could it not have been so arranged? Your answer I suppose, is ready—

I recd. another letter from Mr. Warriner, last evening, saying, that at 10. o'clock on Tuesday Evening, agreeably to my request, he joined Mrs. Norcross and others at Capt. Carew's in my favorite song of "Auld Lang Syne"—and took a glass of wine in memory of *absent friends*—as I did, precisely at that time—and as *you* probably did, *in imagination*—(for *you* are very *temperate*,) You know what pledge I gave you—the same which I have so often given you, before—the *whole* I have to bestow.

It has rained yesterday—to-day—& still continues—the road has become very muddy, & the travelling exceedingly bad—Could it have been imagined that I expected to go to M. this week?—The storm would have been a very seasonable one, indeed—I shall come, the next time, *directly after a storm*, if I can—tho' it is somewhat uncertain when—²

Are you all well, at home? How is Lavinia? I feel some anxiety for her—remember me to her most *particularly*. Just remind her of that beautiful penmanship, in a small neatly bound volume of hers—and tell her not to blush as she reads the tender sentiments [?] there expressed.[3]

Sister Mary returns to So. Hadley to-morrow or Monday—We are all well, and have had a very pleasant time of it, at the T——giving—We have had several marriages in town, on the occasion, and do you believe that it was currently reported, and believed, that you was to come to Amherst, at this time, *to stay*? Don't smile—[4]

The Mt. Pleasant school flourishes, very well indeed—and the *"united head"* of it find no difficulty in making their way in the world—and enjoy the pleasure of each other's society, as much as "heart could wish."

Write me, immediately—tell me every thing about yourself—& friends—Increase your happiness, as the most direct way to add to mine—make my regards to your father's family, and believe that I am, as ever entirely Your Edward

Good night—I wish I could give you the parting kiss.

Please to make your own apologies for this letter—E——What do you think of our improved News-paper? There is one in the mail now for your father.

Saturday Morning.
My Dear Emily, the man by whom I expected a letter from you has just returned, & brought none. I shall look in every mail for one.
E——

1. Mr. Underwood remains unidentified.

2. As this paragraph demonstrates, Edward was still tempted by the providential or demonic symbolism of his Monson journeys.

3. Edward must have written something in Lavinia's album.

4. This rumor may suggest that by Amherst standards the engagement was unusually protracted.

Edward's discouragement is evident in this letter; Emily had not lived up to her agreement to write him more frequently. Yet he insisted, "I will listen to any apology you have to make before I attempt to complain of your want of punctuality."

65
Edward to Emily Norcross
4 December 1827

Amherst, Dec. 4. 1827.

My Dear Emily,

There is a time when "expectation fails," and I would gladly tell you that in relation to your letters it seldom happens: but how different from this is the fact. This is the third of mine since you have replied—but I will listen to any apology you have to make before I attempt to complain of your *want of punctuality.* Mr. Colton is in town—came up on Saturday last, & returns as far as Belchertown this afternoon—and you may suppose that I spend all my time in preparing epistles to yourself, from receiving one almost daily—but I do much besides—my letters, as you will perceive, cost me but little labor, else I could not find time to write so often—I write fast, and almost always in haste, tho' I consider the time spent in conversation with My Dearest Emily, as pleasantly appropriated—& only wish that it could be less interrupted.

It rains again, and there is every appearance of a storm of some continuance—If the weather had indicated a pleasant day to-morrow, and I could possibly have left my office, I should have returned with Mr. Colton. But I can not—Business, this week, is rather fuller than common, and I can not well leave—I intend, however, to visit you in the course of a week or *two—whether it storms or not.*

Mr. Colton has told me some news—that Mr. E. Williams of Spfd. is published to Miss Holbrook[1]—that Mr. Warriner was at Monson again, last week!!—rather often, indeed. And that he has taken the School in the Academy, on his own responsibility. He anticipated making some improvements in the system of instruction which will render the Academy more popular—& increase the numbers of scholars.[2]

My Dear Emily, when will you come and pass a short time with us? Will you, in the month of January? Can you be spared, at home? or are you as *busy* as ever—is all your time occupied in making arrangements for the future—do you visit much?—How is your health—Does Mr. Colton give Chemical Lectures, this winter—shall *you* attend?

Time gradually passes, Dear Emily, and we draw nearer the time when we expect to enjoy the society of each other. The idea has something serious, as well as pleasant in it. We are to try what almost all who have been in a situation to do it, have tried before us—and when so large a portion have succeeded in gaining, not only a comfortable support, but in securing the conveniences of life, what have *we* to fear, more than others. To be sure, we may be sick—we may be unfortunate—but we shall be provided for in some way—We will not anticipate evil—nor forbode misfortune—We will do our duty, with a firm reliance upon the support of that Providence who always takes care of those who act with a proper regard to his purposes—Our chance of success is more than an even one—and with reasonable diligence, I do not fear making my home, the deposit of comforts—and I do not fear that I shall have any reason to regret the manner in which the direction of it is disposed of—but, on the contrary, I anticipate the highest pleasure from the good management which the experience of my dearest friend will ensure.

I expect Mr. Colton, every moment, & I must be ready for him. Will you write by the first mail, if you have not already done it—If you have, don't think it too much if I ask you to write again—The pleasure of reading your letters, ought to be a sufficient reason for your writing—Brother Wm. is now at Boston, after more goods—Sister Mary returned to So. Hadley, yesterday—& we are quite alone—tho' all well.[3] Give my respects again to all the family, and receive, once more, the assurance of the warmest affection, & devoted attachment of your Edward—

I have not heard from Mrs. Coleman lately—how is she—How is Hiram's health?

1. Edward is referring to the posting of wedding banns. Fanny Holbrook and Eleazer Williams were married on 1 January 1828. She was presumably a sister of Eliza Holbrook Norcross.

2. Apparently Warriner had decided to direct a school, perhaps a primary school, that was affiliated with Monson Academy.

3. Edward was "quite alone" in a large family that may have included some boarders. In addition to his mother and father, six of his siblings were probably then living in the Dickinson household. Apparently the absent William and Mary meant more to him than all the others, and it is perhaps significant that only William and Mary had visited Emily at home in Monson, so far as we know. There is no indication that Samuel visited her at home while he was a student at Monson Academy.

Edward received a letter from Emily on 6 December that is no longer extant. It described the progress of Warriner's romance with Olivia Flynt and promised a full " 'disclosure of thought' " when Edward was next in Monson. In his reply, Edward characterized Warriner's pursuit of Olivia as "wild passion" rather than "rational esteem."

66
Edward to Emily Norcross
10 December 1827

Amherst, Monday Morning. Dec. 10. 1827.

My Dear Emily,

Mr. Poindexter of Brimfield has been "suspended" from College for the remainder of this term, and is going to Brimfield, by the way of Springfield, this morning, and will probably pass thro' Monson in the stage on Wednesday morning.[1] I send a short letter by him, to say that I shall probably visit you in the course of the present week, most likely on Wednesday or Thursday, if the travelling will admit. It still continues to rain, & the weather is extremely unpleasant. It is day, one half the year, & night, the other half, at the "*Poles*," but *here*, it is rain, one half, & wind & clouds & snow, the other half, no agreeable variety to me, I assure you, tho' my dress secures me from the wet.— Nobody stirs that is not obliged to do it—and were it not for *internal enjoyment*, we must certainly all yield to the influence of the "horrors." But, it is not so—we can see it rain—snow & hail,—hear it thunder & see it lighten—hear the wind whistle, and the trees crack, and still be in the full enjoyment of comfort & quiet—sit before a cheerful fire, and read some interesting book, & write to our friends, while we bid defiance to the storm that is raging without—come what may. I will be resigned & contented—and will not fear any evil till it actually overtakes me—Then if I can escape, I will.

Your letter was recd. on Thursday evening last [6 December], and gave me much pleasure, I assure you. It seems as if Mr. Warriner was determined to make at least a desperate attempt to gain a "fair" object—and not fail for want of sufficient attention. What would *you* think of a man who should leave all & go 20. miles, one [once?] a week, on business of a nature so pressing?—Would it look like *rational esteem*, or *wild passion*? especially if he had any thing to do at home—

However, I am willing that every man should manage his own matters, so long as he does not interfere with mine. I shall have much to say to you, when we meet. Shall you attend the ordination of Mr. Ware, at Palmer, on Wednesday. Pres. Humphrey is to preach the sermon.[2]

The Mt. Pleasant establishment came very near being consumed on last Tuesday night—the evening on which Mr. [Simeon] Colton left here for Monson—and in consequence of the alarm, our citizens are making exertions to procure subscriptions sufficient to purchase a new Fire Engine—which we much need.[3]

It is now past the time for the stage to arrive—tho' it has not yet come, as it is expected, every moment, I must close—Yes, I must now leave you, again, My Dear Emily, for a short time, tho' the anticipation of meeting again soon, & then for a full, free, & frank "disclosure of thought" as you say—till then, "Good morning"—Give me your hand and receive the parting ———s [kisses or kiss]. Be virtuous & you will be happy: and let your morning & evening prayers mix with mine, that we may be preserved to become *one* in fact, as well as in feeling, and live long in the enjoyment of that mutual happiness which we ought to be calculated to secure—and that each returning day may bring new cause for increasing our mutual attachment. May the best of heaven's blessings, rest upon you, My Dearest Emily, & upon all your friends, and upon me & all my friends, and make us all happy & useful.

Give my respects to your good father & mother, & all the rest of the family—Don't forget *Lavinia*—& little Warren—Ask him if he has got a *medal*, yet?

The stage has come. Good morning.

I am, as ever, entirely Yours.
Edward

Emily—
If I don't come, when I expect to—I shall, as soon afterwards, as I can—

1. George L. Poindexter, a nongraduate of the class of 1831, attended Amherst in 1827–28. He registered for college from Natchez, Mississippi.

2. The Reverend Heman Humphrey (1779–1861) was president of Amherst College from 1823 to 1845. Joshua Kirkland Ware was a graduate of the class of 1824.

3. "Under date of Dec. 27, the *Inquirer* published a notice signed by 'E. Dickinson, secretary pro tem,' of an adjourned meeting of the 'proprietors of the new fire engine'" (Carpenter and Morehouse, *History of the Town of Amherst*, p. 359). Edward continued to interest himself in the "Fire Society" of which he became the secretary, presumably early in 1828.

Edward visited Monson on 13 and 14 December but nothing unusual happened either there or on his journey home. This letter makes it clear, however, that the Norcrosses had established 1 May as the wedding date to which he had agreed. He continued to ask Emily to advance the date, suggesting 1 April, especially since the house he was preparing for their occupancy would be ready by that time. Paternalis-

tically, he also expressed further concern about Emily's active social life, indicating that, for reasons of health, he wished her to confine herself more closely to her home. Still, he concluded, "I will not dictate," a statement that surely implies he could dictate were he inclined to do so.

67
Edward to Emily Norcross
19 December 1827

Amherst, Wednesday, Dec. 19. 1827.

My Dear Emily,

I had intended to write to you, last evening, and send the letter by this morning's mail, but company prevented, and I shall send to Northampton P. Office, so that you will receive it on Friday morning.

I reached home at 6. o'clock Friday evening [14 December] after I left you, and am happy to inform you that I went & returned, the last time, without meeting with any accident, or any circumstance to mar my enjoyment—and the instance is so rare, that I feel peculiarly grateful at my good fortune. Since my return, till yesterday noon, I have spent all the time my business would permit in procuring subscriptions to purchase the new *Fire Engine*, which I told you, I expected to find in Amherst when I returned. We succeeded in buying it—for $300—It is a large, elegant, and as far as we can judge from the little trial we made of it, an excellent one, and an article which we much needed in our village. The subscribers are to meet to-morrow evening to organize a company.

I send you now, as perhaps the most convenient time, the size of the rooms in the house which we expect to occupy, as you expressed a wish to know, when we last met. You will find the minutes [dimensions] at the end of the third page of this letter.[1]

It is now fine sleighing with us, and I can not but expect some of you will take a ride to Amherst, when the road is so good. Your father told me that he should intend to come up & see us, if convenient, when it was sleighing—Will he probably come, & when? Just make it convenient to accompany him, *to see the house, if not to visit me*! I shall propose to your father to have you come to *stay with me, before the first of May*, for I presume, when you are *ready*, you will not object to my proposal, as soon as I am prepared, which can as well be the first of April, as May. What do you think of it? Don't refuse, till you have had time to reflect—for you know it is time for me to have something to say.

We have just heard most interesting intelligence from Greece. A large battle has been fought by sea, and a fleet of 70. ships belonging to the Turks & Egyptians, (who are engaged with the Turks against the Greeks) has been almost totally destroyed—and the loss of men to the Turks & Egyptians immense.² This news is really reviving. That a nation which was once "first in arts and arms" should be reduced to a state of slavery—that they should be compelled to render homage to a race of infidels—that they should pay tribute to a horde of barbarians—that a people so distinguished for refinement & excellence, should submit, as a matter of absolute necessity, to a savage foe, is too humbling to the pride—and too degrading to the spirit of men— rather would I make one desperate struggle, and destroy as many as possible, and as a last refuge from their cruelty, plant a dagger *in my own breast*—than drag out a life of such misery—such vexatious servitude—I hail the dawn of that day which shall reinstate this injured, abused & insulted people upon their former elevation—which shall place them on their once enviable station among the nations, with the most enthusiastic pleasure—It must be a source of the most pure delight to the philanthropist—the patriot—to the lover of the human race, to hear that success attends the arms of this brave portion of our fellow men—It seems as if the "God of battles" had at length, espoused their cause—as tho' He had now come forth to "conquer"—I rejoice at the news of their victories—I glory in repeating & spreading the tale of their triumph—The people of the U. States, the whole Republic of North-America—the nations of Europe—*the whole world* should join in the most rapturous hosannas to the King of Heaven, that he has crowned this nation of pure spirits with such overwhelming success—and defeated so totally, an immense array of the "*enemies of all righteousness*"—Let all the nations shout Hallelujah!—and offer their most unfeigned gratitude to Him who "rides upon the whirlwind & directs the storm."³

My Dear E. do you not feel for the young men who have fled, or been driven from their beloved country to our shores, to escape the slaughter which so indiscriminately fell upon all whom the Turks could reach? Do you not sympathize with them in the pleasure which must fill their breasts when they hear of so animating intelligence? Does not your bosom glow with pleasure, and your heart palpitate with delight to reflect that these young men who have suffered all but the horrors of the "last conflict" [Armageddon?] are once more encouraged to hope that the freedom of which they have been deprived is about to be restored to their countrymen—and that they will once more, in all probability, look upon their native soil with the feelings which naturally fill every mind on contemplating the place of its birth—in reflecting that the land of their nativity is once more free!

My Dear Emily, I feel most deeply on this subject—I want to see you and express to you, how much happiness I have recd. from information in relation to a country in which I have, for years, felt much more than an ordinary interest: for I know your heart too well to believe that you would feel less joy than myself, at such success. But I must waive the subject.

How do you do? How have you been since our last interview? Has your cold left you? Be careful—don't expose yourself by too punctual an attendance upon the meetings of the numerous societies of which you are a member—Do you think it best to attend the *singing society*? I hope you will be persuaded to omit it. Still *I will not dictate*. I fear your zeal in the cause of benevolence will lead you beyond your strength—that you will not keep within the bounds of prudence—You know that I feel much interested in your health, & happiness, as mine is increased or diminished in the same proportion as your own. Give my respects to all—Write me by return of mail on Saturday—Take care of yourself—and believe, My Dearest Emily, that in every vicissitude in life, in prosperity or adversity, my greatest pleasure will arise from the assurance that you are mine, & I am yours—I shall write again, soon.

Edward

Front room below, 17. ft. long, & 15. ft. 2. inches wide—4. windows & blinds. 2 Front chambers—17. ft. long—15. ft. & 4. inches wide—4. windows in each. Dining room, about the same size—2. windows. The bed-room chambers, large enough.

1. Edward had bought or was in the process of buying half of a house belonging to the widow Jemima Montague, who is otherwise unidentified.

2. An account of the battle of Navarino appeared in the *New-England Inquirer* on 20 December 1827. His connection with the *Inquirer* apparently enabled Edward to report this news to Emily in advance of the paper's publication.

3. The last quotation is line 292 of Joseph Addison's poem "The Campaign."

Emily was making some effort to further her education; her busy social life included singing lessons and a course of lectures on American history. Moreover, this is one of her clearest, promptest, and most generous letters.

68
Emily Norcross to Edward
25 December 1827

Monson Tuseday morn

My Dear Edward

It was not my intention to disappoint you when I engaged to write by saturdays mail, but your letter which you supposed would be recieved friday morning made quite an excurtion into the eastern country at least I conclude so as it came from that direction saturday afternoon it was then to late to write. I have therfore been obliged to keep you in suspence untill this morning It is precious time yet I do most cheerfuly allow a small portion to my friend I was happy indeed to learn from your letter as I had before supposed that you reached home pleasently. I thought very much of you dear Edward, concluded you would be much elated at the smile of nature upon you a circumstance somewhat remarkable in your history as far as my knowledge exstends. A season for sweet repose was not I presume unwelcome to you, but fortunate for you my dear E that you are not apparently affected when deprived the priveledge but one sweet consolation yet remains for you, that we shall not long be seperate, but united in one. I will not then be so ungenerous to you. You observed that you had fine sleighing with you, which is quite the reverse with us we have had but little snow and that is rapidly leaveing us. I know not when Father will visit you as he wishes to go to the east as soon as their is sleighing sufficient. I am not surprised that you think you have delayed a long time for me. I will talk with you of new proposeals when we are again so happy as to meet, but untill that period do not flatter yourself at all.

Mr. Williams called for his lady on thursday last in his useual stile I conclude from what I have learnt, do you think they are enviable characters. I suppose Miss H thinks rather than to be stigmatised an old maid she will accept the first offer.[1] I conclude you do [not?] wish me [to] cultivate my musical powers, but I have as yet attended the Society to which you refered, but I do not exspect to attend punctualy hereafter. I will obser[v]e to you that I last evening commenced a course of lectures on American History, any thing for a variety I suppose you will admit Mr Woodbridge is our lecturer from Ware, perhaps you may have seen him as he is a brother of yours by profession Esq Chapman was so polite as to call upon us with the honou[r]able gentleman after the lecture last evening, and do you not suppose that I was quite captivated with him,[2] but no more of this May I now leave you, hopeing that you accept this short letter, as I have had but few moments to write this morning

your devoted Emily

1. Edward mentioned the Williams-Holbrook engagement in Letter 65. Emily apparently considered Williams somewhat affected in manner and did not care for Miss Holbrook.

2. Jonathan Edwards Woodbridge, a grandson of *the* Jonathan Edwards, graduated from Williams College in 1822. Before beginning his legal studies, Woodbridge taught school for a year and then returned to Williams where he served as a tutor for three years. Not long after completing his legal training, which lasted approximately three years, he abandoned the practice of law (which he may never have commenced) to conduct a school. Woodbridge subsequently spent two years at Princeton Theological Seminary, became a Presbyterian minister, and, after his health failed, became associated with the religious press. Later in life he returned to schoolteaching. In Letter 69, Edward characterizes him as a "perfect pattern of pomposity and affectation."

III

"I do not wish for company"

*"Let us prepare for a life
of rational happiness"*

69
Edward to Emily Norcross
1 January 1828

> Amherst, January 1.st 1828.
> Tuesday morning 1. o'clock

My Dear Emily,

It is with peculiar pleasure that I welcome the point at which I pass to another period of my existence, & wish you a most "happy new year." I am now 25. years old! and I most cheerfully devote the first moments of a new year to my dearest friend. Another year, my dearest Emily, has gone. Another period is numbered with those which were, and are not. Are you sensible of the rapidity with which these circles are completed? Can you realize that it is a year since we hailed the dawn of 1827?—Can you feel that we are so much nearer the termination of our earthly career than we were, twelve months ago? But so it is. Another, and still another has passed over our heads, since we were acquainted. We are rapidly hastening to that point beyond which we can not pass—we are fast approaching the period when we shall be counted among those who *have been*—What ought to be our feelings, on such an occasion? Ought we to feel grateful that we have been preserved? Ought we to render our thanks to that Being who has watched over us, and kept us from the dangers to which we have constantly been exposed? Ought we to call to mind the happiness we have experienced in the society of our friends—that they have all been preserved to us—that we have occasion to bless our Creator that while many of our fellow citizens have been removed from the world, none of our immediate connexions have been taken from us—and that we have enjoyed much in the society of those who are most dear to us—that *we* have had many agreeable interviews—and realized the pleasure which arises from the most unreserved communications of mutual confidence, and felt, to the full extent, the truth of the sentiment, that "Friendship's the wine of life"—"Angels, from friendship gather half their joy." [1]

Have we done all in our power to promote each other's happiness? Have we studied the pleasure of each other, more than that of all others besides? Have we felt a proper regard for our friends—Have we done all in our power for their good? Have we endeavoured to advance their interest? Have we exerted ourselves in the cause of benevolence? Could we not have done much more, to advance the cause of truth and true religion in the world? Has not some object of distress escaped our notice—has not some miserable wretch been left without the means of becoming better?—But enough of this.—

How do you do? Is your health good? are you now enjoying yourself as well as usual? You say that you "have commenced a course of Lectures on American history and Mr. W. of Ware is your Lecturer"? And you enquire with much significance, whether "I do not suppose that you are quite captivated with him"?—I can only say, in reply, *I certainly hope not*. Remember that it is an old, and a true maxim, that "all is not *gold* that *glitters*²—all pomp and, show, & froth, is not *sense*—I am so happy as to have a slight acquaintance with the "honorable gentleman"—I know much of him—and his leaving his more important study of his profession to deliver a course of Lectures, merely for the sake of "captivating" a few young Ladies, corresponds well with his former character—Don't say any thing, for the world, from me, but look at him, *critically*—scan him down, & if you are then "*capitivated*" with him, I have no more to say. I will say to you, My Dear Emily, that *I don't like him*—and he has left a character behind him, at Northampton, where he attended the Law School—and is there considered as the most arrant pedant—and a perfect pattern of pomposity and affectation—It is enough for you to know that he is no more than other men of much more modest pretensions—The rest when I see you—Keep these remarks a profound secret—He is *engaged* to a sister of Esq. Bartlett's wife—³

Rev. Mr. Coleman preached for us, last Sunday week, and had something to say to me respecting our friend, the *wise* man—says that all is as it was, and your cousin is yet safe—What do you think of this? Can it be?—⁴

Mr. John Holbrook called on me Saturday afternoon, with a letter from W. [Warriner?] informing me that Mr. Williams was to be married Tuesday, (this day—) His wife was with him, but as I had a court in my office, at the time, I could not see her⁵—Mrs. Eliza, I suppose, has gone to Springfield to attend the *nuptials*—Shall you be there? I presume not. I have expected your father here, since the sleighing has been so good, but know not when to calculate on seeing him. I am desirous of having him visit Amherst for several reasons—hope he will come, soon. Can you find *time* to accompany him? I presume not. When I visit you again, I shall intend to bring Lavinia home with me—probably in about a fortnight—tho' not certain⁶—My father goes to Boston, this week, and my business will keep me much confined—not so much, however, but what I shall leave one day, to see *you*—I should be happy indeed, if I could persuade you to pass a week with us, but have despaired—tho' I feel it to be your duty to yourself, as well as to gratify me to comply with a request so often made, & so reasonable, at the same time. But I will not urge you further—ere long I hope I shall be so happy as to have you under my exclusive protection & care—*1st April, you will be ready*? My business is good, & increasing—Brother Wm's is remarkably good—better than has ever been known in Amherst before—I see that I must close. Write me by Thursday's mail—don't forget—make my respects to all—and believe me yours most devoutly

Edward

It is vacation in College[7] Good morning! ½ past 2.—

I must now retire to rest—I send this to N. Hampton, this morning. Our mail went down, yesterday—

1. The quotations are from *Night Thoughts*, bk. 2, lines 582, 576.
2. The closing quotation marks are omitted here.
3. Possibly Esquire Bartlett refers to Joab or Dwight, who were Amherst inn-keepers in the 1820s. Woodbridge eventually married Catharine Starkweather of Williamstown. According to Calvin Durfee's *Williams Biographical Annals*, Woodbridge could not have married until at least 1835. The original engagement may therefore have been broken.
4. The "*wise* man" is Warriner, who seems to have fallen out of favor with both Emily and Edward.
5. John Holbrook was perhaps Eliza Holbrook Norcross's brother. I have been unable to discover what kind of a court Edward was conducting in his office.
6. Edward may have spoken with Lavinia about visiting him, but I suspect that he was announcing his intention rather than confirming a mutually agreed upon plan.
7. There is a drawing of a pointing hand at this point.

70
Edward to Emily Norcross
3 January 1828

Amherst, Thursday Morning, Jan.y 3. 1828.

My Dear Emily,

I have an opportunity of sending to Monson, and I always write, you know, by every conveyance. The sleighing is about gone—the morning is as warm as spring—nothing but ice & water in the road—but never mind—we shall have more snow, & more good sleighing yet—

Mr. Williams & his Lady passed Tuesday night in town, after being bound in the "*nuptial knot*"—I called & passed an hour with them in the evening, and left them, *in good season*, to arrange their own affairs—not, however, till I had recd. a piece of the *wedding cake* to give hope to my dreams.

Yesterday morning, you know, was rather dark & cloudy & they did not set off on their journey, till late in the forenoon. I wished them "God speed."—

I shall have time to say but few words—The small pox has prevailed, in some measure, at Northampton, & there have been some cases at Greenwich & Hardwick—but we have as yet escaped; & it is said that it has now disappeared from these other places. Have you ever been *vaccinated*? If not, you will find much security in having it done, now. And I hope you will not omit doing what will place you out of the reach of one of the most fatal disorders which prevail to so alarming a degree, in the country.

It is vacation in College—Academy flourishing—Talking much of a new Meeting-house, & have a Parish meeting on Tuesday next to see what can be done respecting it: Newspaper increasing rapidly in subscribers—750. now—I am making preparations for putting my house in repair—shall be ready as soon as proposed in my two last letters— shall not you?—I expect to hear from you on Saturday—I must stop— How are you all?—Have not yet seen your father—and I must leave you by saying that I am as I have, for a long time, assured you I was, Your devoted Edward

How flourishes the Lecturer on Am. [American] History?!

Edward was offended by parts of this letter.

71
Emily Norcross to Edward
5 January 1828

Monson Saturday morn

My Dear Edward

Frequent repetition of my disobedience I trust will not exhaust your patience, which I think has been faithfuly tried, but I presume you would desire me to exclude apoligies, as we are not strangers and most certainly whatever tends to augment your happiness or pleasure I would consider it a priveledge to exert my feeble abilities as far as lies in my power.

The introduction of your letter of wednsday last was perused with deep interest by your friend.[1] Can we realise that another important year has elapsed since our acquaintance, and are there not many interesting and important enquiries to engage our attention of the past.

Unmerited favours of a temporal nature have not been withheld which should awaken in us a sence of gratitude for the numerous blessings we have enjoyed but my dear Edward could we be interested in that religion which will guide and support us in life and our never failing portion in that trying hour when we must be seperated, was this our happy situation I would ask no more, but is there not a hope glowing in evry bosom. More when we meet.

I percieve you are quite solicitous for our Historical lecture[s] most certainly they cannot fail to produce much interest as we have so powerfull a lecturer. His gestures and flourishes are quite graceful do you not think so. Is it not singular that your feelings[?] should have so commanding an influence over mine but it is to strong to overcome, but it is for us to be prudent and not to injure the reputation of others, but let their works prove them

Mr Colton has also commenced a course of Chemical lectures of which he has a respectable class. I do not attend except an ocasional lecture. Lavinia and two brothers go to them you speak of the 1st of April with much confidence[2] I suspect you overlooked the caution I gave you in my letter of depending upon uncertainties, the subject must remain as it is untill I see you.[3] My health is very good indeed as you may suppose from my going out almost evry evening

You proposed Lavinias returning with you when you should again visit me, she wishes very much to go but is quite uncertain you must not therefore think much of it The fine sleighing is all gone and we have but little reason to exspect good going at present. I must leave you dear Edward in much haste

Yours Affectionately Emily

1. Emily is referring to Letter 69, which was written on Tuesday.
2. In Letter 69, Edward had written, "*1st April, you will be ready?*"
3. She means that he should continue to assume that she will not be ready until 1 May, the date that had been agreed upon for their marriage.

Edward was hurt by Emily's refusal to advance their marriage and restrained his anger with difficulty. His tone is occasionally sarcastic, although he claimed to be "amused" by her "decision of character." He was also embarrassed by her unwillingness to be seen with him publicly in Monson, especially while paying social visits to such neighbors as her uncle Rufus Flynt. Nor could he quite relinquish the hope that she would come to Amherst to see their house, if not to visit him.

Emily's ambivalence about her impending marriage contributed to her unwillingness to be seen in public with Edward. She must have been attempting to defend her Monson friendships against this ambivalence, which also indicates a high level of anxiety about her status in that community. But if she felt too conflicted to permit herself to be seen in public with him in Monson, there was virtually no chance that she would be capable of interacting with his family and friends in Amherst at this time.

"I am determined to bring you out, a little," Edward asserted. "You may expect an invitation to ride with me, when you see me again, if the going is comfortable." But he was equally determined to keep her in and described himself as "in constant anxiety that you will expose yourself so much that you will destroy your health." Edward's desire to control her movements was growing stronger.

72
Edward to Emily Norcross
10 January 1828

Amherst. Thursday Eve. 1/2 past 11. Jan.y 10. 1828.

My Dear Emily,

I have a pile of letters lying by me on my table which I have been obliged to write this evening, to send out in the mails of to-morrow morning—But altho' it is somewhat late, and I have been very closely occupied till this solitary hour, yet, I have now locked my door, drawn my curtains, and prepared myself for an hour of social pleasure with you. I expect to visit you on Tuesday or Wednesday next, if nothing should prevent—otherwise, as soon afterwards as convenient—and shall expect Lavinia to return with me. The "*caution*" in your letter "to the contrary notwithstanding"—and having recd. several polite invitations to visit at Capt. Flynt's with you, I shall endeavour to fulfil a promise, which I never yet could induce you to assist me in performing—I intend, also, to call at Doct. Carter's *with you*[1]—for, I think, if you intend to be seen with me at all, you can not have much delicacy in accompanying me to a neighbor's house, after I have shewn myself *publicly* to the good people of Monson, for nearly the space of two years, with no particular *business* to make my visits so frequent, except what I have transacted with you. I begin to be plain, you see. Don't you think it is time?—

My father is now at Boston, and will probably remain there for several weeks. It is possible that I may go down myself, but by no means certain.

I rise at 6.o'clock in the morning, and after "making my bed," & sweeping my room, (two very agreeable things for a *man* to do,) walk a mile & back before sunrise—then study & attend to business till 11. o'clock at night—on ordinary occasions, and as much later as circumstances require—Many of *your letters* are written after that time.

I was much pleased with the *moral* part of your letter and shall endeavour to profit by the good advice which you gave in a few words, in relation to the Lecturer—I am happy to receive useful hints from any quarter but they come with a peculiar force from you—and will doubtless have a salutary effect—tho' I must confess, that I was rather amused at the decision of character, and the resolution in relation to some particular things proposed in my previous letters, which your letter exhibited—and I will plainly tell you that I laughed most heartily, tho' "all alone", to see the air of *authority* & *independence* which you assumed—and I am sure that I have nothing to fear from the exercise of a freedom & frank avowal of sentiment which the fact that "we are not strangers" induced you to exert.—You say, you "think I overlooked a caution which I gave you, respecting a dependance upon uncertainties"—certainly not, Emily—I read it, & *recollected* it, too, but thought I would write as tho' I cared nothing about a caution, having so little foundation in good earnest—and you say further, "all must remain as it is, till I see you—" rather *decided*, I confess, but rather laughable. Nothing gives me more real amusement than, once in a while, a little variety of manner, a style, a sentiment— and when it comes from one so dear to me, as you are, and used with the discretion which always characterizes *all* you do, it is doubly gratifying—But enough of this till we meet. There is now a prospect of a little addition to a light snow that fell, last night—and I can not but hope that we shall soon have more good sleighing—You may expect an invitation to ride with me, when you see me again, if the going is comfortable—I am determined to bring you out, a little—you have refused & excused yourself long enough, and it is now high time that you should be a little less reserved in your appearance with me—Have I not reason to fear that you will think it best to remain at Monson after we are married? Don't you think you have had *your way* about long enough?—I see you are disposed to smile in your turn, at my assumption of a little "brief authority." So, if you please, we will offset, the one against the other, thus far—But to be serious—I expect a carpenter every day, to begin the work on our house—and I have made such arrangement respecting it, that we can occupy it as soon as we please after the "*1st April*"—I find that by making some repairs, which will not be very expensive the house can be made, not only very comfortable, but quite handsome, and I shall fix it in such a manner that I think we shall both be suited, so far as that is concerned: tho' I have no wish, as we are just setting out, to go into an expense which will not be considered as perfectly prudent & economical—I had rather begin prudently & run no risk of embarrassment in consequence of unnecessary expenses—In this, I know you all agree with me. I should be very glad to have you see it before much is done to the inside, that you may have a voice in the style of making the repairs & improvements, and do not quite relinquish the expectation that I shall be able still to induce you to think it best for you to see Amherst once more before you become an inhabitant. But this I must leave with you, as I always have done. I was happy indeed to hear that your health was so good—tho' I can't say that I approve of your being "*out almost every evening*"—I am in constant anxiety that you will expose yourself so much that you will destroy your health. You *must be a little more careful*, Emily—I can not feel easy to think, every evening, whether it "rains or shines," you are exposing yourself to the night air—I can not but feel afraid that you are *out*, whether I know it, or not. The "*Lectures*," I suppose, are interesting! I hope I shall be so happy as to hear one, when I am in town—what evening, do they come?—I see that my hour is almost spent—my sheet filled, & my weary limbs feel the want of rest. I can say no more—Give my respects to all—and receive the entire devotion of yours

Affectionately—Edward

My Dear Emily—give me the parting ——— [kiss]

Good night—

1. Perhaps the Doctor Cullen Carter who was practicing in Monson in 1837 but who is otherwise unidentified.

Edward visited Monson on Wednesday and Thursday, 23 and 24 January. There is no indication in his subsequent correspondence or in Emily's that he succeeded in bringing her out, "a little." However, he did succeed in bringing out her more sociable sister Lavinia. In fact he returned to Amherst about sunset on Thursday with Lavinia, whom he to some extent viewed as a substitute for her sister. Lavinia, however, was not happy in Amherst, as the following letter, written by her to Emily, indicates. Perhaps she sensed that she was being used as a pawn in a lovers' quarrel.

73
Lavinia Norcross to Emily Norcross
27 January 1828

Amherst. Sunday Eve. Jan. y 27. 1828[1]

Sister Emily

I expect Edward will tell you not to send after me this week but you know I did not expect to stay but a few days and therefore I am not prepared to and I think Cousin Lorin had better come for me Wednesday the present week if convenient[2] but I will leave it with Edward he insist[s] on my staying and he will tell you not to send for me but perhaps you can act your judgement and I think you will think I had better return this week—

Lavinia

1. The heading is in Edward's hand.

2. Loring Norcross was born on 7 October 1808. He was the son of Joel Norcross's brother William and Oril Munn. Loring's father died in 1813; his mother remarried in 1816. In November 1834 Loring and Lavinia were married. They were first cousins. Contemporary responses to this marriage of near relatives were not enthusiastic. See Bingham, *Emily Dickinson's Home*, pp. 26–27.

Edward read and deliberately misinterpreted Lavinia's letter. Clearly, she wanted to return home on Wednesday but was intimidated by Edward, who was determined to have her stay until the following week. In part because of her age—she was not quite sixteen—Edward ignored the somewhat pathetic tone of her letter and focused exclusively on her phrase, "I will leave it with Edward." Edward's stratagem was unintelligent and unsuccessful, but one sympathizes with his desire to extract some concession from the Norcrosses and especially from Emily. Despite his fondness for Lavinia, in this situation he viewed her as a pawn in his contest with the Norcrosses. As I have already suggested, Lavinia had her way. Similarly, in 1834 she successfully opposed her father's wishes in order to hasten rather than to delay her own marriage.

The first lines of Edward's letter were written on the same sheet of paper as Lavinia's, following hers.

74
Edward to Emily Norcross
27 January 1828

My Dear Emily,

You will see that Lavinia & myself have joined in a letter to you—in which she says she will leave the question of returning this week or next, *with me*—and you know that I am unwilling that she should leave us before next week, at the earliest, tho' I did not intend to have her go so soon as that, till I heard of her arrangement with Loren— You must not, therefore, send before next week—as I intend to carry her to Northampton, & some other of the neighboring towns, where my business will lead me, this week, if the going will admit—besides she will have had no opportunity to visit or become acquainted with the young Ladies here, unless she stays longer—In short, I expect you will regard my wishes, in regard to her visit & not send till next week—then, I shall have some expectation of being favored with a *call* from *yourself*—agreeably with my invitation. It has snowed considerably to-day, and now hails so fast, that we have once more, a little prospect of sleighing. Lavinia & I got home quite comfortably, about sunset, on Thursday, having suffered but little inconvenience from the cold—as the *Taverns* are frequent.

Yesterday I went into my house with Lavinia, and showed her all except the cellar, & the chambers over the kitchen & wood-house—& she will tell you what she thinks about it—the joiners will probably finish the chambers in the course of the present week—and I shall have the repairs on the other parts of the house, made, as soon as the weather is warm enough to work to advantage—I want you should come & examine it yourself—perhaps you might suggest some alterations or some improvements which would render it more pleasant—I want to make it as much so as possible.

I did not say as much as I intended, to you about being married the 1.st April, tho' I conclude it will make but little, if any difference with you, whether it is then or the 1.st May—should like to have you write about it in your next. Will your father go to Boston, this week? When will he return? How is his health? It is not certain yet, whether I shall go or not. If I do, it will be as soon as next week.

Judge Howe's death creates considerable sensation in this vicinity and throughout the state—and it is truly melancholy to reflect, that a man at his age (only 42.) who had raised himself to so high a station—who had acquired so much reputation, and was fast gaining additional honors, and rising to higher & still higher eminence, should be cut off in the midst of his usefulness.[1] The moral is truly a serious one—It is not a light matter to lose a man who has just become what he desires to be, & what is needed in the business of the State. His place can not be filled for a long time so ably as he filled it himself. It takes much time and close study & practice to become familiar with the laborious & intricate duties of a judge. It is the most trying of all labors, and nothing will so quickly wear out a man as engaging in earnest in the discharge of the duties of that office—It is observed always, that a judge seldom lives to a great age—It is not to be expected. Their salaries are large, so that they may save a competency for the support of their families if they should be taken away, themselves.[2]

Judge Howe united in his character many excellencies, and few men were more hospitable, kind & benevolent, and few men knew better how to relieve the wants of the destitute than he. But he is gone! and we can only say of him, as of others, *"he has been."*

I suppose you are now wading in the snow to or from some meeting as you have something to lead you from home every evening!—I should like to examine you on the subjects to which your attention is so much called, of late—perhaps I could judge of your proficiency—and I might possibly give you some useful hints as to the best course to be pursued in making so many studies profitable, at the same time.[3] Let us examine a little—Singing School—Chemical Lectures—Historical Lectures—Bible Class—Concerts—Missionary, Charitable & Female Bible Associations—Cent & Tract Society—and others of a name & description which do not now occur to me. Let me say in a word, My Dear Emily, that while I think that all these combined will not produce so much solid good as a much less number, with more time to reflect upon them will produce—still I would have you act your pleasure entirely, in regard to your attendance upon any or all of them—only preserve your health—If they add to your happiness, they will promote mine—and I am glad indeed to discover in you so much earnestness in the cause of benevolence, and so great a desire to aid every thing which has for its object the improvement of society, or the melioration of the condition of any portion of our fellow men—Go on in the ways of well doing, and you will render yourself doubly dear to all the truly virtuous and worthy—while you will, at the same time, add to to [sic] the interest which you already hold in my esteem. A woman, you know, gives a character to her house & family, if possible, more than her husband, and when she is what she should be, amiable, virtuous, prudent & intelligent & benevolent, she can hardly fail to draw blessings on herself and on her household. I have given my affections to you & recd. yours in return—and now My Dearest Emily, let us resolve, in the presence of the Being who knows all our thoughts & actions, that we will exert ourselves to promote the happiness of each other & that of all around us—and let our prayers ascend for each other, morning & evening, that we may individually experience that change which we believe must take place, before we can be recd. into the abodes of the pure spirits who dwell in the presence of the Eternal! Respects to all the family—Lavinia appears to be contented, so far—Write soon—and accept the entire devotion of Yours most affectionately—Edward

I watched with a cousin of mine that is sick, Friday night, & with my visit to M. I feel rather dull, this evening—a stupid letter indeed—but what is written, is written—& must be sent.

    1. For Samuel Howe, see also Letters 8 and 89. Howe died on 20 January.
    2. Edward seems to be thinking of himself as a future judge.
    3. In her somewhat spirited letter of 5 February, Emily objected to Edward's plan to examine her so that he might help to direct her education.

Edward was offended by what he viewed as Lavinia's abrupt departure, especially since Loring arrived without a note for him from Emily. In her letter, Lavinia had asked that Loring arrive on Wednesday; he arrived on Tuesday; Emily apparently realized that Lavinia had not felt free to express herself in Edward's presence. By the close of this letter, however, Edward felt somewhat mollified. Writing soothed him, and he feared Emily's displeasure more than she feared his.

75
Edward to Emily Norcross
30 January 1828

Amherst, Wednesday Morning, Jan.y 30th. 1828.
My Dear Emily,

    It seems that you did not "find time" to say a few words to me by your Cousin Loren? But you know me too well to believe that I will neglect writing to you, on that account. Why did you let him come so soon? We had not half finished our visit with Lavinia—I wrote you, in a letter which you probably recd. this morning, not to send till next week. I yesterday carried Lavinia & Lucretia to Northampton—came round by Mr. Gilbert's[1]—and was intending to have them go to S. Hadley Canal, to see Sister Mary to-day or to-morrow; when to our surprise, as soon as we had returned from Northampton, Loren presented himself—and tho' I am always glad to see him, the pleasure

with which I should have recd. him would have been much increased
had he not come with the intention of carrying away Lavinia—I am
almost disposed to say that she shall not go, but she thinks it best—
tho' I do not think she has been homesick; & could she have stayed
long enough to have become more acquainted, & visited some more
of the neighboring towns, I think she would have been contented to
stay—However, she concludes to go—and I have consented by receiv-
ing her promise to come & stay a month, next Spring. It is now fine
sleighing, tho' there is but little snow, and there could not be a more
pleasant day to ride—were you here, I would have a sleigh-ride with
you—and will you believe me when I tell you, that I had some expec-
tation of seeing you here, when I returned! I do not relinquish the
idea, yet. Your father will probably come soon. I want much to have
him come, & you with him. I think I shall not go to Boston this
winter, unless some business should render it necessary, as my busi-
ness requires my attention at home. I want much to hear from you by
letter. Can you not write by Thursday's mail? Or will your attendance
on the Lectures prevent? I think my house & myself will be ready by
the *1.st April*; or as soon as the ground is settled. Expect you will be
ready.—When will your father go to Boston? and how long will he be
absent.

I think very much of you, My Dearest Emily, every day—and of the
prospects before us. Could I be assured that my success will be equal
to my wishes—that I shall be able by diligence & close attention to
business, to gain the reputation which is so desirable to a man in
public life—and could I know that all my exertions would result in
your happiness and my own united—and could I know that I should
be able to make myself what you may hope I may become, I should
feel my pleasure much increased. You have a right to expect that I
shall do all in my power for you & myself—and you have a right to
expect much from me—I owe it to you to try to make myself a reputa-
tion of which you will not be ashamed—and I have a constant induce-
ment to press onward in the cause of honorable exertion—I know you
feel interested in my Success, & every thing connected with my under-
taking—and I feel a peculiar pleasure, as I have more than once before
assured you, in having a tried friend in whom all my secrets are safely
reposed—and with whom I can, at all times, hold such unreserved
social intercourse—I want you here, where that pleasure need not be
so interrupted—My most earnest wishes will attend you for success &
pleasure in all you do—Preserve your health—do not be too zealous
in acquiring miscellaneous knowledge—and do not mix too many
subjects to-gether—but I need not caution you—Your good sense will
guide you right—I have nothing to fear from the exercise of your

sound discretion—I most cheerfully submit all that belongs to your department to your management. Loren is almost ready, & I must stop—try to write by Thursday's mail—Give my love to all the folks—& receive, for yourself, the entire devotion of your affectionate Edward

Good morning—Love to Lavinia—

Loren & she will tell you the rest.—

1. "Mr. Gilbert" is unidentified but may have conducted a tavern.

76
Edward to Emily Norcross
31 January 1828

Amherst, Thursday Afternoon
Jan.y 31. 1828.

My Dear Emily,

Don't you think it rather queer that I should *"find time"* to write to you, every day? and hear from you about once in a month? Certainly, it is rather curious, but no matter for that—when I have so good a chance to send, ten minutes devoted to you is not lost—I was glad that Lorin & Lavinia had so good a time to return—I am sure we miss Lavinia at our house to-day. Tell her that I am quite lonesome without her, & should like to have her return & finish her visit. Give my love to her—The sleighing is almost gone—and we must once more wade thro' the mud for one or two, or perhaps more days—rather hard, but it is so common, that I don't think much of it—The Southern Stage has this moment arrived, & if the letter sent by Lorin to Lavinia, is in to-day's mail, I shall inclose it in this—¹

Tell Wm. that I have not as yet recd. a number of the "New England Farmer" which I can send him—as soon as I do get one, he shall have it.²

Mr. Lyon has just now returned from Greenfield where he went yesterday—& called on me—while he is at dinner, I write—as soon as he stops [arrives], I must stop. Let me hear from you, as soon as consistent—My business is as good as usual, tho' rather dull for a week past—However, when it is a little poorer, I am certain that it will soon improve—always look at the bright side, you know. I must stop—don't let it be known that you hear from me so often—I will not trouble you again, immediately—Success to the Historical Lecturer—& *your party for his benefit*! I should like to attend.[3] In the greatest haste—Your devoted Edward

Don't forget my respect to Lorin & all the family—

1. Loring must have told Edward that he had sent Lavinia a letter which would arrive after her departure.

2. The *New England Farmer and Horticultural Register* was a magazine that was published in Boston from 1822 to 1846.

3. Despite her mockery of Woodbridge in Letter 71, Emily continued to attend his lectures, and Edward could not have been pleased. He disliked Woodbridge personally but also viewed him as a representative type. Woodbridge, he believed, gratified his libido at the expense of his career. Such men generally aroused his scorn, especially since he himself would have liked to visit Monson more frequently but could not do so without neglecting his business. Edward heard about the lectures not from Emily but from Loring, who was "very social and genial in his nature" (Joel Warren Norcross, *History and Genealogy of the Norcross Family*, p. 109).

Ignoring Edward's displeasure over the (from his point of view) abrupt termination of Lavinia's visit, Emily continued to express her gratitude for Edward's frequent letters, praised his faithfulness, apologized for not having written sooner, described herself as having been almost "homesick" during Lavinia's absence, and assured Edward that she had asked Lavinia, who had returned safely, for all the Amherst news. Acknowledging Edward's doubts about the progress of her continuing education, she teased him good-humoredly about his plan to examine her on the historical and chemical lectures she had been attending, and reserved for herself the "priviledge" of selecting her own subject for the upcoming test. She also explained that Joel Norcross had intended to come for Lavinia himself, which would have pleased Edward, who had been trying unsuccessfully to lure him to Amherst. But Joel Norcross had acceded to the wishes of Lavinia and Loring and had presumably postponed his visit for a later time. Rejecting Edward's plan to advance the date of their marriage, Emily observed tactfully, "It is unpleasent for me to decide in opposition to your feelings which I so much regard" and promised that, if he agreed to the later date, "I shall never make any other objection," a formidable promise indeed. As I indicate in the notes to this letter, there are other covert indications that she was finding Edward's manner overly controlling.

77
Emily Norcross to Edward
5 February 1828

Monson Tuseday morning

My Dear Edward

It is highly gratifying to me to see you disposed to give me frequent inteligence from you. I think it a good specimen of your faithfulness, but dear Edward you would like an equal return I presume, which you certainly deserve but I fear that you will ever have reason to say that I have been deficint [?] I exspected to have written Saturday last, but Father and Mother went out on a visiting tour which rendered it necessary for me to be very much engaged dureing their abscence I was therefore much disappointed Sister Lavinia reached home Wednesday evening, perfectly safe, and much gra[t]ified with her visit I was happy indeed to see her, as she so seldom leaves home that I could not realise at all how much her abscence would affect me I was almost inclined to be homesick. I suppose you would have given me liberty to ask her as many question[s] as I wished, as I considered myself particularly interested. I presume that you will rejoice with me at the close of our Historical and Chemical Lectures. I felt myself very much relieved you seem disposed to doubt however whether I have made much progress in the various branches in which I have been engaged. This is hard judgeing but as it is from you I will endeavour to think of it occasionally, but were you to examine to me, I would like the priviledge of selecting my own subject, to which you would not object I trust, but to be sincere dear Edward I think your sentiments correct, and I would hope not to deviate from them should I become a subject to your athourity.[1] My Father has not gone to Boston yet but will probably go very soon his health is quite good at present, he intended to have gone for Lavinia as he was desireous of visiting you, but as Cousin Lorin was so much disappointed he concluded to relinquish the idea untill some future time supposeing that Lavinia would be much better pleased to see Cousin Lorin than himself. It appears that you have not forgotten the 1st of April which is fast approaching or at least you wish to remind me of it. It is unpleasent for me to decide in opposition to your feelings which I so much regard yet may I not hope that you will be perfectly willing to let me stay untill the time which was first appointed I shall never make any other objection. As you gave me the priviledge of giveing my direction with respect to any alteration to be made in the house which you exspect to occupy[2] I will say to you that I would like very much to have the blinds in the front room turn like ours perhaps you have noticed them. The lower part of the blind only I think it a great improvement, but perhaps you may think this is asking to much, but you are not obliged to gratify me. I have something more to add with regard to the painting but will defer it untill I may see you again which I suppose will not be many weeks shall I leave you dear Edward, but it is for a short time, which is the only consolation. I shall have much to disclose to you at our next meeting

Lavinia wishes to be remembered to all of you I have written in my useual haste as you will judge by this letter.

From one who will ever remain
your Emily

1. In "should I become a subject to your athourity," Emily's use of the conditional tense underscores her hesitation.

2. In the phrase "the house which you exspect to occupy," Emily's pronoun is another indication of her lack of enthusiasm for married life.

Evidently Edward had not yet received Emily's letter, which was written on the same day as his. He could barely contain his anger and concocted yet another scheme to get her to Amherst and to stay overnight, arguing cogently but not persuasively, "The request is certainly reasonable, and I shall consider any attempt to evade it, without some more substantial reason, than your pressing business *(as you seem to be at leisure, every evening to go out) as unfair & unreasonable!"*

78
Edward to Emily Norcross
5 February 1828

Amherst. Tuesday noon. Feb.y 5. 1828.

My Dear Emily,

Do I need an apology for writing the *fourth time*, without having *once* heard from you? I shall make none, except that I have an opportunity to send. And I have resolved to give you *one more* invitation to come & *stay over night* in Amherst—and when I say that it will not be quite convenient for me to go to Monson myself, you will think it proper, I presume, that I should propose this way—Let Wm. bring you as far as Belchertown on Wednesday next week—about noon, & I will go there in the afternoon, by 2. o'clock, & wait upon you to Amherst, and after you have stayed one or two days, (which is as long as I dare propose, for *you* to be absent from home,) I will return with you to Monson—Will this be agreeable to you? I shall conclude it will, unless I hear to the contrary, before Wednesday next—& go to Belchertown for you—"*rain or shine.*" The request is certainly reasonable, and I shall consider any attempt to evade it, without some more substantial reason, than your *pressing business* (as you seem to be at leisure, every evening to go out) as unfair & unreasonable! I think I have borne your numerous refusals with exemplary patience, & you ought to think that I begin to "*be in earnest.*" I have given you frequent hints respecting your "*punctuality*"—and can only say, that a little more regard to that *most important of all qualifications*, would add very much to the virtues which already make so essential a part of your character—I think more of it, perhaps, than you are aware. Does your father intend to visit Amherst? If so, when?

Are you well? Tell Lavinia that I should be glad to have a letter from *her*, & will answer it, immediately[1]—Give my love to her, & all the family, & receive for yourself the affectionate regard of Your

Edward

More, soon. Till then, "Good bye"—
I shall be at B. [Belchertown] after you—Don't "give me the slip"—If you do—[2]

1. No such letter has been found.
2. Unless Edward is threatening to break off the engagement, this is an idle threat. Emily did give him the slip.

79
Edward to Emily Norcross
8 February 1828

Amherst, Friday afternoon, Feb.y. 8. 1828.

My Dear Emily,

Your letter of Tuesday morning, was recd. last evening, and I was glad indeed that you have been able, after two weeks' time, & reading three of my letters, to get sufficient leisure to "pen a short reply:"[1] tho' I must confess that I do not understand the reason why you are not willing to yield a little, in respect to the time of our marriage, when I have already waited a year longer than I ever intended to wait—However, I find that my arguments are without much weight, and I shall not press them against so decided an expression of your will in relation to it. The time, I suppose will come, & my claim upon you will then be good—& I hope you will find no new excuse for delay—as you promise "you will not make any other objection"—You say that your father intended to have come after Lavinia—I have desired very much to see him here, and since receiving yours last night, I have thought of proposing to have [him] come up with you on Tuesday next, and leave you till the last of the week, when I will return with you—Will it not be convenient? I have no idea of receiving any thing but *actual sickness* as an excuse for not complying with my proposal to visit Amherst next week, in one or other of the ways which I have devised. Unless I see you Tuesday, or hear from you to the contrary, I shall be in Belchertown by 2. o'clock in the afternoon of *Wednesday next*, to accompany you to Amherst. If I had not important business with you, I would not urge it so much, after being refused times without number, and I had almost said, without good reason, too—However, you may rely upon it, that I shall not be satisfied with "*no*," for an answer, this time, let the going be what it may. I am glad that you have *dared* to say so much as to express a wish respecting the *Blinds*, and I shall soon expect to know what you allude to about the *Painting*—You need not fear that you are "asking too much," as you suggest, or that you will not be gratified. I shall certainly consult your wishes in relation to the matter, as far as I can induce you to express them. My new chambers are nearly finished, ready to plaister [?], and paint, and I shall show you the whole house next week, and you may feel perfectly right in suggesting any improvements which you may like to have made. I shall feel a pleasure in making them. I want your father should examine the house, also—I had already told the man who is to make the Blinds, how I wanted those for the front room. Lavinia can tell you how the house will appear. I shall, if possible, have it *ready* by *the 1.st April*, and if you had rather "*stay*" at home than to come, 4. weeks longer, I shall submit.

Mary's school ends to-morrow, & I expect her home to-morrow night. Lucretia is now with her, this week, on a visit, & will return with her in the stage.

I have been afflicted with one or two severe attacks of the toothe-ache, this week—broken of my rest, and, at times, almost "*maddened with pain*"—I am not entirely free from it, now, but feel an occasional *twinge*—a *jump*, which actually shakes my head. But I can bear it, tho' reluctantly, I assure you.

Tell Lavinia that I feel quite sorry that we can not have her company, longer—she has promised to stay a month, next spring[2]—Give my compliments to her—and Lorin, and remember me to all the family. You are right in supposing that I rejoice with you, at the close of your Lectures—*You must not go out in this mud.* It is not prudent, and I must lay my commands upon you. I would say much more, but the man by whom I am to send this to N. Hampton P. Office (as our mail has passed) will soon go, and I must reserve the more important matters till I meet you here, next week—I shall then have a plain talk with you—

The weather is as warm as spring—and the roads as muddy as March—I hope the ground will *"settle"* soon—Don't you?—We are all well & want very much to see you. I must stop—and merely add, that I remain as ever, Yours most Affectionately—
                                                                Edward

My Dear E. I wish you would imitate my example in giving me intelligence from you, as often as you hear from me—I would not then complain of neglect.

  1. Actually, Emily's letter (77) was a longish one and does not include this phrase.
  2. It is not clear that this visit occurred.

Emily's letter arrived in time to prevent Edward from attempting to meet her in Belchertown. But this was also a time of crisis in their relationship.

80
Emily Norcross to Edward
9 February 1828
                                            Monson Saturday Morn
My Dear Edward
    One more invitation. I suppose then you concluded if so I must be resigned. Your true sincerity I never would presume to despute. Yet there are, and have been reason[s], to prevent me from acting in compliance with your wishes. Perhaps you will say they are all trifling, I am sensible that my feelings are unlike many others at least those within the bounds of my observation, but it is not necessary for me to explain to you why, except that when I am differerently [sic] situated I shall enjoy myself much better.[1] My dear Edward will your patience admit one more refusal hear me for a moment and perhaps I may be so fortunate as to convince you that it is inconvenient for me to visit you the next week. My Father leaves to Boston Monday morning and I should be quite unwilling to to [sic] go from home while he is absent. And after he returns I must necessarily be much engaged And may I hope that you will make no other arrangements untill I may see you I have merely written a few words to you, which I trust you will accept. From your devoted Emily.

1. Emily is either being disingenuous or feeling somewhat ashamed of being a drudge at home. In all probability, her problem was primarily psychological rather than practical, as Edward himself had concluded. Nevertheless, in this letter she feels excessively burdened by her responsibilities to the Norcross household. Perhaps the most disturbing aspect of this letter is her unwillingness or inability to explain her motivation to Edward. But this has been a marked characteristic of her correspondence with him.

81
Edward to Emily Norcross
18 February 1828

Amherst. Monday Afternoon
Feb.y 18. 1828.

My Dear Emily,

I have an opportunity to send to N. Hampton and say a few words to you, in reply to your letters which I have recd. since we last met. I was very much disappointed that you could not feel willing to gratify me so much as to comply with my invitation to visit me. I will not express my feelings till I am so happy as to meet you again—which may possibly be on *Wednesday* of the present week, if my business & the going will admit. Tho' it is rather uncertain—I shall want to see your father, will he be at home? Has he returned from Boston?—We are all well—& presume you are—Give my particular respects to all your friends and receive my most devoted attachment to yourself—

My house will be finished by the 1.st April[1]—& I shall be ready— Hope you will—at any rate shall say something pretty decided about it when we meet—I may come on Wednesday of this week—may come on Saturday Eve. & to pass the Sabbath—and I may not come less than [before] 3. weeks—all depends on affairs at home—Till then, "good bye"—receive, my heart's devotion—and my constantly increasing attachment—in the greatest possible haste, as the bearer of this to N.H. is ready to start—Give the parting ——s—

Yours entirely
Edward

1. In some previous letters, Edward said "our house," as he does in Letter 82, where the word "our" is underlined.

Despite his discouragement, Edward visited Monson on 23 to 25 February. Joel Norcross arrived in Amherst soon after Edward's return, although they did not travel together. According to Emily's Let-

ter 84, her father's visit at that time had not been prearranged, so that Edward must have been "somewhat surprised" at seeing him. It is interesting that after so many months of delay Joel Norcross took off on this trip impulsively.

82
Edward to Emily Norcross
27 February 1828

Amherst Feb.y 27. 1828.

My Dear Emily,

Your father returns this morning, & while his horse is harnessing, I write a few words. We have been over all *our* house, and examined it, thoroughly—he has proposed some alterations, with which I am much pleased—he saw Wid. Montague, & will tell you all about her & the house, and what he thinks of our prospect of having a comfortable house—It storms, & he thinks of starting, tho' I have tried to induce him to stay till fairer weather—There seems to be some connection between a storm, & any communication between Am. & Monson—Is this a bad omen?—I don't believe so—Never mind—there must be fair weather, bye & bye—or the other people must suffer as well as ourselves—I am resigned & contented—I can say only a word more. Let me hear from you as soon as sometime next week—Give my respects to all the family—

My cold is not yet quite cured—something of a cough remaining—tho' I think I shall get rid of it, soon. I can only add—Good morning, My Dear, and remain as ever, yours most devotedly—receive the most precious of all tokens of affection, the parting ———s—and believe, so long as you & myself are one, that it will ever afford me the highest happiness to promote our mutual enjoyment & comfort.

I am Yours—Edward

Edward was reassured by Joel Norcross's visit. He now proposed the second week of April as a compromise for the wedding date.

83
Edward to Emily Norcross
2 March 1828

Amherst. Sunday Afternoon. March 2. 1828.

My Dear Emily,

I have a little time between meeting & tea, and I shall devote it to you, altho' it is the Sabbath. Your father left here in the rain, and tho'

I was very sorry to have him start in a storm, yet as it happened, had he not gone when he did, he would have found himself on "bare ground," the next morning. Did he reach home safely? How is his cold? Did he not increase it by his unpleasant ride? I hope not. I could not write much by him, as my time was partly occupied, & my cold was too uncomfortable to allow me much pleasure from writing letters, even to you. I am now quite well, & experience no inconvenience except an occasional cough in the evening. Your father went with me, over the whole of the house which we expect to occupy, & proposed several alterations which will render it much more comfortable than it would otherwise have been: and I think, when they are made, you will feel willing to try it! The family expect to leave it, on Tuesday, if the weather is such that they can[1]—and my men are going to work repairing that part, immediately—I hope to have it completed in 3. or 4. weeks—and to move into it *with you*, the *second week in April.* Your father thought of going round by Springfield home, to see about your *stove*—said he should inform me when it was ready, that I might send for it, by sleighing, if there was any, and that Mr. Cotton was to bring up your *chairs*, by snow, so as not to injure them[2]—I am expecting to see him, as soon as there is sufficient snow to make it safe for him to set out. It snows now, very much as it did, when I was at Monson, last Sabbath—and I hope for enough to take a *sleigh-ride*, as you know my sleigh-rides, this winter, have been generally enjoyed *on wheels?*— I did not think to say any thing to your father about our *publishment.* Are you willing to have it put up, a fortnight from to-day, the 16.th March? I think that a proper time, and unless you object, I will direct the Town Clerks in Amherst & Monson to do it, then.—

Mr. Newman, Mary's friend, came in town last evening, and is at our house to-day—He will stay a few days, till some business which he has here is finished, & return to Andover. I would persuade him, if I could, to remove to Amherst, & open a Book-store, so that we could have Mary near us. I am much attached to her, and am unwilling to lose her society, tho' I must submit, I suppose.[3]

My business grows better—had three trials yesterday—and an office full of men, all day—am employed in several a week, for some weeks to come—which, I presume, you are glad to hear.

Does your father intend to change houses with Hiram, this spring? Has he yet come to any conclusion respecting it?—and will his determination have any effect upon the time of our marriage?—

Are you all well? Has your mother perfectly recovered her health? Has Lavinia's cold left her? You must be careful of your own health. You feel so much confidence in your ability to brave all kinds of weather, & attend your various meetings, whether it storm or not, that I am much concerned, lest you should injure your health. Will you not hear me, once, and be persuaded not to go out in the wet & mud—in damp, chilly weather. I feel great anxiety—Your *resolution* leads you to undertake some things, which I fear may prove a lasting injury to you. Be careful, is all I can say, and as you regard my happiness, I hope you will regard my advice. I am rather opposed, My Dear, to so many *evening* assemblies, tho' I thought of the beautiful Saturday evening (last night) which you again had to attend your "Bible Class," & was happy, I assure you in reflecting that a night which had generally been so unfavorable, during the winter, should be so pleasant a second time, for you to attend a meeting from which I hope you will receive much benefit.

The time draws near, My Dear Emily, when we expect to unite our fortunes, and pass the remainder of our lives in each other's society. Are we sensible of the importance of having correct views on the subject, which, of all others, most intimately concerns our individual & mutual happiness? Do we possess that yielding, complying disposition which will induce each to conform to the reasonable wishes of the other? Have we determined that we will forego individual for mutual happiness, when the former is inconsistent with the latter? Are we prepared to say to each other, that we will be faithful & kind & true, in prosperity & adversity, in sickness & health?—Are you satisfied, after a more particular acquaintance with me, & an opportunity to learn my character, at home & abroad, to place yourself under my guardianship for life? Do you feel safe under my protection? Are you willing to run the risk of sharing the happiness which a successful attention to my profession may produce—or dividing with me the unpleasant feelings which a failure in all my attempts at reputation might bring upon us? We ought to be honest, My Dear Emily, with each other, & with ourselves—We ought to examine ourselves & see whether our attachment is founded in a similarity of tastes & dispositions—whether it exists in our respect for the good qualities which we suppose to exist in each other, or whether it arises from something which will cease to exist after a short intimacy—I will plainly tell you what I think of my own disposition, and what I think of yours. I am naturally quick & ardent in my feelings, easily excited, tho' not so easily provoked—decided in my opinions—determined in accomplishing whatever I undertake—hard to be persuaded that I am wrong, when I have once formed my opinion upon reflection,—sometimes unyielding and obstinate—rather particular—like to have every thing in the [proper] place, & done at the right time[4]—have a little nervous irritability in my constitution—am rather high-spirited, at times—tho' generally moderate—like to have things go pretty smoothly, & have business enough to keep me occupied. I now come to you. I think you are resolute—decided—rather particular—want to see every thing go on well—& see every body happy. I think your disposition to be good—that you are kind—benevolent—patient in trouble—able to endure in sickness—that you will deprive yourself of comfort & repose to render a friend more comfortable—and I think, too, that your feelings are somewhat easily excited, & that your vivacity might, in case of emergency, approach to spirit—Is this a correct picture?—Of the many good qualities which I think you to possess, it may not be proper here to speak. I do not flatter, My Dear, when I say, that I find in you just what I have long wished to find a Lady to possess, and that in giving the whole affection of my heart, to you, I feel a pleasure which never before my acquaintance with you, could I say sincerely, that I felt. I am not what you deserve—but my attachment to you is such, that I shall use my utmost exertion to promote the cultivation of those virtues from the exercise of which I have reason to expect much solid enjoyment—Be as honest with me, in your letter, as I have been with you. Make my respects to all the family—Write me by the mail of *Thursday* without fail—tell me about our *publishment*—and let me hear about your health, & every thing respecting yourself: and believe that it gives me the highest pleasure to call myself, Your Most Affectionate Edward

I am employed in a case which is to be tried before Wm. Bridgman Esq. (Doct. Bridgman,) on Saturday of this week, at 1. o'clock—and expect to be at Belchertown at that time.[5]—Good night.

My father has not yet returned, tho' we expect him, this week—My compliments to Eliza—

I have much more to say, but no room. Must defer it till the next time.

1. Edward is referring to the current tenants.

2. Mr. Cotton is associated with Monson but otherwise unidentified.

3. Mark Haskell Newman was a native of Andover, where he owned a bookstore. After moving to Amherst, he moved to New York City where he amassed a fortune in the publishing business.

4. A tear in the paper around the seal accounts for the reading in brackets.

5. William Bridgman (1784–1864) was a leading physician in Hampden County. His law practice may have been restricted to Hampshire County.

Emily was also reassured by her father's visit to Amherst but contin-
ued to insist on the first of May for their wedding. In response to
Edward's somewhat abstract description of their characters in Letter
83, she responded, "You cannot fear but what I am perfectly satisfied
but for myself your experience must judge."

84
Emily Norcross to Edward
6 March 1828

Monson Thursday Morning

My Dear Edward

Although the business of the morning useually occupies my atten-
tion yet your request I think deserving the first claim I conclude you
were somewhat surprised at seeing my Father so soon after you left. It
was quite unexspected to me yet I was very anxious that he should go.
We gave ourselves much trouble in consequence of the storm the day
he came home, as he was much afflicted with a cold, but he returned
with but very little inconvenience, quite fortunate I think that he came
as he did, as there was no snow visible the next morning.

He observed to me that he visited the house that you exspect to
occupy and thought with the alterations and repairs you were make-
ing it would be quite pleasent and comfortable. I suppose [you] are
sufficiently aquainted with my Father to know that he is plain in his
remarks, perhaps you had some specimens of it when visiting you yet I
trust you were prepared for it, as it is designed for the best.[1] You
mentioned that your cold had left you which I was very happy to hear
I was fearful your ride home would not benefit your health at all yet
you have said nothing of the result. Sister Lavinea has been indisposed
for a week, so much so that we [have] been obliged to call for medical
aid yet it gives me pleasure to say that she is recovering. I cannot
neglect to mention that Mr Warriner has again call[ed] upon us, much
to my surprise. He appears in high spirits I recieved a short visit from
him yesterday afternoon, he was desireous that I should visit at Uncle
Flynts in the evening as he exspected to give an exhibition of his
musical powers but fortunately I had a good apology as I had the
night previous watched with our sick neighbour I was therfore unable
to go out.[2] I think him very inquisitive he made some enquiries for
you yet I did not consider myself obligated to tell him more than I
pleased. We cannot I think doubt his friendship. I would therefore
ever wish to treat him with respect. As regards the change with our
family and Hirams it is now decided. We exspect to move the 1st of
April, unpleasant as it is to me I must submit, but my dear Edward I

suppose it is for the best, and as I have but a few days to spend at home I[t] matters but little with me. And my dear are you not willing to gratify me in one particular, which is not to think of being married untill the 1st of may I am certainly sincere in what I say to you and may I presume that you will not be unwilling to hear me as I have often said to you that this was the last objection you would recieve from me.[3] It will make but little difference yet it is unpleasant for me to oppose my dear friend. Do think of this as my feelings are familiar to you I must leave you soon yet there are many things I intended to say to you. As respects my acquaintance with you, you cannot fear but what I am perfectly satisfied but for myself your experience must judge. Much remains upon this subject. My dear Edward much as I think of you I must bid you Good Morning yet the period is close at hand when I shall anticipate [?] much happiness with you. I now leave you yet my thoughts will not cease to act. This haste you must excuse Yours dear Edward

1. Emily's description of her father as perhaps overly blunt but well intentioned is her only direct reference to the character of either of her parents in the course of this correspondence.

2. Warriner was a soloist with the Springfield Handel and Haydn Society, of which Eliza Norcross was also a member.

3. Emily seems to be suggesting that after they are married she will comply almost mindlessly with all of Edward's requests. Given this view of her duty as a wife, it is no wonder that she sought to prolong their engagement. It is also possible that she is using the word "objection" in a more limited sense and referring only to their wedding, but her fears were, I think, more pervasive.

In Letter 83, Edward had asked whether Joel Norcross intended to exchange houses with Hiram "and will his determination have any effect upon the time of our marriage?" Although Emily answered the first question, she ignored the second. Again, her unwillingness to explain her motives is striking.

85
Edward to Emily Norcross
6 March 1828

Amherst. March 6. 1828.

My Dear Emily,

Mr. Field, of Monson, has just called on me & says that he is going to return immediately, & while he sits in my office, I write a few words. He is in search of a place to establish himself in business—[1]

The family left my house, yesterday—and I have several men at work there. I expect to hear from you to-night or Saturday. Has Mr.

Cotton gone to Boston? Your father thought some of sending by some team from Amherst to bring your crate of crockery, directly here, to save transportation. I suppose, however, he has concluded differently, or I should have heard before now.

My health is now very good. (Mrs. Hunt was confined with a Son, on Tuesday evening, & is quite comfortable.) Don't mention it![2]—We are soon to have a new public house—and a young man has just come in town to establish himself as a Physician—all kinds of business are [?] rather increasing, and the place becoming by degrees, of increasing importance—[3]

My Sisters have a party, this afternoon—should be extremely happy to have your company!—I suppose we must be deprived of that a little longer. Take care of your health, above all things.

Are you all well? Write immediately, if you have not already done it. Make my regards to all the family, and believe me, tho' in the greatest haste

Yours most devotedly Edward

I suppose you recd. my letter by yesterday's mail.

1. Mr. Field of Monson is unidentified. In Letter 87, he is described as about to move to Amherst.

2. It is unclear why Edward wishes to keep this birth a secret. He may be referring to the wife of Reverend William W. Hunt (1796–1837), who was himself in poor health.

3. The new physician is unidentified. For a discussion of the rapid growth of the town of Amherst between 1810 and 1830, see George R. Taylor, "The Rise and Decline of Manufactures and Other Matters," in *Essays on Amherst's History*, ed. Theodore P. Greene (Amherst: The Vista Trust, 1978), pp. 43–77. The town's population increased from about 1,900 in 1820 to a little over 2,600 in 1830, a 37 percent increase. Taylor describes a corresponding building boom during what he calls "Amherst's Golden Age from about 1810 to 1837" (p. 70).

86
Edward to Emily Norcross
19 March 1828

Amherst. Wednesday Morning. March 19. 1828.

My Dear Emily,

I have omitted to write, some days longer than I intended—and it is now too late to send by our mail, but I expect Francis Warriner is going to Springfield to-day, & I shall probably send by him.[1] Your letter was recd. and also one from your father, last Thursday.[2] I shall be obliged to say all I do in much haste, as my time is very much occupied—business in the office, the week before Court—and the men at work on my house, take up all my attention. I hope to finish the inside, in the course of this week & next, ready to occupy (1.st April!) and the outside, all except painting, which will be done as soon as the weather will admit. I have had all my cupboards, closets painted *red*, am painting the rooms *white*, & the floors, *slate*. Does that suit you? What color would you like to have the *kitchen*, & floor? Would you not have it a *light yellow*, & the floor, *yellow*—instead of *slate*? Will you have the Pantry, buttery, painted *red*? I hope it will be repaired so that you will feel *contented* when you come to stay.

Do you like light or dark *paper*, on the walls, the best? I think, on the rooms which have *four* windows & are very light, that I had better have *dark* paper, & on those which are not so light, *light* paper—Don't you think so?

I intended to have gone to Springfield to-day, but the going is so bad, I conclude not to go. Your father wrote me that he expected to be there, this week, & should send me word about the *stove*—he thought it had better be *set up*, before we moved, to have it well tried—I think so, too.

I suppose, from your wish not to be married till the *1.st May*, that you chose not to be *published*, at the time proposed. When will it be agreeable? Why not on the last Sabbath in this month—the 30.th inst. You once said to me that you was not particular about it. *It must be done*. Why not *then*, as well as at any other time?—

I want you should write to me by the mail of Saturday respecting the *painting & papering*, in answer to my enquiries—and also, in relation to the *publishment*. I shall want to send word to your *Town-Clerk (who is he,)* to attend to it—and there will not be time unless you write by that mail—and the painting etc. I must know about—also.

Do you expect *to move*, the 1.st week in April, the week after next? If so, I may visit you, the week after that—next week is Court at Northampton, & the week after, (the 1.st week in April) at Greenfield, both of which Courts my business makes it necessary for me to attend—After that, I shall be at liberty, & shall visit you as soon as agreeable & convenient to you & the family.

Write me about it, won't you?

My father did not return from Boston till last week—after an absence of 10. weeks—Came home in good health—[3]

Mr. Newman staid in town a week—quite a visit!—tho' he had considerable business to employ him a part of the time—[4]

I am equally surprised with yourself, at the renewal of our friend

W's visits at Monson. How stands the matter, now? I recd. a letter from him after his return, speaking of you—making enquiries respecting our plans etc—But, as you say, "I did not feel obliged to tell him more than I pleased," tho' you need not fear but what I shall be disposed to treat him "with respect."

You have probably heard that Messrs. *Hayden, Webster* & *Bond* of Waterbury, Conn, have *failed* in business—after making a loss, in the *short time of two or three years,* of more than $20.000 Dollars!!! Rather unfortunate—I am sorry for Mrs. H.—But so the world goes—They enjoyed it while they could—A little more economy might have saved them, still.—A warning to all young men, to be prudent & industrious.

Has Lavinia recovered? I feel much interest in her, and was happy, indeed, to hear that she was improving in her health? Hope she is now well—Make my particular respects to her—

We have had a great snow—two or three days sleighing, tho' it is now about gone—Understand there is to be a great Concert at Springfield, this evening. Do any of your friends attend? I presume you do not. At least, I hope so.—

As to the time of our marriage? I suppose you have fully made up your mind, for the 1.st May. I suppose you will be ready, *then*—

The time is close at hand, My Dear, when we expect to form the most intimate & the most interesting of all earthly relations—Let us prepare for a life of rational happiness. I do not expect, neither do I desire a life of *pleasure*, as some call it—I anticipate pleasure from engaging with my whole soul in my business, and passing the time which can be spared from that, in the enjoyment which arises from an unreserved interchange of sentiment with My dearest friend—May we be happy & useful and successful, and each be an ornament in society—and gain the respect & esteem & confidence of all with whom we are, in any way, connected. I must close—But tho' absent from me, My Dear, you are not forgotten—Make my respects to all the family, and accept the assurance of my constantly increasing attachment and affection. Don't fail to write by Saturday's mail. Will you not come to Amherst, with me when I visit you, next?—Think of it—In much haste, as you will see.

Yours entirely Edward

1. Francis Warriner (1804–66), a member of the Amherst College class of 1830, was a younger brother of Solomon Warriner, Jr.

2. Joel Norcross's letter to Edward has not been found.

3. 1828 was a pivotal year for Samuel Fowler. He represented Amherst in the Massachusetts legislature (hence his stay in Boston), was an unsuccessful candi-

date for Congress, and attempted, also unsuccessfully, to establish a law school in Amherst. In the next few years, his fortunes declined rapidly and in 1833 he emigrated to Ohio, together with his wife and some of their children, where he died in 1838. For a discussion of Samuel Fowler's career, with its "sad ending," see Sewall, *Life of Emily Dickinson*, 1:28–43.

4. A notice signed by Edward that appeared in the *New-England Inquirer* on 10 April 1828 announced that "the Notes and Book Accounts of Mark H. Newman, are in the hands of the Subscriber for collection," as "Mr. Newman has removed from Amherst."

News from Monson that Lavinia was still unwell prompted Edward to write again on the same day. He described himself as feeling "constant anxiety about some of you, lest you should be unwell, and suffer from too much exposure."

87
Edward to Emily Norcross
19 March 1828

Amherst. Wednesday Afternoon. March 19. 1828.

My Dear Emily,

I wrote to you by the mail of this morning, and you will receive my letter on Friday morning—still, I have always a word to say to you. My health is now perfectly good, and I learn by Mr. Field, who you probably know, expects to move into Amherst, the 1.st April, that Lavinia is still unwell, tho' recovering. I feel much concerned for her, her health is so delicate—Take the best care of her, won't you, My Dear, and tell her from me to use the utmost caution about taking cold—She must be careful—I think very much of her, indeed, and can not think of having her suffer by ill health—I can say nothing, but, do all you can to cure her—Are you well? Don't expose yourself to the wet & cold—How is your mother's health? I feel constant anxiety about some of you, lest you should be unwell, and suffer from too much exposure—

You are then to exchange houses with Hiram, the 1.st April—I have said something in my other letter respecting my house—time of publishment—(30.th March) and shall expect a letter to be mailed for me on Saturday—giving an answer to my enquiries—Don't fail to do it— Perhaps you had better direct to me at *Northampton*—as the letter will reach there *Monday*, & I shall be there at Court, *Tuesday* Morning—and the mail will not come to Amherst till Tuesday night—I shall say no more now, as Mr. Field is waiting—I send a letter also to your father, respecting our *publishment* & other things—He will perhaps consult you. I requested him to do it—presuming that you would have no objection.[1]

Remember me particularly to all the family—& write by Saturday's mail—direct to Northampton—

My house gets along well—In much haste

Your affectionate Edward

1. Edward's letter to Joel Norcross has not been found.

88
Emily Norcross to Edward
22 March 1828

Monson March
Saturday Morn

My Dear Edward

I recieved a letter from you yesterdays mail also one by Mr. Fields and I conclude you exspect an answer without delay I never intend to disappoint you when in my power to comply yet I was fearful I should be under the necessity of doing it this morning as Sister Lavinea remains quite ill. She is this morning under the unpleasant operation of a blister upon her side which is quite tedious. She looks sorrowful indeed, yet I think it will be a great benefit to her our Physician does not aprehend her situation alarming still we have experienced much anxiety for her I trust however from her present appearence that her disease is checked and that she will soon begin to recover. In relation to our publishment my dear Edward I know what my wishes are, and you will now allow me to express them, but perhaps you may think that I do not make one effort to meet your proposals my dear are you willing to defer it untill you visit me as there is no necessity of doing it untill that time. My father conversed with me upon the subject and I know he would prefer you to wait untill then, yet he would not wish to interfere with our plans. Think of this my dear, as I trust you have some patience reserved. You may think from my management that I suppose the fountain inexhaustable, but I will not long disappoint you, as it affords me no pleasure. My things from Boston reached home quit[e] safe as far I have learnt. I have been very much engaged since then, as I wished to accomplish as much as possible befor we move. I have much to occupy my time and attention the present Spring. My mind is often completely confused when I allow myself to dwell upon the subject, but I useually lay it aside with the reflection that it will result in our happiness.[1] When we meet again I shall say much which time now forbids. You wish me to say what colour I would prefer, for the floors. Slate is rather to dark. I presume your painters know what is suitable, light led colour or somthing similar would answer for the chambers and the space below. The floor in the front room you [should] not paint at all as a [?] carpet sets much better without it The middle room floor a very little darker than the chambers the kitchen as you please.

I shall let you suit your own taste as respects the paper and I will engage to be satisfied, do not be in to much haste as ther is sufficient time. I suppose you are to be abscent next week and week after, my best wishes for your success. My health is very good, yet there [are] many complaining around us

Mrs Newton still continues² I shall anticipate meeting you the next week after we move, if convenient, untill then I must leave you. I send this to Northampton as you requested

Yours Emily

1. By "the subject," she means something like her marriage or the impending change in her life.

2. For Mrs. Newton, see Letter 62. Emily may mean that her ailing neighbor is still living.

Ironically, Edward thought that he was preparing for a life of rational happiness and persisted in trying to hold Emily to her promise to be married by 1 May at the very latest. Describing her delaying tactics as "artful," he admonished her, "I hope that you will soon be less disposed to try experiments upon my faithfulness." But by this time in their courtship, Emily's experiments upon his faithfulness seem less artful and more neurotic than he supposed.

89
Edward to Emily Norcross
27 March 1828

Northampton March 27. 1828.
Thursday Morn.

My Dear Emily,

I am now in Mr. Mills' office, for the purpose of replying to your letter which I received on my arrival here on Tuesday morning, as I expected—I am extremely sorry to hear of Lavinia's continued illness—and could I do anything to hasten her recovery, tell her that there is nothing which I would not most heartily undertake to relieve her of the pain which she suffers. I am much interested in every thing relating to her, and shall depend on your skill in nursing, to do all that can be done for her speedy restoration—Give my particular regards to her—& tell her that I shall hear of her convalescence with great pleasure. I feel safe to have her in your careful hands—knowing that you will do all that can be done—Exert yourself for her, won't you?

I had all my floors in my house painted *slate*, the *first* time, before receiving your letter—and I immediately directed the 2.d coat to be light lead color, as you requested—one chamber is papered—and all the inside will probably be completed in the course of the next week—shall begin to paint the outside, this week or next. My blinds are also in a good state of forwardness, and will all be ready in season—and I think the whole will be in readiness to occupy *before the 1.st May*, tho' I see you are determined so to manage in relation to our *publishment*, that there is no *possibility* of effecting our union previous to that time—rather *artful*, My Dear—however, I still have a *little* patience, tho' I think the repeated delays & disappointments to which I have been subjected have had some tendency to diminish the capital stock—It is not *inexhaustible*, as you suggest—I hope that you will soon be less disposed to try experiments upon my *faithfulness*.[1]

I suppose you expect to move, next week—1.st April—and unless I hear from you to the contrary, in the *course of the next week*, I shall intend to visit you, on Tuesday or Wednesday of the week after—about the 8.th or 9.th of April—and shall intend to be *published the sabbath after I see you*, and married the *1.st day of May*. To that you have more than once promised *never to object*—I shall, therefore calculate upon it—as you have set your own time. I shall be at Greenfield Court, a part of next week—probably not more than two or three days—think I may get home by Thursday—"Fast-Day."

Mr. Gilbert, who has been at Monson, came here on Monday and has joined the Law-School[2]—Mr. Woodbridge also, the "Historical Lecturer," has been in town two days, and has this morning started to the Western part of the state.

The business of the Court will not take up all the week, & I shall probably be able to leave this evening, or to-morrow morning—and shall go as soon as I can, on account of seeing to the work about my house.

Mr. Mills' health remains about the same, and he has considerable hope that warm weather will restore him to comfortable health—I intend to call & see him to-day. He has always been a good friend to me, and there is hardly any man whom I should more rejoice to have recover, and again engage in business than him—He was the flower of our Bar, and the most distinguished Lawyer that we had.[3]

Judge Strong, who presides at the present term of the Court, delivered a handsome eulogy upon the memory of Judge Howe, whom all so much lament, and said much calculated to induce all young men to imitate so bright an example, that they may deserve the same honors which circle around his tomb[4]—My Dear Emily, could you but feel the grief which shrouds the friends of a man who is removed in the midst of life and in the sure path of constantly increasing usefulness and honor—could you realize the sorrow which clouds the brightest prospects when so *pure a light* is extinguished and did you know the loss which the profession sustain[s] in the death of a man so every way what he ought to be, you would sympathize with your dearest friend—and join me, most sincerely in the prayer which even my hard heart pours out that his pure spirit may shed its light upon all those who are following him in the same path, and who desire to emulate the virtues which he so eminently possessed & cultivated.

My Dear, I must soon close, as the Court has already opened—and I must attend. Will it not be convenient for you to write me again, before I visit you? Should be glad, you know to hear from you, at all times—If you can, will you write as soon as the Tuesday's mail of next week—so that it will reach me on Thursday—

Give my respects to all the family—and present my most affectionate regards to Lavinia—She must not be sick—I want much to see her.

Mr. Field expects to move to Amherst, the 1.st of April, you know? I suppose, from your letter, you are much engaged—presume you will be prepared by the *1.st of May*, without any *further delay*—as I shall expect, unless something very extraordinary takes place, to finish on that day what I have been so long in arranging. You ought to expect me to show some *earnestness*—and ought not to expect me to yield to any further proposition for *delay*. I shall esteem it *unreasonable*, tho' I do not fear it—in the least.

My Dear, you are constantly in mind, tho' absent from me—and I anticipate very much pleasure in the prospect of soon being able to enjoy with you all the comforts of domestic life—let us do all in our power to prepare ourselves to render the relation which we so soon expect to form, one of rational enjoyment, and let us not forget to supplicate the favor of that Being who holds the destinies of all in his hands, and day & night implore his protection & blessing. Let us be virtuous & we shall be happy.

My Dear, I must leave you, tho' but for a short time—My heart is with you & my first wish is that you may be happy.

Write, if you can, next Tuesday—and believe me, as ever,
Your most affectionate friend
Edward

1. In his letter of 19 March, Edward had asked Emily to express her preference about the colors he had selected for the floors, cupboards, wallpaper, and so forth. She wrote on Saturday morning, 22 March, as he had requested. Therefore, it is curious that Edward had already instructed his painters to apply slate-colored paint to the floors. Perhaps a second coat produced the final light lead color she desired, but she had also asked that the parlor floor remain unpainted. There may have been a touch of malice in his speed. Previously, Emily had expressed a preference for the blinds, and it is unclear whether Edward followed her instructions. In Letter 79, he told her that she had written after he had already commissioned them, but his instructions may nevertheless have coincided with or anticipated hers. Obviously she was difficult to work with because she participated only sporadically in planning for their home.

2. "Mr. Gilbert" is unidentified. Presumably he became a law student rather than a member of the faculty.

3. Mills died in May 1829; the law school apparently closed shortly thereafter.

4. Solomon Strong (1780–1850) was judge of the court of common pleas and a former member of Congress.

90
Edward to Emily Norcross
3 April 1828

Amherst. (Fast) 3.o'clock P.M. Ap. 3. 1828.
My Dear Emily,

My first determination, on learning from Cousin Albert that you had not written me by him,[1] was, not to write to you, but I soon repented, as I am not composed of materials which will suffer me to neglect what I am assured will always afford my friend pleasure—to know that I am in the enjoyment of the most perfect health—and that my Spirits are good—and my business flourishing and to receive a kind remembrance from one whom you know values you more than all else besides—My Dear, how do you do? Have you got rested since your removal? How did your Mother bear the change? And how is Lavinia? Albert says she is much better—and I can assure you that I am rejoiced to hear it—I can not think that so intelligent and interesting a young female should be deprived of health, at so interesting a period of life—She is very dear to me—Make my kindest regards to her—I have sent her a small present—don't tell of it.

I expected not to return till last evening, but came early in the afternoon, & saw Albert, as he passed thro' Am. on his way to Sunderland with Mr. Graves.[2] He came as far as here this morning, and attended meeting with me, forenoon & afternoon, and will carry this to you this evening.

I shall intend to visit you next Tuesday, if I can—and shall then expect you to fulfil your promise to visit some of our friends with me—and did I suppose that it would be of any avail, I should give you an invitation to return with me, & see the house etc. but that, I suppose, is out of the question—*1.st May, I shall call for you—to be married.*

Albert is waiting & I must be short—My Dear, take good care of your health—the time is near when I hope to call you mine. Be virtuous & benevolent & kind—and may the best of heaven's blessings rest on you forever—Give me the parting ——s—and receive, tho' in haste, my sincere love & affection—Shall I hear from you before I see you?—Good afternoon, My Dear—Love to all the family—In much haste

Yours entirely Edward

1. Albert Norcross was Loring's younger brother.

2. In all probability "Mr. Graves" is Colonel Rufus Graves (1758–1845), the close friend of Samuel Fowler. Born in Sunderland, Graves was a graduate of the Dartmouth College class of 1791. According to W. S. Tyler, "He had *Amherst College on the brain,* and some of his cooler neighbors really believed he was beside himself." Unsuccessful in his own business ventures, he was an indefatigible fund raiser for the College before his move to Ohio in 1834. He died there at the age of eighty-six. Thus there are numerous parallels between the careers of Samuel Fowler and Rufus Graves, though Tyler implies that Graves died a fulfilled rather than a broken man. See *History of Amherst College,* p. 118 and passim.

Edward visited Monson on 8 and 9 April, but this letter says nothing about his visit. By the time Emily wrote her next letter, however, the couple had already agreed that they would be married on 6 May. While he was in Monson, the Norcrosses must have persuaded him to agree to this final delay. They were reluctant to give up Emily, and she was reluctant to leave.

91
Edward to Emily Norcross
18 April 1828

Amherst. Friday Morn. April 18. 1828.

My Dear Emily,

I did not intend, when I left you last, to postpone writing so long, and nothing but the daily and hourly expectation of having an opportunity to send by the man who was to bring the Crate & Box of Looking Glasses has prevented—I can not tell, as I have not been able to see him, when he will go, tho' I suppose, soon—

My health is perfectly good, tho' I am very much fatigued with the numerous duties which I am obliged to perform—Yesterday I escaped very narrowly being much injured—by a horse running with me in a waggon, tho' I was so fortunate as to come off with no personal injury except a slight sprain of one of my ancles—It is not serious, as I can walk quite comfortably. My waggon was considerably broken, and my horse ran 6. miles before he was caught—and I can assure you that I am grateful indeed that I suffered so little, when so much exposed—

My house etc. are nearly done, much to my gratification—

Your stove arrived safely from Springfield, and is well set, and so far as I can discover, will operate as we could wish—it draws perfectly—and boils well. It is not the rusty thing which your father, in his peculiar way of producing an agreeable surprise in having things prove much better than he represents, would have us believe—but one of the neatest, & best looking stoves that I ever saw—it is much liked by all who have seen it, and I think will prove exactly what you want—the fire place I have filled up—

As to the company who will go with me to Monson, I can not now tell you definitely—tho' I will write again soon, probably from *four* to *six* or more of my friends will accompany me—Have you consulted Elvira? What does she say? Shall I write to Mr. Allen? Will it not be agreeable to you, that Mr. Coleman & his wife should be invited? They have always been very polite to me, and I should like to be so to them. Has Olivia yet returned from Belchertown? How is her health?—

I can not have milk of Mrs. Montague, as you proposed, but shall be obliged to keep a cow—as I now think—and I think you will need a *girl* to assist you—I can now engage one, if you conclude to have one, and I never had any other expectation, till I last met you—You must direct about it, as you think best—

Mr. Field & family & Miss Newell, I have had the pleasure of seeing—they came the day I returned from Monson—I think he may do well, if he is industrious—Mr. Gilbert has removed to Masonsville, N. York—and his son Harvey is married & has taken the house of his father—[1]

I heard, this week, that Loren was in Boston with Capt. Flynt—Brother Wm. & Mr. Field start to-morrow—after goods—[2]

There is an uncommon degree of building & repairing going on in Am. this Spring, and never was business more lively—property is fast increasing in value—I hope it will continue—

My Dearest Emily, I must close, as the stage will soon arrive. I can only say, as you see that I have written in much haste, that I shall write again, very soon—in the mean time, let me ask how you & all the rest do?—and assure you of the importance of having a right sense of the duties which we are soon to take upon ourselves—My Dear, my heart is with you, and you are constantly in mind—I can only give you the parting hand, this morning, & leave the expression of a more ardent attachment till another time—Make my regards to all—and receive once more the renewed expression of the affection which you know I feel for you—

In much haste, Good morning—Your devoted Edward

What think you of having a party accompany us as far as Belchertown—and have a party from Amherst meet us there? Will you think of it & inform me?

Let me hear from you immediately—

1. Mr. Field and his family were originally from Monson but had moved to Amherst, as in Letters 85 and 87. Miss Newell was probably from Monson but is otherwise unidentified. Mr. Gilbert and his son Harvey were from Amherst, where Harvey owned a distillery.

2. Alpheus and Stillman Field were William Dickinson's business partners. Mr. Field from Monson may have been one of their relatives. In any event, it is unclear which Mr. Field accompanied William to Boston on his buying trip.

This is one of Emily's more determined and coherent letters, yet her tone was far from flattering as, for example, when she stated, "I suppose we are to be married a week from Tuseday next yet I cannot be positive as I know not what will be the situation of our friends." (Her cousin Julia was seriously ill.) Predictably, Emily wanted the wedding celebration "to be managed with as little noise as possible." Although weddings tended to be smaller, less formal, and less costly in the 1820s than they became during the post–Civil War period, Emily's desire to dispense with attendants was unusual, as was her reluctance to be escorted from Monson to Amherst by their mutual friends. Wedding tours, or honeymoons, were not common practice among the middle class until the 1840s.

92
Emily Norcross to Edward
24 April 1828

Monson April 24th
Thursday Morning

My Dear Edward

Perhaps I have not answered your letter as soon as you exspected, but I suppose you are sensible my present engagements are numerous. I imagine sometimes you may think it strange that I find so much to occupy me, but my dear Edward I think I could convince you. I regret that you still belong to the unfortunate society. I think you had better withdraw your name, for the present.[1] I should judge however that your spirits were not much depressed I have but little time this morning to converse with you I will therfore speak of a few particulars. As respects Mr Allen and Elvira I can give you but little encouragement yet I have not consulted them as they are now in deep affliction. You was I believe aquainted with Cousin Julias ill health It is painful for me to say that her case is hopeless but I suppose it is thought she can never recover. It is a grevious affliction to the family yet it is what others have been called to endure, but we are not naturaly disposed to think that we may share with others untill experience teaches us the painful lesson. Under the present situation of the family I have thought it would not be proper to say any thing upon the subject. No matter if we do not abide by the ceremony I presume you are not so diffident but what you would consent to stand by my side for a short time even if we had no company to stand up with us. I shall not be particular I suppose we are to be married a week from Tuesday next [6 May] yet I cannot be positive as I know not what will be the situation of our friends I shall exspect you near the middle of the afternoon with what friends you wish to accompany you should nothing prevent. You proposed a party to meet you in Belchertown My dear I would wish you to be gratified, but give me liberty to say that I wish the proceedings to be managed with as little noise as possible. It is uncertain whether we have company to go with us from Monson as it must depend very much upon circumstances

You need not think I should neglect Cousin Maria and Husband as I think much of them Cousin Olive returned very soon after you left I think her health some what improved. I recieved a visit from her a few days since I have many friends call upon me as they say to make their farewell visit. How do you suppose this sounds in my ear But my dear it is to go and live with you. You speak of haveing a girl. I shall not consent to it at all. I think there can be no difficulty in obtaining the milk we should wish to use at least may I hope that you will [make] no other arrangements untill I see you. My Father has concluded not to send my things untill the day after I go as it will be more convenient then. Except the crate should we have an opportunity I make but one objection to his arrangements, that is I do not like to trouble your friends more than is necessary. I presume the chairs will be sent up next week. I must now leave you once more by saying that you must not be disappointed should the time of our marriage be altered. Yet there is nothing to prevent except the situation of Uncles family as they now experience a day of trouble we wish to do all in our power for them, but should there be a change I will give you seasonable notice.[2]

I have written in very great haste do therfore excuse me

From your affectionate Emily

1. Emily is referring to the incident with the runaway horse described in Letter 91 in which Edward narrowly escaped a serious injury. "I regret that you still belong to the unfortunate society. I think you had better withdraw your name, for the present" is another example of her humor. Unless I am mistaken, however, she is being unsympathetic. Presumably she had concluded that Edward was inclined toward self-pity. Her tart tone was perhaps intended to brace him up.

2. Amos Norcross was the father of Elvira and the ailing Julia. Julia died in Monson in 1850 at the age of forty.

93
Emily Norcross to Edward
29 April 1828

My Dear Edward

As there remains a few words I wish to say I will accept the present opportunity. May I hope that you have recieved my letter before this, as you seemed some what disappointed when I last heard from you at the delay. Most certainly my dear I am sensible that delays are very dangerous at present[1] I mentioned to you that father would not send any thing of mine untill after I had left. He has since concluded to send one team before that time and the othere after I go. As he wishes me to be there to take care of them, all I wish of you is to lay them in your part of the house and let them rest untill I come My dear will you do me the kindness to write a line to Cousin Maria and Husband with my best respects, wishing the pleasure of their company, one evening of next week. I leave it with you as I have no opportunity of sending directly to them As respect[s] Wm Town and lady I would prefer you not to send to them I would much rather recieve a visit from them after we ar settled² I have some serious hours dear Edward but I have not time to express my feelings to you this eve[n]ing. Cousin Julia is yet quite low, but rather better, they now have hopes of her

In much haste yours entirely but once more I leave you I think it best that we stand up alone as I do not wish for company

1. Given that there were arrangements for the wedding and for their house-keeping still to be made, Emily may be referring to delays in their correspondence. Or she may be referring to the fact that her "Crate & Box of Looking Glasses" had not arrived when Edward wrote Letter 91. She may also have been feeling guilty about having caused Edward to wait so long to marry her.

2. William Towne and his fiancée Frances Robinson were mentioned by Edward in Letter 51. When Edward was in Monson in early April, he must have suggested inviting them to the wedding, because Towne's name does not appear in Letter 91.

Gallantly, Edward acceded to Emily's request to dispense with wedding attendants, remarking, "No, My Dearest Emily, I shall never fear to stand by you, alone." He could afford to be generous: the battle was fought, the victory almost won. Emily's battle, one senses, was just beginning.

94
Edward to Emily Norcross
29 April 1828

Amherst. Tuesday Eve, April 29. 1828.

My Dear Emily,

I expect Mr. Cutler, about whom I have so often spoken, as the man whom I expected to bring your crate etc, to go to Monson to-morrow, & he will bring it when he returns, together with any thing else which you choose to send.¹ I recd. your letter [92] on Saturday, & regret to hear such painful tidings from your Cousin Julia—I can but hope, yet, that she may recover, if she is still alive—I can do no more—do all you can for her—

I made my arrangements to have your goods come to-day, but suppose that the alteration in your arrangements was not made without wise reasons—As to *troubling my friends*, as you say, you need not fear that—it will give them pleasure to do any thing for us, which will render us more comfortable, or ease the burden of our commencement of keeping house—I suppose there will be many little things wanted which I have not thought of, but I shall procure every thing which occurs to me as necessary—The house has been cleaned by a black woman, but I suppose it will have to pass thro' other hands again, under your own inspection—I told her, that if there was *one speck* left on the windows, they would be all taken out & washed anew!—So you see, I have done my duty—I have had flat stones laid on the bottom of part of my cellar—and have been busy for the last four weeks, I can assure you.

I go to Court to-morrow morning—and expect my case to be tried some day this week. I did not go to-day, as my business at home made it extremely inconvenient—and I expected your *chairs* here besides— When will they come—I shall leave word with my brother, to take care of them, if they come, in my absence. As to a party meeting us, at Belchertown, I shall relinquish the idea, as you seem opposed to it, & I care little about it, tho' I should like very well to have some company from Monson as far as Belchertown, if circumstances will admit—I am not particular—

I shall leave the management of the ceremony entirely with you till I meet you—and if not convenient for any company to stand on our right & left, I am not "so diffident but what I would consent to stand by the side of My Dear, for a short time"—unsupported by friends— No, My Dearest Emily, I shall never fear to stand by you, *alone*—tho' if you choose to comply with the custom, on such occasions, I pre-sume there will be enough present to constitute a respectable side-company.

I wish that your father would request Mr. Ely to attend [officiate], as I may not reach Monson in season to make it perfectly convenient for me to call on him for the purpose, myself—and if you find a favorable opportunity to apologize to Mr. Colton for my neglect to call upon him when last in town, should like to have you—as he may think it strange that I should visit M. several times without seeing him—tho' I have called at his house, every time except the last—I have recd. my *certificate* of publishment in Amherst, & suppose there is one ready for me in Monson—

I am expecting to go on Tuesday next, after you, My Dear—and shall calculate to reach there from 2. to 3. o'clock in the afternoon—if agreeable, with my friends, probably six in number, unless I hear from you to the contrary—I hope there will be no occasion for delay, as my business is all arranged with reference to that time, & it will be more convenient for me then than afterwards—Will your brother Wm. & Mary [Fanning?] come up with us. (I am here interrupted by Prof. Worcester, who wishes to see the paper on my rooms, and I have been over the whole house with him[2]—) and I have had many calls of a similar kind from Gentlemen, as well as no small number of Ladies—

Why they all feel so much interest in seeing my house, I know not, except that they would like to call and see the new occupant, at a proper time—My Dear, do you realize that you are coming to live with me? May blessings rest upon us—and make us happy—May we be virtuous, intelligent, industrious and by the exercise of every virtue, & the cultivation of every excellence, be esteemed & respected & beloved by all—We must determine to do our duty to each other, & to all our friends, and let others do as they may. "A conscience void of offence towards God & man"³ will secure us a permanent happiness.

My Dear, I must stop, as I have very much yet to do, this evening. Will you therefore excuse me. I suppose you recd. my letter [91], on Sunday Evening last.

Is your health good? Are the family all well?—We are all well & my health never was better—and you are right in supposing that my spirits are not depressed—tho' I am very much fatigued with the court labors which I have passed thro' lately—

Make my warm regards to all friends—tell Lavinia, that I do not forget her, in particular—and give me the parting hand till we meet to become *one for life*—

Your affectionate Edward

Mr. Field informed me this evening, that he was going to Monson, next Monday—

P.S. 10. o'clock. I have just been down to the house, as Cousin Thankful Smith is there this evening, and find the evening most beautiful.⁴ If we had been married this evening, it would have been as pleasant a time as could have been—I found one of our Peach trees in blossom. The weather has grown much warmer, within one or two days, and appears now like being fine weather—I always enjoy such pleasant moonlight evenings very highly indeed—it seems as if I could not prize them enough—and could not feel happy enough amid such beauties. But enough—Will you write by Mr. Cutler—

Edward

1. Cutler, an Amherst merchant, is perhaps also mentioned in Letter 63.

2. As previously stated (Letter 60, n. 2), Samuel Melancthon Worcester was [co]editor of the reorganized *New-England Inquirer*. According to Edward Hitchcock, he was "always genial and gentlemanly in his feelings, frank and unsuspicious" (*Reminiscences of Amherst College*, p. 30).

3. Acts 24:16, slightly misquoted.

4. Thankful Smith was the daughter of Samuel Fowler's sister Anna and her

husband Oliver Smith. Thankful continued to visit the Dickinsons in later years, as when she intruded on the poet in March 1852. See *Letters of Emily Dickinson*, 1:186.

95
Edward to Emily Norcross
2 May 1828

Amherst. Friday Eve. May 2. 1828.

My Dear Emily,

Your father's team arrived here this evening, with a load of goods, all safe, apparently, tho' none of them will be opened till you come yourself—I sent for the crate by Mr. Cutler, who I supposed would be in Monson on Wednesday, but Mr. Cotton, who came up on that day with the chairs, carried the letters, which I had prepared to send by Mr. Cutler[1]—The chairs, so far as I can perceive, came with very little, scarcely any injury—I was absent.

I was at Northampton Court only two days, Wednesday and Thursday—as my affairs at home were rather pressing. I saw Mr. Coleman there, and gave him a written invitation for himself & Maria to attend our wedding on Tuesday Eve of next week. He said he expected to be in Monson to-day, and intended to go to New York next week—but would be happy to accept the invitation which I presented in our joint names—probably Maria will be there, if he is not. I had concluded, before I heard from you, not to invite Wm. Towne & Lady to visit Monson, next week—He is expected in town, however, next week, on his way to Albany etc. and we shall probably see him—

I was rather amused with William's allusion to the "Shad Pedlar"—and would like to have enjoyed the joke, myself—in the "land of steady habits."[2]

The time is short, My Dear, and we shall probably soon have occasion to enter upon the serious duties of life—Are we prepared? But I am to[o] tired to "moralize," and, as Wm. says, I am much disposed to retire into the arms of Morpheus, (the god of sleep) and take a potion of "tired natures sweet restorer" "balmy sleep."[3] My Dear, once more, good night—love to all, and every [?] blessing on yourself—I can only add, that I am Yours

entirely & forever—Edward

Your teamster *would not go to our house*—

Saturday Morn. My Dear, it storms some this morning, preparatory, I hope, to fair weather, next week. Will the rest of your goods come on Monday, or not till after you come yourself.

1. Letter 94 was hand delivered by Cotton. Edward may also have written to William or Joel Norcross but these letters have not been found.

2. In his lighthearted letter of 29 April, William had described being mistaken for a "Shad Pedlar" as he returned in his wagon with a load of wooden goods after "a tour to the Shakers." The "land of steady habits" is not a phrase employed by William, who had stated, "This is truly a busy Season with Farming But in addition to the common concerns of the Farm an other small affair in which you somehow or other seem to have some little interest claims a share of our attention this spring." Throughout this courtship correspondence, Edward employs quotation marks to set off phrases that are in varying degrees interpretative paraphrases. Contextually, the "land of steady habits" is Monson.

3. In his letter, William had written, "Emily has just come in, Says she shall write you herself the 'Order of the Day', which saves me the trouble & moreover gives me an opportunity of retiring into the arms of Morpheus." "Tired nature's sweet restorer, balmy sleep" is the opening line of *Night Thoughts*.

POSTSCRIPT:

A REGULAR FAMILY

96

Edward to "Mrs. Emily N. Dickinson Amherst" 23 September 1828

Northampton Sept. 23. 1828.

My Dear Emily,

The Hon. Mr. Bliss of Springfield has spoken to me to-day, about boarding his son. Says he & Henry Morris are coming to Amherst to-day, & he will try to get in, at our house. You know my opinion respecting it, and I leave it entirely with you to manage as you think best. The work, you know, comes upon you, and it is wholly immaterial with me, what you conclude. Mr. Bliss feels quite anxious to have him in some *"regular family."*[1]

Will you do exactly as you choose, and you will gratify me, as you always do.[2]

I shall be at home to-morrow. Let one of my Sisters stay with you to-night, without fail.

Yours as ever,
Most affectionately
Edward

1. Richard Bliss prepared for college at Monson Academy, attended Yale in 1827–28, and graduated from Amherst in 1831. His father George was a business associate of Joel Norcross's. Henry Morris also prepared for college at Monson and graduated from Amherst in 1832. He and Richard appear to have been cousins. Henry Morris subsequently had a distinguished career as a lawyer and jurist. He married Solomon Warriner's sister Mary in 1837. Perhaps half the students at the College boarded in private homes.

2. Emily's decision remains to be determined; subsequently, however, Edward and Emily were eager to have male boarders to protect her during his absences. See Leyda, *The Years and Hours of Emily Dickinson*, 1:8.

EPILOGUE

But were they happy? Yes and no. Edward Dickinson fulfilled many of his professional ambitions. He exerted himself and was rewarded for it. He reestablished the family name and perhaps even the family honor in Amherst. He was an important though not a commanding figure in Massachusetts politics and for a brief period of time had some modest influence on the national scene. He was respected by almost everyone who knew him, yet he had few intimates. The poet reported, "Father says in fugitive moments when he forgets the barrister & lapses into the man, says that his life has been passed in a wilderness or on an island—of late he says on an island."

Both the outer and the inner life of Emily Norcross Dickinson are more difficult to assess. She raised three highly individualistic children and ran a beautifully well-appointed home. Her physical health was good until her husband died, her mental health less sound. It is painfully apparent in the courtship letters that hers was not a strongly articulated personality, and she never achieved a clearly defined identity, except as a dependent. "I loved him so," she mourned after her husband's death, perhaps romanticizing the reality.

Together as marriage partners, the Dickinsons were not inspiring role models, if their children's behavior is any evidence. Yet Emily Dickinson's first known poem is a valentine written to her father's law clerk in 1850, which satirizes some of the actual courtship conventions of America in the midnineteenth century and invents some others. In the outrageous world of Dickinson's verse, marriages are arranged by fond fathers—for their sons. Dickinson courted her brother in a letter of 1851 that is designated as Poem 2 in the standard edition of her work. Another comic valentine followed in 1852, the first of her poems to be published during her lifetime. The fourth poem in the now-standard Johnson edition of Dickinson's poetry has nothing to do with courtship and is concerned with a sort of eternal voyage or a voyage to eternity or perhaps with an eternal homecoming. The situation to which the poem alludes is nicely obscured. The fifth poem, "I have a Bird in spring," emerged out of a quarrel between Dickinson and her brother's fiancée Susan Gilbert, whom she was courting while they were engaged in a romantic friendship of ambiguous erotic import. In this fifth poem, the last known poem of her literary apprenticeship, Dickinson seems to be repressing her vision of tragic selfhood. According to the hackneyed speaker of Poem 5, the world has an Emersonian balance in which loss is assuredly recompensed by gain.

Whatever its elements of pathetic and even tragic dependency, Dickinson's life depended on her ability to, as she once put it, "entertain" herself. Some of the entertainment was grisly and Dickinson was not always entertained, but this venture was mandated in part by the emotional remoteness of both of her parents. Thus the Dickinson household both encouraged and discouraged the self-reliant stance on which so much of her poetry depends. Even her sister Lavinia—pretty, popular Lavinia—could not bring herself to become anyone's wife, preferring instead to fulfill herself, to the extent that she did, as a dutiful daughter and formidably devoted sister. And Austin's marriage was eventually a famous disaster. To repeat. The Dickinsons' marriage tended to reinforce rather than to transcend the gender stereotypes of their day. This much is clear from their courtship letters, where one looks in vain for the lighthearted or tender notes of passionate comradeship. Yet together as parents the Dickinsons provided their children with a collective space of their own, which enabled the poet Emily Dickinson, after many false starts, to select her own society. For this much at least, lovers of literature are in their debt.

SELECTED CHRONOLOGY

1803	1 January	Edward born in Amherst to Lucretia Gunn and Samuel Fowler Dickinson; eldest of nine children
1804	3 July	Emily born in Monson to Betsy Fay and Joel Norcross; eldest daughter in a family of nine children; three of them died before her courtship; a fourth gravely ill at that time
1813		Samuel Fowler builds the house on Main Street, the Homestead, said to be the first brick house in Amherst
1814		Edward enters Amherst Academy
1819		Edward enters Yale but spends part of his freshman year at Amherst Academy because of his father's inability to pay the bills
1823		Emily attends girls' boarding school in New Haven; Edward graduates from Yale; returns to Amherst to join his father's law practice
1825–26		Edward appointed a major in the Massachusetts Militia; attends Northampton Law School
1826	January	Edward serves as marshal at a military court in Monson; meets and is captivated by Emily Norcross; her father one of the town's wealthiest men and leading citizens
	8 February	Edward writes the first of his courtship letters
	1 March	Emily writes the first of her responses
	4 June	Edward writes formal marriage proposal
	September	Edward opens law office in Amherst after considering other locations
	30 October	Emily more or less accepts his proposal
1827	20 August	Emily visits Amherst for the first and only time before her marriage, accompanied by her brother William
1828	Winter-Spring	Strain between Emily and Edward; in March, Lavinia Norcross visits Amherst in her sister's place

	6 May	Marriage of Emily and Edward in her parents' home
1829	26 February	Emily's married brother Hiram dies
	16 April	Birth of William Austin Dickinson; Emily Elizabeth Dickinson (the poet) to her brother in her first extant letter in 1842: "There was always such a Hurrah wherever you was."
	September	Emily's mother dies of tuberculosis at the age of fifty-two; described in an obituary notice as pious and self-effacing
1830	Fall	Edward Dickinson, his wife, and small son move into the Homestead, a now divided house
	10 December	Birth of EMILY ELIZABETH DICKINSON
1831	6 January	Remarriage of Joel Norcross to Sarah Vaill; Emily Norcross Dickinson's response unrecorded though her sister Lavinia protests
	3 July	Emily Norcross Dickinson admitted to church membership, applying by letter
1833	28 February	Birth of Lavinia Norcross Dickinson; the poet on her sister in 1873 while her parents were still very much alive: "She has no Father and Mother but me and I have no Parents but her."
	April	Poor and broken-spirited, Samuel Fowler Dickinson leaves Amherst to direct the manual labor required of students at Lane Theological Seminary in Cincinnati; his wife and several children follow shortly thereafter
1834	4 November	Lavinia Norcross marries her first cousin
1835	May	Edward's sister Catharine writes to him that their father's "spirits are completely broken down & probably will never rise again."
	August	Edward appointed treasurer of Amherst College; holds the position continuously for almost forty years
1836	Summer?	Samuel Fowler and family move to Hudson, Ohio; he takes a position as treasurer at Western Reserve College; subsequently leaves his accounts "in a sorry mess."

1838	Winter	Edward begins two-year term in Massachusetts legislature; furthers the cause of Amherst College; writes notes to the children urging them to be good and to obey their mother; promises to bring presents
	22 April	Death of Samuel Fowler at the age of sixty-one; wife and remaining daughter make plans to return to Massachusetts
1839	19 December	Lucretia Gunn Dickinson, Edward's mother, writes a pathetic letter to him asking for help, which was apparently not forthcoming
1840	April	Edward and his family move to more spacious quarters on North Pleasant Street; they own the entire house
	11 May	Lucretia Gunn Dickinson dies in Enfield where she had been living, perhaps with a cousin
1842	January	Edward begins another term in the Massachusetts legislature
1843	15 September	Ann Shepherd writes to her sister, describing a visit from Mrs. Edward Dickinson: "She was as usual full of plaintive talk."
1846		Joseph Lyman, a friend of Austin's, lives with the Dickinsons; subsequently describes their home life at that time as close to idyllic. "[Mrs. Dickinson] was a rare and delicate cook in such matters as crullers and custards and she taught the girls all those housewifely accomplishments."
	5 May	Death of Joel Norcross at the age of sixty-nine; Emily Norcross Dickinson's reaction unrecorded
1847–48		Emily Dickinson attends Mount Holyoke Female Seminary; rooms with one of her Norcross cousins; suffers from homesickness and from the confinements of institutional living but does well in her studies; does not return the following year because her parents want her at home
1850	January	Lavinia Dickinson has begun attending Ipswich Female Seminary; says she has a "great aversion to writing," but her roommate says "Vinnie writes all the funny letters that go from this room."

	4 March	Emily Dickinson sends first extant poem, to her father's law clerk
	May	The poet alarmed by her mother's ill health which she describes as almost unprecedented
	8 August	Austin graduates from Amherst College
	11 August	Edward Dickinson admitted to church membership by profession of faith
	September	Austin teaching school in Sunderland; the poet misses him greatly
1852	17 December	Edward elected to the United States House of Representatives on the Whig ticket
1853	March	Austin begins attending Harvard Law School; secret engagement to Susan Huntington Gilbert, the poet's closest friend
1854	13 January	Emily Dickinson writes to the Reverend Edward Everett Hale inquiring about the death of her friend Benjamin Franklin Newton, once her father's law clerk
	Summer-Fall	Austin graduates from law school; crisis in erotically charged friendship between Emily and Susan Gilbert
1855	February	Edward serving in Congress but has been criticized by his political enemies for spending too much time in Amherst; Emily visits him in Washington and stops off in Philadelphia on her way home; stays there with her mother's cousin Maria Flynt Coleman and her husband Lyman; through them, probably meets the Reverend Charles Wadsworth, pastor of the Arch Street Presbyterian Church of which they are members
	Mid-November	Dickinsons move back to the Homestead, which Edward has repurchased and refurbished
1856	1 July	Austin marries Susan in Geneva, New York; none of the Dickinsons attend the ceremony; Edward thwarts their plan to move to the Midwest; builds the Evergreens for them as a wedding present and takes Austin into his law practice as an equal partner; probably embezzles money from the estate of his orphaned nieces to do so; during part of this year Mrs. Dickinson in

		Northampton for water cure, suffering from chronic depression
1857		Virtually undocumented year in the life of the poet; probably a time of great mental anguish
1858		Emily Dickinson writes first Master letter; in another letter comments on the severity of her mother's depression; socializes with Austin and Sue and some of their friends in the Evergreens but is becoming more reclusive; begins making packet copies of her poems
1861	19 June	Birth of Edward (Ned) Dickinson, Austin and Sue's first child; perhaps at about this time the poet writes second Master letter
1862		Emily Dickinson probably writes third Master letter and composes some 366 poems; writes to Thomas Wentworth Higginson in April in response to his *Atlantic Monthly* essay "Letter to a Young Contributor"; sends him poems to evaluate; he praises her poetry but advises her to "delay 'to publish,'" which she does; describes her family in several letters written to him at this time: "My Mother does not care for thought . . . Father, too busy with his Briefs—to notice what we do—He buys me many Books—but begs me not to read them—because he fears they joggle the Mind. They are religious—except me—and address an Eclipse, every morning—whom they call their 'Father.'"
1863	12 July	A neighbor observes that Mrs. Dickinson is "quite herself again."
1864	Late April	Emily Dickinson begins seven-month stay in Cambridge for treatment of serious eye problem; lives in a boardinghouse with her orphaned cousins Louise and Fanny Norcross, who are among her closest friends
1865	April	Returns to Cambridge for eye treatment; suffers from photophobia and depression; continues to be enormously productive as a poet
1866	14 February	"The Snake" published in the *Springfield Republican*, thanks to Sue and Samuel Bowles; Dickinson is outraged and protests an apparently minor editorial change; one of only eleven poems

		known to have been published during the poet's lifetime; reprinted in *The Republican* three days later
	29 November	Birth of Martha Dickinson (Bianchi), Austin and Sue's second child
1869	11 May	"I do not cross my Father's ground to any House or town."
1870	16 August	Thomas Wentworth Higginson visits the poet in Amherst; meets and dislikes her father; does not meet her mother
1871	Spring	"Father was very sick. I presumed he would die, and the sight of his lonesome face all day was harder than personal trouble. He is growing better, though physically reluctantly. I hope I am mistaken, but I think his physical life don't want to live any longer. You know he never played, and the straightest engine has its leaning hour."
1874	16 June	Death of Edward Dickinson, aged seventy-one, while serving in the Massachusetts legislature, in Boston, after suffering a stroke, perhaps compounded by medical malpractice; Austin prostrated by grief; Vinnie takes charge of the elaborate funeral, which the poet does not attend; yet she dreams about her father every night for more than a year after his death; "His Heart was pure and terrible and I think no other like it exists."
1875	15 June	Mrs. Dickinson suffers a stroke on the eve of the first anniversary of her husband's death; nursed continuously thereafter by Emily and Vinnie
	1 August	Birth of (Thomas) Gilbert, Austin and Sue's third child
1878–84		Emily Dickinson's Indian summer romance with her father's recently widowed friend Judge Otis Lord
1882		Mabel Loomis Todd, recently arrived in Amherst, engages in serious flirtation with Austin's son Ned but soon becomes fascinated with Austin, as he is with her; in subsequent years they sometimes met and made love in the Homestead, apparently with the approval of Vinnie and Emily

	14 November	Emily Norcross Dickinson dies at the age of seventy-eight after many years of invalidism; her last words: "Dont leave me, Vinnie."
1883	5 October	Poet leaves the Homestead for the first time in many years to attend the deathbed of her nephew Gilbert; becomes violently sickened and suffers from prolonged nervous exhaustion for months thereafter
1884	5 September	Helen Hunt Jackson asks to be Emily Dickinson's literary executrix
1885	12 August	Death of Helen Hunt Jackson
1886	15 May	Death of Emily Dickinson from Bright's disease at the age of fifty-five; her funeral attended by Higginson who reads Emily Brontë's poem beginning "No coward soul is mine."
1886	Summer	Vinnie turns packet copies of the poems over to Sue for editing
1887	January?	Vinnie recovers the poems in Sue's possession
	February	Vinnie persuades Mrs. Todd to edit some of the poems
	November	Mrs. Todd begins transcribing the manuscripts in her possession; subsequently succeeds in interesting Higginson in the project
1890	12 November	Publication of *Poems by Emily Dickinson Edited by Two of Her Friends*; a selection of 115; despite mixed reviews, the sales were brisk

SELECTED BIBLIOGRAPHY

Amherst College Biographical Record of the Graduates and Nongraduates, Centennial Edition, 1821–1921. Edited by Robert B. Fletcher and Malcolm O. Young. Amherst: Trustees of Amherst College, 1939.

Baym, Nina. *Woman's Fiction: A Guide to Novels by and about Women in America, 1820–1870.* Ithaca: Cornell University Press, 1978.

Bernhard, Mary Elizabeth Kromer. "Portrait of a Family: Emily Dickinson's Norcross Connection." *New England Quarterly* 60 (1987): 363–81.

Bianchi, Martha Dickinson. *Emily Dickinson Face to Face: Unpublished Letters with Notes and Reminiscences.* Hamden, Conn.: Archon Books, 1970.

Bingham, Millicent Todd. *Emily Dickinson's Home: Letters of Edward Dickinson and His Family.* New York: Harper and Brothers, 1955.

Capps, Jack L. *Emily Dickinson's Reading, 1836–1886.* Cambridge, Mass.: Harvard University Press, 1966.

Carpenter and Morehouse. *The History of the Town of Amherst, Massachusetts.* Amherst: Press of Carpenter and Morehouse, 1896.

Cody, John. *After Great Pain: The Inner Life of Emily Dickinson.* Cambridge, Mass.: Harvard University Press, 1971.

Dickinson, Edward [Coelebs, pseud.]. "Female Education." *New-England Inquirer,* 22 Dec. 1826; 5 Jan., 26 Jan., 23 Feb., 20 April 1827.

Dickinson, Emily. *The Letters of Emily Dickinson.* Edited by Thomas H. Johnson. 3 vols. Cambridge, Mass.: Harvard University Press, 1958.

——. *The Poems of Emily Dickinson.* Edited by Thomas H. Johnson. 3 vols. Cambridge, Mass.: Harvard University Press, 1955.

Dickinson Family Papers. Houghton Library, Harvard University, Cambridge, Mass.

Dictionary of American Biography. 1928–1937.

Emerson, Ellen Tucker. *One First Love: The Letters of Ellen Louisa Tucker to Ralph Waldo Emerson.* Edited by Edith W. Gregg. Cambridge, Mass.: Harvard University Press, 1962.

Gay, Peter. *The Bourgeois Experience Victoria to Freud: Education of the Senses.* New York: Oxford University Press, 1984.

History of Monson Massachusetts. Compiled by Monson Historical Society, 1960.

Hitchcock, Edward. *Reminiscences of Amherst College: Historical, Scientific, Biographical, and Autobiographical.* Northampton: Bridgman and Childs, 1863.

Kaplan, Justin. *Walt Whitman: A Life.* New York: Simon and Schuster, 1980.

Leyda, Jay. *The Years and Hours of Emily Dickinson.* 2 vols. New Haven: Yale University Press, 1960.

Longsworth, Polly. *Austin and Mabel: The Amherst Affair and Love Letters of Austin Dickinson and Mabel Loomis Todd*. New York: Farrar, Straus and Giroux, 1984.

Martin, Wendy. *An American Triptych: Anne Bradstreet, Emily Dickinson, Adrienne Rich*. Chapel Hill: University of North Carolina Press, 1984.

Mossberg, Barbara Antonina Clarke. *Emily Dickinson: When a Writer Is a Daughter*. Bloomington: Indiana University Press, 1982.

New-England Inquirer (Amherst), 1826–28.

Norcross, Joel Warren. *History and Genealogy of the Norcross Family*. 2 vols. 1882. Manuscript, New England Historic Genealogical Society, Boston, Mass.

The Northampton Book: Chapters from 300 Years in the Life of a New England Town, 1654–1954. Northampton: Tercentenary History Committee, 1954.

Nye, Russel B. *George Bancroft: Brahmin Rebel*. New York: Alfred A. Knopf, 1944.

Pollak, Vivian R. *Dickinson: The Anxiety of Gender*. Ithaca: Cornell University Press, 1984.

Rothman, Ellen K. *Hands and Hearts: A History of Courtship in America*. New York: Basic Books, 1984.

St. Armand, Barton Levi. *Emily Dickinson and Her Culture: The Soul's Society*. New York: Cambridge University Press, 1984.

Sedgwick, Catharine Maria. *Hope Leslie; or, Early Times in the Massachusetts*. Edited by Mary Kelley. New Brunswick: Rutgers University Press, 1987.

Sewall, Richard B. *The Life of Emily Dickinson*. 2 vols. New York: Farrar, Straus and Giroux, 1974.

_____. *The Lyman Letters: New Light on Emily Dickinson and Her Family*. Amherst: University of Massachusetts Press, 1965.

Taylor, George R. "The Rise and Decline of Manufactures and Other Matters." In *Essays on Amherst's History*, edited by Theodore P. Greene, pp. 43–77. Amherst: The Vista Trust, 1978.

Traubel, Horace. *With Walt Whitman in Camden*. Vol. 1. Boston: Small Maynard, 1906.

Tuckerman, Frederick. *Amherst Academy: A New England School of the Past, 1814–1861*. Amherst: Printed for the Trustees, 1929.

Tyler, W. S. *History of Amherst College during Its First Half Century, 1821–1871*. Springfield, Mass.: C. W. Bryan, 1873.

Whicher, George Frisbie. *This Was a Poet: A Critical Biography of Emily Dickinson*. New York: Charles Scribner's Sons, 1939.

Wolff, Cynthia Griffin. *Emily Dickinson*. New York: Alfred A. Knopf, 1986.

INDEX

CVCA Royal Library
4687 Wyoga Lake Road
Stow, OH. 44224-1011